sharp VOCAB

D1446074

Related Titles

Sharp Grammar
Sharp Math
Sharp Writing

sharp
VOCAB

Building Better Vocabulary Skills

PUBLISHING

New York

This publication is designed to provide accurate and authoritative information in regard to the subject matter covered. It is sold with the understanding that the publisher is not engaged in rendering legal, accounting, or other professional service. If legal advice or other expert assistance is required, the services of a competent professional should be sought.

© 2008 by Kaplan, Inc.

Published by Kaplan Publishing, a division of Kaplan, Inc.
1 Liberty Plaza, 24th Floor
New York, NY 10006

All rights reserved. The text of this publication, or any part thereof, may not be reproduced in any manner whatsoever without written permission from the publisher.

Printed in the United States of America

August 2008
10 9 8 7 6 5 4 3 2

ISBN-13: 978-1-4195-5036-2

Kaplan Publishing books are available at special quantity discounts to use for sales promotions, employee premiums, or educational purposes. Please email our Special Sales Department to order or for more information at *kaplanpublishing@kaplan.com*, or write to Kaplan Publishing, 1 Liberty Plaza, 24th Floor, New York, NY 10006.

Contents

Introduction

Dear Reader,

Do unknown vocabulary words you overhear in a conversation or read in a book (or see on a test!) make your head swim? Do you struggle to get through a reading passage because of just one difficult phrase? Do you keep quiet because you're afraid of misusing certain words? Is it frustrating to know how good your essays, papers, and test scores would be if you only had a larger vocabulary? The answer may very well be yes to all of these. Even if you can only relate to just one, then this book is for you. Just buying *Sharp Vocab* puts you on the road to a better vocabulary!

After reading *Sharp Vocab*, not only will you sound more intelligent when talking with family and friends and not only will you better understand what you are reading, you will find that word knowledge will enhance your professional life, whether it is as a student or an employee. An extensive vocabulary can help you score better on exams, get promoted, or simply save you time when solving everyday problems.

Improving your vocabulary can seem like a tedious process. But learning about word use and meaning doesn't have to be boring. Allow us to introduce the **Building Block Method.**

This teacher-approved method was devised by the experts at Kaplan to make learning vocabulary as painless as possible. It is proven in several areas of study, including math, grammar, and writing!

Like any other book, you'll begin with the basics—in this case, word roots—and move on from there. The final chapter is "Fifty-Cent Words You Can Actually Use," fifty-cent words being the extravagant terminology often found in crossword puzzles and on GRE exams. Speaking of exams, there are also chapters dedicated to words commonly found on both the GRE and SAT exams. If your goal is scoring higher on a test, this is the book for you. Since *Sharp Vocab* contains more than 900 vocabulary words, the test makers will be hard-pressed to ask you about a word not contained within these pages.

Within *Sharp Vocab*, vocabulary words are often presented in a context that involves situations you might find in your day-to-day life. Some words come with an explanation pertaining to their origin while others are explained using synonyms (words with the same or similar meaning) and/or antonyms (opposites). Not only will you read about these words using varied examples, you will be tested on them in a variety of methods, which is also a part of the Kaplan approach.

There's no smarter way to learn. So get started—a vastly improved vocabulary is only a few building blocks away!

HOW TO USE THIS BOOK

We recommend reading through cover to cover, but if you only have a few days for practice with this book, there are chapter headings to help you find your desired subjects or targets. Within each chapter, you will find Kaplan's systematic approach for improving your vocabulary. Each chapter has been specifically designed with memorization in mind. Each chapter contains five key components as the means to this end:

1. Building Block Quiz

You'll begin each chapter with a short quiz. The first ten questions are a preview of sorts, testing your knowledge of the material to be covered in that chapter. The last two questions will cover material from earlier lessons, so if you get these questions wrong, it's time to go back and review! Taking this quiz helps reinforce what you've already learned, while targeting the information you need to focus on in each chapter. Plus, you'll get even more review from the answer explanations, which tell you why each answer choice is right or wrong.

2. Detailed Lessons

Each chapter focuses on one specific subject area, which will help in the memorization process. Association is one way we can enhance our ability to absorb information. With detailed explanations of the chapter concepts, a multitude of relevant examples, and a variety of strategies to help you remember what you need to know, you will find your vocabulary growing by the minute! Just to make sure you don't forget anything, we will also help you to review the fundamentals from previous chapters, looking back while moving forward.

3. Plentiful Practice

Repetition is the key to mastery. So be prepared to practice, practice, practice! You'll find everything from simple matching exercises to exercises that ask you to apply the skills you're learning to practical, real-life situations. By "learning from all sides," so to speak, you're much more likely to retain the information. And remember, don't start a new chapter if you haven't mastered the earlier material—you'll be building on a weak foundation.

4. Chapter Quizzes

At the end of each chapter, you'll find a 20-question Chapter Quiz to help you practice what you've learned and assess how well you remember the new vocabulary. These quizzes, broken down into true/false and multiple-choice formats, cover material from the chapter and will help to make sure that you've mastered the words before you move on.

5. Cumulative Test

Finally, the book concludes with a 25-question *Sharp Vocab* Cumulative Test covering words from all of the chapters. It will further reinforce your mastery of new vocabulary words and allow you to see how much you've learned.

With a system as easy as this, a fantastic vocabulary is well within your reach. All you have to do is take the first step. Good luck!

CHAPTER 1

Word Roots

The keys to unlocking unfamiliar words

This first chapter is special because it not only teaches you the most important word roots out there, but it is also an introduction to many of the new vocab words featured in the following chapters!

BUILDING BLOCK QUIZ

DIRECTIONS: Circle the choice that you think best defines the word root.

1.	**ver**, as in verisimilitude:	very	false	true
2.	**prox**, as in proximity:	far	approximately	near
3.	**mal**, as in malevolent:	good	bad	nice
4.	**cap**, as in capitulate:	seize	full	capsize
5.	**am**, as in amorous:	love	hate	hug
6.	**belli**, as in belligerent:	beautiful	war	peace
7.	**dic**, as in contradiction:	speak	play	promise
8.	**anti**, as in antipathy:	for	against	feelings
9.	**inter**, as in intermission:	between	through	besides
10.	**omni**, as in omniscient:	all	none	rarely

BUILDING BLOCK ANSWERS AND EXPLANATIONS

1. **Ver** means *true,* and has its origins in the Latin *veritas,* which means truth. Also, for those of you who speak Spanish, *verdad* means truth. **Ver**isimilitude means the appearance of being true or real.

2. **Prox** means *near.* Hence, **prox**imity means to be near something: the right answer, the correct location, or something else. *Approximately* is a trick answer, as it contains the word root but is not a definition. *Far* is an antonym.

3. **Mal** means *bad.* Since the second part of the word, *volent,* relates back to a Latin word for *will* (as in to will or wish bad things upon someone else), **mal**evolent means wicked and spiteful. *Good* and *nice* are its antonyms.

4. **Cap** means *seize.* If you **cap**itulate, it means you are giving in to whoever is trying to seize you or your possessions.

5. **Am** means *love.* To be **am**orous is to feel loving. And although you might want to hug someone you feel amorous toward, *hug* does not define the root. *Hate* is an antonym.

6. **Belli** means *war* and can be found at the beginning of many hateful and violent words: **belli**cose (warlike) and **belli**gerent (aggressive), for example. *Beautiful* and *peace* are contrary to all things **belli**.

7. **Dic** means *speak* and contra**dic**tion means to speak against another person or against one's own logic. *Play* and *promise* are irrelevant.

8. **Anti** means opposite or *against.* When a person displays **anti**pathy, he or she is in opposition to something. Although when you are **anti**-something you have feelings against it, *feelings* is not a definition. *For* is an antonym.

9. **Inter** means *between.* An **inter**mission, for example, is a break between acts during a play. Often, **inter** is used to indicate something done or communicated between people or groups of people. Be careful not to confuse **inter** with intra, which means *within. Through* and *besides* are incorrect definitions.

10. **Omni** means *all.* When **omni** is used to indicate all it is in a grand sense; not as in she ate all the pizza or he stole all the money, but as in **omni**scient, which means all-knowing. *None* and *rarely* are virtual antonyms.

Now that you've tested your skills, it's time to learn some word roots! When you're reading them over, try to absorb not only the definition for each word root, but also the example words provided. You'll find that, in the least, the words share the meaning that comes from the word root.

PART ONE

a-, an- not, without
Examples: asymmetrical, anonymity

ac-, acr- sharp, sour
Examples: acuity, acumen

ali-, altr- another
Examples: alien, altruism

am-, ami- love
Examples: amorous, amity

ambi-, amphi- both
Examples: ambidextrous, amphibian

ante-, ant- before
Examples: antecedent, antediluvian

auto- self
Examples: autonomous, automobile

bene-, ben- good
Examples: beneficent, benign

bio- life
Examples: biology, biodegradable

cap-, capt-, -cept, -cip- take, seize
Examples: capacious, capitulate, precept

chrom- color
Examples: chromatic, chromosphere

circum- around
Examples: circumlocution, circumvent

with, together
Examples: cohesion, collaborator

-gno-, -cogn- know
Examples: agnostic, ignoble

MEMORY TIP

If you've ever taken a **bio**logy class, what did you *learn* about? You learned about life, right? **Bio**logy is the study of *life,* and in many high schools the class is now called *Life* Science.

Practice 1

DIRECTIONS: Match the word root (left column) with its definition (right column).

1. **a**   without

2. **ac**   know

3. **ante**   color

4. **chrom**   before

5. **gno**   sharp

PART TWO

contra- against
Examples: contradiction, contrary

cosmo-, -cosm world
Examples: cosmopolitan, cosmos, microcosm

demo-, dem- people
Examples: democracy, pandemic

dia- across
Examples: diameter, mediate

dic-, dict- speak
Examples: dictate, contradiction

dis-, dif-, di- apart, away
Examples: disheveled, dissemble, disclosure

ex-, e- out, out of
Examples: exorbitant, extrude, expropriate

fac-, -fic, -fect, fy-, fea- make, do
Examples: facile, prolific

frag-, frac- break
Examples: fragment, refract

gen- birth, class, kin
Examples: genealogy, genocide

MEMORY TIP

You will note that oftentimes these word roots don't just appear at the beginning of the vocabulary words. The **dic** in contra**dic**tion comes in the middle, for example. **Dic** has to do with spoken words and **contra** means *against*. If someone contradicts himself, he has gone against something he said previously.

---

grad-, -gress step
Examples: graduation, digress

grat- pleasing
Examples: ingratiate, gratuity

in-, ig-, il-, im-, ir- not
Examples: incorrigible, intrepid, inviolable

inter- between, among
Examples: interlocutor, interlude

intra-, intr- within
Examples: intrapersonal, intramural

MEMORY TIP

Many math teachers use the example of a pizza to teach **frac**tions. The word root **frac** means *to break,* which makes sense, as a pizza is broken down into slices and distributed to everybody at the dinner table.

Practice 2

DIRECTIONS: Match the word root (left column) with its definition (right column).

6.	**dia**	within
7.	**frac**	pleasing
8.	**grat**	across
9.	**inter**	between
10.	**intra**	break

PART THREE

jour- day
Examples: journal, sojourn

lec-, -leg-, lex- read, speak
Examples: lecture, illegible

liter- letter
Examples: literacy, alliteration

mal- bad
Examples: malevolent, malfeasance, malediction

MEMORY TIP

"Means Anti-Love." Remember that fun little mnemonic device, and you will remember what **mal** means. Any word with **mal** in it is a negative word.

---

man- hand
Examples: *manhandle, mandate*

morph- shape
Examples: *amorphous, anthropomorphic*

mut- change
Examples: *mutability, immutable*

neg- not, deny
Examples: *abnegate, negligible*

nom-, -nym- name
Examples: *autonomous, eponymous*

nov- new
Examples: *novice, novel*

ob- against
Examples: *obdurate, obfuscate, obstreperous*

omni- all
Examples: *omniscient, omnipotent*

-path-, pass- feel, suffer
Examples: *apathetic, empathetic*

phon- sound
Examples: *telephone, cacophony*

plac- calm, please
Examples: *implacable, complacent*

MEMORY TIP

Rather than envisioning something, when you see the root **phon** think of the *sound* your cell **phon**e makes when it rings. Do you have a favorite song programmed in? Is it something funky or just a plain old ringing telephone? Regardless, thinking of your **phon**e ringtone will remind you that **phon** means *sound*.

Practice 3

DIRECTIONS: Match the word root (left column) with its definition (right column).

11. **leg**	against
12. **mut**	read
13. **neg**	change
14. **ob**	calm
15. **plac**	bad

PART FOUR

pot- power
Examples: impotent, despotism

-prox-, prop- near
Examples: approximate, proximity

rid-, ris- laugh
Examples: ridicule, deride

sacr-, sanct- holy
Examples: sacred, sanctimonious

scrib-, script-, scriv- write
Examples: scribble, proscribe

sequ-, secu- follow
Examples: sequence, non sequitur

syn-, sym- together
Examples: synergy, synonymous

tim- fear, frightened
Examples: timid, timorous

urb- city
Examples: urban, urbane

vac- empty
Examples: vacate, vacuous

ver- true
Examples: verisimilitude, veracious, aver

> **MEMORY TIP**
>
> When you first pull the **vac**uum cleaner out of the closet, the bag inside should be *empty*. And when you're done **vac**uuming, you should throw out that bag and put in a new one. One that is also . . . *empty!* Think of that empty **vac**uum bag, and you will be sure to remember that **vac** means *empty*.

Practice 4

DIRECTIONS: Match the word root (left column) with its definition (right column).

16. **prox**   holy
17. **rid**   laugh
18. **sanct**   write
19. **scrib**   near
20. **tim**   frightened

PRACTICE ANSWERS AND EXPLANATIONS

Practice 1

1. **A**, as in **a**nonymity, is synonymous with *without*.

2. **Ac**, as in **ac**uity, is synonymous with *sharp*.

3. **Ante**, as in **ante**cedent, is synonymous with *before*.

4. **Chrom**, as in **chrom**atic, is synonymous with *color.*

5. **Gno**, as in a**gno**stic, is synonymous with *know.*

Practice 2

6. **Dia**, as in me**dia**te, is synonymous with *across.*

7. **Frac**, as in re**frac**t, is synonymous with *break.*

8. **Grat**, as in in**grat**iate, is synonymous with *pleasing.*

9. **Inter**, as in **inter**lude, is synonymous with *between.*

10. **Intra**, as in **intra**personal, is synonymous with *within.*

PRACTICE ANSWERS AND EXPLANATIONS *(cont'd)*

Practice 3

11. **Leg**, as in il**leg**ible, is synonymous with *read.*

12. **Mut**, as in **mut**ability, is synonymous with *change.*

13. **Neg**, as in ab**neg**ate, is synonymous with *deny.*

14. **Ob**, as in **ob**durate, is synonymous with *against.*

15. **Plac**, as in im**plac**able, is synonymous with *calm.*

Practice 4

16. **Prox**, as in **prox**imity, is synonymous with *near.*

17. **Rid**, as in de**rid**e, is synonymous with *laugh.*

18. **Sanct**, as in **sanct**imonious, is synonymous with *holy.*

19. **Scrib**, as in pro**scrib**e, is synonymous with *write.*

20. **Tim**, as in **tim**id, is synonymous with *frightened.*

CHAPTER 1 QUIZ

Take your time, not only when answering the questions, but also when reading the answer explanations that follow. Set a goal for yourself—80% (16 correct answers) is recommended. If you don't reach that goal, go back and read through the chapter again. Good luck!

DIRECTIONS: For questions 1–11, circle T for True or F for False. For questions 12–20, circle the synonym.

1. **T F   phon**—sound

2. **T F   ob**—for

3. **T F   urb**—city

4. **T F   vac**—full

5. **T F   pot**—power

6. **T F   ac**—dull

7. **T F   altr**—against

8. **T F   ambi**—both

9. **T F   auto**—mechanical

10. **T F   nym**—without

11. **T F   man**—hand

12. **cap**, as in capitulate:	give	take	flee
13. **circum**, as in circumvent:	around	between	throughout
14. **dem**, as in demagogue:	statistic	people	list
15. **gen**, as in genealogy:	birth	clothing	science
16. **morph**, as in anthropomorphic:	changing	shape	animalistic
17. **a**, as in asymmetrical:	combined	without	congruent
18. **chron**, as in chronological:	time	uncommon	sensational
19. **cosmo**, as in cosmopolitan:	round	literature	world
20. **jour**, as in sojourn:	day	rush	bother

CHAPTER 1 QUIZ ANSWERS AND EXPLANATIONS

1. **True. Phon** is synonymous with *sound*. Just think of the sound of your best friend's voice coming through your cell **phon**e.

2. **False. Ob** is synonymous with *against,* so for is an antonym. Just think, you wouldn't try to **ob**struct something (keep it from happening) if you weren't against it.

3. **True. Urb** is synonymous with *city*. Just think of **urb**an (in the city) and sub**urb**an (just outside of the city).

4. **False. Vac** is synonymous with *empty,* so *full* is an antonym. One example of the word root in use is **vac**uous, which means empty-headed and unintelligent.

5. **True. Pot** is synonymous with *power.* To be **pot**ent is to be powerful.

6. **False. Ac** is associated with *sharp,* as in how something offends the senses. Something **ac**rid has a sharp odor, for example. *Dull* is an antonym.

7. **False. Altr** is synonymous with *another,* not with *against* (that word root would be **anti**). **Altr**uistic is a good example, as it refers to one who does nice things for another person.

8. **True. Ambi** is synonymous with *both*. A person who is **ambi**dextrous can complete tasks with both hands equally well.

9. **False. Auto** is synonymous with *self,* not with *mechanical*. For example, something that is **auto**matic will perform a task by itself.

10. **False. Nym** is synonymous with *name*. Think of ano**nym**ous, which means without a name. The word root meaning without is **a**.

11. **True. Man** is a word root for *hand,* as seen in the words **man**handle (to beat up with the hands) and **man**date, which is usually a document granting permission that has to be signed by hand.

12. **Cap** is synonymous with *take. Flee* does not fit and *give* is an exact antonym.

13. **Circum** is synonymous with *around. Between* and *throughout* are tempting, because both also deal with direction, but both are wrong.

CHAPTER 1 QUIZ ANSWERS AND EXPLANATIONS *(cont'd)*

14. **Dem** is synonymous with *people*. A **dem**agogue is a leader of the people, even if she is not a good leader. *List* and *statistic* are irrelevant choices.

15. **Gen** is used to signify kin or *birth*. Although **gen**etics, which is the study of heredity (the traits acquired at birth), is a science, *science* is incorrect. *Clothing* is irrelevant.

16. **Morph** is synonymous with *shape*. Anthropo**morph**ic refers to human characteristics, like shape, attributed to gods or animals. You might be tempted by *changing,* because the word **morph** is often used to mean changing—but what it really means is to change shape. *Animalistic* is a distracter.

17. **A** is a word root that means *without*. *Combined* is not synonymous with **a,** and *congruent,* which means similar, is an antonym.

18. **Chron** is synonymous with *time,* or in order (as in **chron**ological order). *Uncommon* and *sensational* are unrelated.

19. **Cosmo** means *world* and in the case of **cosmo**politan, worldly or international. The world may be *round,* but that answer is unrelated. *Cosmopolitan* may be a magazine, but *literature* is unrelated, too.

20. The word root **jour** means *day,* so *rush* and *bother* are irrelevant answers. A so**jour**n is a temporary stay.

CHAPTER 2

School Days

The basic vocabulary to get you through
social studies, science, and math

BUILDING BLOCK QUIZ

This "building block" quiz tests the information you will learn in this chapter, plus two word roots from the previous chapter. By answering the 12 questions below, you will get a sense of how closely you'll have to study this chapter in order to master the vocabulary you'll need to find your way around the classroom!

DIRECTIONS: Fill in the blanks, using the most appropriate of the four multiple-choice answers. The correct answer will always fit into the sentence grammatically.

1. Matt's math teacher suggested he review all of the _____ before his calculus test.

   (A) algorithms   (B) refract

   (C) punctuation marks   (D) archipelagos

2. On their cruise last summer, the Smiths took a boat around the _____, visiting more than a dozen islands.

   (A) cartographer   (B) amorphous

   (C) savannah   (D) archipelagos

3. The weatherman ruined the bottoms of his favorite pants as he walked among the waterlogged, _____ ruins.

   (A) simian   (B) diluvial

   (C) sarcastic   (D) potable

4. Jen waited until her father made sure the water was _____ before taking a drink.

   (A) arboreal   (B) diluvial

   (C) archipelagos   (D) potable

5. The science teacher knew that his students would love the _____ exhibit at the zoo.

   (A) arboreal   (B) simian

   (C) stubborn   (D) aerate

6. They all agreed that calling a town with a nuclear reactor Wellsville was a real _____!

   (A) turgid   (B) stratify

   (C) concave   (D) misnomer

7. Although Jerry said the spilled milk looked like a dog, everyone else at the table told him it had a(n) _____ shape.

   (A) potable   (B) diluvial

   (C) amorphous   (D) misnomer

8. To make sure her product was accurate, Nandi consulted a(n) _____ before opening her mapmaking business.

   (A) cartographer   (B) placebo

   (C) adjunct   (D) acclivity

9. Even if the pills were a(n) _____ and simply made of sugar, Kevin was glad they made his mother feel better.

   (A) placebo   (B) simian

   (C) acclivity   (D) archipelago

10. Because he loved studying plant life, Harvey knew he wanted a(n) _____ job at the nature preserve.

    (A) calamitous   (B) circumnavigate

    (C) asymmetrical   (D) arboreal

11. **Contra**, as in **contra**diction, is synonymous with _____.

    (A) day   (B) against

    (C) letter   (D) bad

12. **Leg**, as in il**leg**ible, is synonymous with _____.

    (A) read   (B) take

    (C) change   (D) fear

BUILDING BLOCK ANSWERS AND EXPLANATIONS

1. A. Since **algorithms** are key to solving math problems, (A) is the only possible answer. *Punctuation marks* and *archipelagos* have nothing to do with math, as the former relates to exclamation points and semicolons while the latter is a set of islands. To *refract* is to deflect sound or light; besides, the word doesn't fit grammatically in the sentence.

2. D. **Archipelagos** are large groups of islands, making (D) the correct answer. The other three answers don't fit into the sentence structure, and their meanings have nothing to do with islands. *Savanna* is another geographical word, but it means treeless plains. *Amorphous* means shapeless and a *cartographer* is a mapmaker.

3. B. Anything that is **diluvial** has to do with a flood. The hint of waterlogged ruins makes (B) the perfect choice. You might be tempted to choose *potable,* but since that has to do with safe drinking water, it really isn't an appropriate choice. *Simian* has to do with apes, and *sarcastic,* which means mocking and ironic, is used to describe a person.

4. D. **Potable** has to do with water that is safe for drinking, making (D) the correct choice. *Diluvial* also has to do with water, but refers to a flood. Since Jen wasn't interested in drinking a flood, (B) is not correct. *Arboreal* has to do with trees and *archipelagos* are groups of islands, so neither word applies.

BUILDING BLOCK ANSWERS AND EXPLANATIONS *(cont'd)*

5. B. There might be an *arboreal* exhibit (one that features trees) on display somewhere. But at a zoo, you are looking at animals and not plant life. Reading in context, the students are going to love the apes in the **simian** exhibit. To *aerate* is to ventilate and to be *stubborn* has nothing to do with zoos or exhibits.

6. D. Wellsville is no name for a town with a nuclear reactor; with one leak that town certainly will not be well! Thus, the name is completely unfitting—it is a **misnomer**. In addition, **misnomer** is the only choice that is a noun, so *turgid* (an adjective meaning pompous), *stratify* (a verb meaning to divide), and *concave* (an adjective meaning curved inward) cannot be correct.

7. C. Although someone might drink spilled milk, **amorphous**, which means without clear shape, is a better answer than *potable,* which means safe to drink. As everyone else contested Jerry's claim about how the milk looked, the answer is apparent. A carton of milk is not enough to cause a flood, ruling out *diluvial,* and *misnomer* is a noun, so it does not apply.

8. A. Cartographers are expert mapmakers, so it makes sense that Nandi would want to consult one. *Adjunct* is something connected to something else; even though that something can be a person, it is too much of a stretch to be correct. *Placebo* is also a noun, but it refers to a fake medicine (often administered in research studies). *Acclivity* describes an upward slope, so it is not a possible choice, either.

9. A. After reading the whole sentence you can establish a contrast. Despite taking a **placebo**, or a false remedy, Kevin's mother felt better and he was glad. She did not take a group of islands (*archipelago*), nor did she take a *simian* (ape), or an *acclivity* (upward slope), although those would be interesting things to take!

10. D. Nobody wants a *calamitous* (disastrous) job. *Asymmetrical* is also an adjective, but it means uneven, so it does not fit in the context of the sentence. *Circumnavigate* doesn't work, either, as it means to go around. The hint is that Harvey wanted a job at a nature preserve. Since trees are a part of nature, **arboreal** is the only correct answer.

BUILDING BLOCK ANSWERS AND EXPLANATIONS *(cont'd)*

11. B. Contra means *against*. *Bad* is close, but it isn't always wrong or bad to be against something. *Day* and *letter* are irrelevant choices. If you chose incorrectly for this question, you might want to go back to chapter 1 for some review on word roots.

12. A. Leg is synonymous with *read* and i**leg**ible means unreadable. *Take, change,* and *fear* are all unrelated. If you chose incorrectly for this question, you might want to go back to chapter 1 for some review on word roots.

PART ONE

acclivity n. (uh KLIHV ih tee)—an incline or upward slope, the ascending side of a hill
*Climbing up the **acclivity** of Mt. Sizemore took Gemma and Daniel twice as long as they expected.*

aerate v. (AYR ayt)—expose to air
*One of Rob's jobs at the golf course was to **aerate** the greens in order to keep them looking healthy.*

arable adj. (AHR uh buhl)—suitable for cultivation
*The class's community service project was to make the land **arable** for a student garden.*

arboreal adj. (ahr BOHR ee uhl)—relating to trees; living in trees
*The squirrel is an **arboreal** mammal, spending much of its time running up and down trees.*

MEMORY TIP

Although you may not celebrate Arbor Day, a celebration of *trees*, keep in mind that it does appear on calendars. As **arboreal** relates to *trees*, thinking of Arbor Day might just help you to memorize the meaning of this word.

archipelago n. (ahr kuh PEHL uh goh)—a large group of islands
*In some of the Swedish **archipelago** villages, boat taxis are the only form of transportation.*

ballast n. (BAAL uhst)—a structure that helps to stabilize or steady
*Bags of sand are often used as **ballast** in hot air balloons.*

cartographer n. (kar TAH gruh fer)—someone who makes maps
*Early **cartographers** often had to remake their maps when explorers returned with more and more information about unknown lands.*

circumnavigate v. (sir cuhm NAH vi gayt)—to travel completely around
*Bobby dreamed of **circumnavigating** the globe in a hot air balloon.*

conflagration n. (kahn fluh GRAY shuhn)—large, destructive fire
*After the **conflagration** of the night before, Midtown Mall was nothing but a pile of ashes.*

contiguous adj. (kuhn TIHG yoo uhs)—sharing a boundary; neighboring
*The two houses had **contiguous** yards, so the families shared the landscaping expenses.*

cataclysmic adj. (kaat uh KLIHZ mihk)—severely destructive
*The hurricane was **cataclysmic** and resulted in a lot of damage, even though it raged overhead for no more than an hour.*

despotism n. (DEH spuh ti zuhm)—dominance of a nation through threat of violence
*According to some historians, the **despotism** of Stalin outweighed that of Hitler.*

diffuse v. (dih FYOOZ)—to spread out widely, to scatter freely, to disseminate
*Although the fan helped to **diffuse** the cigarette smoke in the club, Meghan could still smell it on her clothes when she got home.*

diluvial adj. (dih LOO vee uhl)—pertaining to a flood
*After the hose on the washing machine broke, Hank's laundry room looked absolutely **diluvial**.*

Practice 1

DIRECTIONS: Read the three choices, then circle the one most closely related to the word in bold.

1.	**aerate**:	expose	provide	descend
2.	**ballast**:	stabilize	explode	effect
3.	**contiguous**:	perpendicular	neighboring	contagious
4.	**despotism**:	threatening	delivery	stabilizing
5.	**diffuse**:	to threaten	to spread	to describe

Your Words, Your World

Don't have time to sit around repeating these words to yourself, over and over again, in order to remember them? Well, you don't have to! The following exercise tests your knowledge of the material . . . without requiring that you take a test! So your job now is to really *think* about what you read, and to really think about the questions that follow.

Diluvial—The word **diluvial** relates to *flooding*. Right now, in your mind, imagine the scene on the news: cars washed up on curbs, mailboxes down on their sides, telephone poles in the middle of the road, and a rowboat on a roof. Can you see the muddy fields? Can you see cars floating down the street instead of driving? Think of this scene, and then think of the word **diluvial**.

Conflagration—As unpleasant as it may be, the easiest way to remember this word is by picturing a destructive fire. Can you feel the heat? See the huge flames? Hear the sirens and see firefighters rushing to put it out? Envision this scene when you hear or see the word **conflagration**.

PART TWO

adjunct adj. (AHD juhnkt)—something added, attached, or joined
*An **adjunct** professor only works part of the time, so she is not given the same full-time status as other faculty members.*

aggregate n. (AA grih giht)—a collective mass, the sum total
*When Gerry finally calculated his debt, it came to an **aggregate** of $3,549.*

algorithm n. (AAL guh rith uhm)—an established procedure for solving a problem or equation
*The accountant used a series of **algorithms** to determine the appropriate tax bracket for her client.*

amorphous adj. (ah MOOR fuhs)—having no definite form
*The spilled milk was **amorphous** as it spread across the kitchen floor.*

antediluvian adj. (ahn tee dee LOO vee uhn)—prehistoric, ancient beyond measure
*The **antediluvian** fossils were carefully displayed at the Peabody Museum.*

asymmetrical adj. (ay sim EH tri kuhl)—not corresponding in size, shape, position, etc.
*The customer refused to pay when she realized the hairstylist had given her an **asymmetrical** haircut.*

dominant adj. (DOM uh nent)—most prominent, exercising the most control
*At feeding time, Marley showed himself to be the **dominant** puppy in the litter and got the majority of the food.*

encroach v. (en KROHCH)—to impinge, infringe, intrude upon
*As the human population expands, we continually **encroach** on natural habitats like the rain forests.*

extrude v. (ehk STROOD)—to force out or shape something by pushing it through a small opening
*Dr. Langley watched with fascination as the volcano **extruded** rock and molten lava.*

> **FLASHBACK**
>
> You will recall that the word root **ex** means *out* or *out of*. It makes sense then that when something is **extruded** it is *forced out*.

misnomer n. (mihs NOH muhr)—an error in naming a person or place
*Greenland is a **misnomer**, since the countryside is mostly icy, not green.*

oration n. (ohr AY shun)—lecture, formal speech
*As class valedictorian, Paulina delivered an impressive **oration** at graduation.*

placebo n. (pluh SEE boh)—a substance with no medical value that is given as medication
Dr. Howell was in charge of seeing whether volunteers who swallowed the sugar pill placebo felt better afterward anyway.

potable adj. (POH tuh buhl)—suitable for drinking
Though the water was deemed potable, it tasted terrible.

prominence n. (PROH mih nens)—importance, eminence
The Homeland Book Store prided itself on having had several authors of prominence give readings over the past year.

trajectory n. (truh JEHK tuh ree)—the path followed by a moving object, whether through space or otherwise; flight
The trajectory of Stephen's long home run was nearly interrupted by a pigeon.

Practice 2

DIRECTIONS: Consider the definition and then circle T for True or F for False.

6. **T F** **antediluvian**—any structure to help impede a flood

7. **T F** **encroach**—to infringe upon

8. **T F** **extrude**—to give something form by pushing it out

9. **T F** **oration**—ability to fly

10. **T F** **trajectory**—path followed by a moving object

Your Words, Your World

Aggregate—What's more fun, totaling up the **aggregate** change in your car, jacket pocket, and that jar on your dresser; or totaling the **aggregate** debt you owe your friends for the movies, dinner, and chipping in for gas?

Prominence—Someday will you rise to **prominence** because of what you learned in school, or will you rise to **prominence** despite what you learned in school? Do you think learning more and more vocabulary words will help you rise to **prominence**? We sure do!

Asymmetrical—Is it worse to wear pants that are **asymmetrical** to your width or a shirt that is **asymmetrical** to your height?

PART THREE

austere adj. (aw STEER)—stern, strict, unadorned
*Larry signed up his kids for karate class, hoping the **austere** sport would teach them the discipline they lacked.*

axiom n. (AKS ee uhm)—premise, postulate, self-evident truth
*Halle lived her life based on the **axioms** her grandmother had passed on to her.*

biodegradable adj. (by oh de GRAY duh buhl)—capable of being decomposed by microbial action
*In earth science, Geraldine learned that fallen leaves are **biodegradable**.*

botanist n. (BAH tuhn ihst)—scientist who studies plants
*As a **botanist**, Giselle was able to spend hours studying orchids.*

coagulate v. (koh AAG yuh layt)—to clot; to cause to thicken
*Hemophiliacs are people who can bleed to death from a minor cut because their blood doesn't **coagulate**.*

concave adj. (kahn KAYV)—curving inward
*The **concave** shape of the bowl held the spaghetti better than a plate.*

delineate v. (de LIN ee ayt)—to explain, depict, describe
*Coach Goldberg **delineated** the strategy to his team the day before the championship game.*

evanescent adj. (ev ihn ESS ihnt)—momentary, transient, short-lived
*George paused for a few seconds to enjoy his busy graduation day, knowing that the feeling of accomplishment would be **evanescent**.*

inherent adj. (ihn HEHR ehnt)—involving the essential character of something, built-in, inborn
*When Tanisha finally saw the **inherent** benefits of memorizing her vocabulary words, she made them a part of her everyday life and did very well on her tests.*

posit v. (PAH ziht)—to assume as real or conceded; propose as an explanation
*Ms. Franics told the math students that before proving the math formula, they needed to **posit** that x and y were whole numbers.*

prototype n. (PRO toh typ)—early, typical example
*Jim and his team were relieved to have finally completed the science project **prototype** so they could go on to building the real model.*

recapitulate v. (ree kuh PIHCH yoo layt)—to review by a brief summary
*Before handing out the final exam, Mrs. Thompson **recapitulated** ten of the major moments in the history of the United States.*

refract v. (rih FRAAKT)—to deflect sound or light
*Angela's crystal necklace **refracted** the rays of sunlight so they formed a beautiful pattern on her wall.*

regurgitate v. (ree GURJ uh tayt)—rush or surge back; repeat without digesting
*Yolanda's mother tried to convince her that she couldn't just **regurgitate** facts; she needed to understand the material to do well on the test.*

remission n. (reh MIH shuhn)—a lessening of intensity or degree
*Dr. Logan told Herman the good news that his cancer had finally gone into **remission**.*

secrete v. (suh KREET)—release fluids from body; produce from a source
*Mr. Mackling explained to John he should start wearing antiperspirant because his body was beginning to **secrete** sweat.*

simian adj. (SIH mee uhn)—apelike; relating to apes
*Scientists say that early humans were more **simian** in appearance than modern humans.*

soluble adj. (SOL yuh buhl)—capable of being solved or dissolved
*Sugar is **soluble** in cold water, but it dissolves more easily in hot water.*

stratify v. (STRAA tuh fy)—to arrange or divide into layers
*Dr. Schliemann found a graduate assistant who was willing to help her **stratify** the layers of soil around Mt. St. Helens.*

turgid adj. (TURH jihd)—pompous; pretentious, dull
*Although Mr. Schneider was the smartest teacher on staff, he was also the most **turgid**, making students not want to take his class.*

Practice 3

DIRECTIONS: Fill in the blanks, using five of the ten words provided below.

evanescent   concave   stratify   biodegradable

botanist   austere   coagulate   axiom

recapitulate   inherent

11. Professor Knight based his theory on the _____ that what goes up, must come down.

12. One effect of cancer is that, depending on the treatment, blood can no longer _____.

13. Laura defended her littering by saying that everything she had thrown out the window was _____.

14. Since liquid is _____ in a test tube, Mr. Frome had to show his students how to measure it from the bottom of the curve and not the top.

15. Anna thought taking AP Biology was one of the first steps to becoming a _____.

Your Words, Your World

Posit—I'm willing to **posit** that everybody you know would rather order a couple of pizzas than eat liver and onions. Am I right? What is something that you would **posit** about your best friend without question?

Recapitulate—My friends and I used to spend hours on the phone at night, **recapitulating** what had happened in school that day . . . and I don't mean in class. Sound familiar?

Stratify—When a school is several stories tall, the floors are always **stratified** so that the science labs are at the top. What about at your school? Why do you think that is?

PRACTICE ANSWERS AND EXPLANATIONS

Practice 1

1. By definition **aerate** means to *expose,* usually to air. *Provide* is close, but not as appropriate. When something *descends* it travels downward, which has nothing to do with **aerate**.

2. **Ballast** *stabilizes.* Although something that is used for **ballast** will have an *effect* on the object being stabilized, this answer is not a synonym. Neither is *explode,* which really has nothing to do with **ballast**.

3. **Contiguous** is synonymous with *neighboring.* Something *perpendicular* might be **contiguous**, but specifically, that perpendicular thing is at a right angle to something else. *Contagious* may sound and look like **contiguous**, but has to do with catching diseases.

4. **Despotism** is synonymous with *threatening.* Although a despot may have a *stabilizing* effect on a country, the word is not a good synonym. *Delivery* is not associated with **despotism** or threatening.

5. **Diffuse** is synonymous with *to spread. To threaten* and *to describe* are unrelated verbs.

Practice 2

6. **False. Antediluvian** is ancient and has nothing to do with floods. Careful—the vocab word *diluvial,* which is very similar, is the word relating to floods.

7. **True.** To **encroach** is to infringe upon.

8. **True.** To **extrude** is to give something form by pushing it out.

9. **False.** An **oration** is a formal speech, not the ability to fly.

10. **True.** A **trajectory** is the path followed by a moving object.

Practice 3

11. An **axiom** is an old saying, and there's nothing professors like more than old sayings.

PRACTICE ANSWERS AND EXPLANATIONS *(cont'd)*

12. When blood **coagulates** it clots, which is the body's way of putting a stop to bleeding.

13. Throwing something **biodegradable** (able to be broken down by natural elements) out the window may still be considered littering in some places, so Laura had better be careful.

14. If you've ever seen contact lenses, you know what **concave** is. When measuring amounts of liquid, use the lowest point of the downward curve.

15. A **botanist** studies plants, so Anna should like biology, although dissecting frogs might not be what she bargained for.

CHAPTER 2 QUIZ

Take your time, not only with the questions, but also when reading the answer explanations that follow. Set a goal for yourself—80% (16 correct answers) is recommended—and if you don't reach that goal, go back and read through the chapter again. Good luck!

DIRECTIONS: For questions 1–10, circle T for True or F for False.
For questions 11–20, circle the synonym.

1. **T F** **soluble**—impossible to solve

2. **T F** **stratify**—to divide into layers

3. **T F** **turgid**—pretentious

4. **T F** **prototype**—typing with just two fingers

5. **T F** **recapitulate**—to give in

6. **T F** **evanescent**—short-lived

7. **T F** **inherent**—to be given something

8. **T F** **austere**—stern

9. **T F** **prominence**—unimportant

10. **T F** **aerate**—expose

11. **to explain**:	delineate	coagulate	recapitulate
12. **to assume as real**:	inherent	posit	encroach
13. **without definite form**:	amorphous	prototype	turgid
14. **added or attached**:	diffuse	adjunct	inherent
15. **to infringe**:	encroach	despotism	austere
16. **sharing a boundary**:	diffuse	coagulate	contiguous
17. **disastrous**:	calamitous	simian	amorphous
18. **to spread widely**:	diffuse	soluble	evanescent
19. **an incline**:	decline	acclivity	delineate
20. **a formal speech**:	oration	amorphous	ovation

CHAPTER 2 QUIZ ANSWERS AND EXPLANATIONS

1. **False.** **Soluble** is capable of being solved, and the opposite of impossible.

2. **True.** To **stratify** is to arrange or divide into layers.

3. **True.** **Turgid** is pretentious.

4. **False.** **Prototype** is an early or typical example and has nothing to do with typing.

5. **False.** To **recapitulate** is to review by a brief summary. This is a confusing one, because it contains the word *capitulate,* which does mean giving in. Just another example of how tricky vocab can be!

6. **True.** **Evanescent** is momentary, transient, short-lived.

7. **False.** **Inherent** is involving the essential character of something, not to be given something. Careful not to confuse **inherent** with an inheritance.

8. **True.** **Austere** is stern.

9. **False.** **Prominence** is important; to say *unimportant* would be incorrect.

10. **True.** To **aerate** is to expose to air.

11. To explain is synonymous with **delineate.** *Coagulate* is to clot, as blood does when forming a scab, and to *recapitulate* is to review.

12. To assume as real is to **posit.** *Inherent* means built-in, as in human nature, and *encroach* means to intrude.

13. **Amorphous** means to be without definite form. *Prototypes* are models or examples, so they have a definite form. *Turgid* means pompous.

14. Added and attached are both synonymous with **adjunct.** *Diffuse* means to spread out and *inherent* means built-in.

15. To infringe is to **encroach;** *despotism* (tyranny) is a noun and *austere* (severe) is an adjective.

CHAPTER 2 QUIZ ANSWERS AND EXPLANATIONS *(cont'd)*

16. **Contiguous** means sharing a boundary. *Diffuse* means to spread out and *coagulate* means to clot.

17. Disastrous is synonymous with **calamitous**. *Simian* is apelike and *amorphous* is without definite shape.

18. To **diffuse** is to spread widely, which might be confused with *soluble* (to dissolve or solve), but the two definitions are not synonyms; also, **diffuse** is a verb and *soluble* is an adjective. *Evanescent* is also an adjective, and means brief or passing.

19. An **acclivity** is an incline. *Decline* is the obvious opposite, while *delineate* (define) does not fit.

20. An **oration** is a formal speech and not an *ovation,* which is a round of applause. *Amorphous,* or without definite shape, is also incorrect.

CHAPTER 3

The Job Market

Words to know for your résumé,
interviews, and thank-you letters

BUILDING BLOCK QUIZ

By answering the 12 questions below, you will get a sense of how closely you'll have to study this chapter in order to master the vocabulary of the job market. If you choose incorrect answers for the final two questions, you'll want to go back to chapter 2 for some review.

DIRECTIONS: Fill in the blanks, using the most appropriate of the four multiple-choice answers. The correct answer will always fit into the sentence grammatically.

1. Dean Higgins was pleased when Myles chose to _____ to his request and describe the details of the fight.

   (A) ascent   (B) assent
   (C) rudeness   (D) disagree

2. Frances was _____ with her hands, so it only made sense that she was a fantastic typist.

   (A) abrupt   (B) disagree
   (C) adept   (D) polite

3. In his senior year, Chris stopped being so _____ and started answering questions in class and going to parties.

   (A) agree   (B) different
   (C) diffident   (D) callous

4. Tanner came from a(n) _____ family and could afford the best, but chose to drive an old, beat-up pickup truck.

   (A) affluent   (B) impoverished

   (C) allergic   (D) flattering

5. With three younger siblings, Jake often felt that the _____ of cooking and cleaning was unfairly placed upon him.

   (A) only   (B) onus

   (C) apelike   (D) first and foremost

6. The announcement that the music store would be closing in five minutes was _____ and so Helen decided to take her business elsewhere.

   (A) dimpled   (B) unskilled

   (C) shy   (D) brusque

7. Del couldn't believe that his _____ gambling debt was over $500.

   (A) importunate   (B) aggravate

   (C) responsible   (D) finances

8. When he started making fun of several students, the class advisor's graduation speech became quite _____ and very few people applauded when he was done.

   (A) stylish   (B) indecorous

   (C) flood-ridden   (D) aristocratic

9. Paul's _____ at the dinner table embarrassed Vicky in front of her friends, and she was sure to let him know afterward.

   (A) repay   (B) kindness

   (C) intrapersonal   (D) insolence

10. Although Mrs. Lovell's background was very _____, she actually understood the lives of her poor students well enough to be a school favorite.

    (A) burden (B) diluvial

    (C) patrician (D) happenstance

11. Mr. Perkins was disliked as he was a(n) _____ disciplinarian.

    (A) rich (B) austere

    (C) despite (D) unreturned

12. As a child Hillary had loved dinosaurs, so it only made sense that she was interested in _____ studies.

    (A) pester (B) antediluvian

    (C) double (D) despotism

BUILDING BLOCK ANSWERS AND EXPLANATIONS

1. B. To **assent** is to agree and Myles, much to Dean Higgins's relief, agreed to share the information. *Ascent* means climb, and is a trick answer. *Rudeness* and *disagree* wouldn't make sense in the context of the sentence, as they are negative words, and a positive word is required.

2. C. Frances was skilled, or **adept**, with her hands, so typing came easily to her. *Abrupt* sounds similar to **adept**, but since it means sudden, it does not fit. *Disagree* and *polite* don't sound right, nor do they fit grammatically.

3. C. Be careful—*different* may sound like **diffident**, but since it doesn't mean shy, it doesn't fit. Chris became more outgoing, so he was no longer **diffident**. He was not *callous* (insensitive) and *agree* does not work in the context of this sentence.

4. A. The word *but* establishes contrast. The best example of contrast is an **affluent** (wealthy) guy driving an old pickup truck. This automatically rules out *impoverished* as an answer. *Allergic* and *flattering* are adjectives, but they don't make sense here.

BUILDING BLOCK ANSWERS AND EXPLANATIONS *(cont'd)*

5. B. Jake had his own life to live but was helping out his family by bearing the responsibility, or **onus**, of so many chores. The other words and phrases—*only, apelike,* and *first and foremost*—are off base.

6. D. An announcement may be described as *shy* and *unskilled,* but those adjectives would apply more to the announcer than to what the announcer says. Helen, feeling either rushed or offended by this **brusque**, or abrupt, announcement, decided not to make a purchase. The fourth choice, *dimpled,* is an adjective that does not make sense in the context of the sentence.

7. A. Although it might *aggravate* Del to have gambled and lost, the blank needs to be filled with **importunate**, which means urgent. Debt like this certainly isn't *responsible* and although the subject of this sentence is *finances,* the word is a noun and doesn't fit.

8. B. To be **indecorous** is to be improper—the only way to describe the advisor's comments. They weren't *stylish,* even though he was probably trying to be cool, and they weren't *aristocratic* because wealth had nothing to do with his jokes. *Flood-ridden* isn't relevant to this dud of a speech.

9. D. Vicky wasn't angry about *kindness,* and both *repay* and *intra-personal* just don't make sense at that point in the sentence. Reading in context, only **insolence** (rudeness or disrespect) works. Paul needs to work on his manners!

10. C. A background can be **patrician** if it is snobby and upper class. Once again, contrast hints at the answer as Mrs. Lovell's poor students liked her despite her aristocratic roots. *Burden* is a noun that cannot be used to describe an upbringing. *Diluvial* relates to a flood and *happenstance* is something that happens by accident.

11. B. Mr. Perkins was an **austere**, or stern, disciplinarian, so nobody liked him. It doesn't matter whether he was *rich* and neither *despite* (careful not to confuse this with *despot!*) nor *unreturned* fits into the sentence. If you chose incorrectly for this question, you might want to go back to chapter 2 for some review.

BUILDING BLOCK ANSWERS AND EXPLANATIONS *(cont'd)*

12. B. Antediluvian makes the most sense as it is synonymous with *prehistoric*. To *pester* is to bother, *double* is two or twice, and *despotism* is tyranny—none of those work in the context of the sentence. If you chose incorrectly for this question, you might want to go back to chapter 2 for some review.

PART ONE

adept adj. (ah DEPT)—very skilled
*Lisa was so **adept** at computer programming that three different companies offered her a job.*

abeyance n. (ah BAY ens)—temporary suppression or suspension
*Michelle's evening routine was in a state of **abeyance** as she put everything on hold to wait for the phone call from the college recruiter.*

assent v. (ah SENT)—to express agreement
*Many recent college grads **assent** to low pay and benefits just to land their first job.*

auspicious v. (aw SPISH iss)—having favorable prospects, promising
*Tamika thought that the boss inviting her out to lunch was an **auspicious** start to her new job.*

bombastic adj. (bohm BAA stihk)—ostentatious and lofty in style, but ultimately meaningless
*The CEO's speeches were **bombastic** and all of Linda's coworkers told her not to take them too seriously.*

circumvent v. (suhr kuhm VEHNT)—to go around; avoid
*Laura was able to **circumvent** the hospital's rules, slipping in to see her mother after visiting hours had ended.*

commensurate adj. (cah MEN suhr eht)—proportional
*Steve was given a salary **commensurate** to his knowledge and experience.*

concord n. (KOHN koord)—agreement
*The board of directors was in **concord** that Stanley was the man to hire for the job.*

conventional adj. (kuhn VEN shun uhl)—typical, customary, commonplace
***Conventional** wisdom says that a getting good job today requires having a college education.*

digress v. (diy GREHS)—to turn aside, especially from the main point; to stray from the subject
*The company CEO tended to **digress** when trying to make a point to the employees.*

flippant adj. (flih puhnt)—marked by disrespectful lightheartedness
*Haley's **flippant** explanation for the mistake angered her supervisor, and she was immediately put on probation.*

importunate adj. (ihm pohr CHUH niht)—troublesomely urgent; extremely persistent in request or demand
*Tanya's **importunate** need for money compelled her to ask her family for help.*

incisive adj. (in SY sihv)—perceptive, penetrating
*Dr. Rhode's **incisive** analysis of the patient's chart helped him to better understand the situation.*

Practice 1

DIRECTIONS: After reading the three choices, circle the one that you think is the *antonym* of the word in bold.

1. **abeyance:**   proceed   wait   anticipate

2. **auspicious:**   promising   pessimistic   fortunate

3. **bombastic:**   modest   pretentious   ignitable

4. **circumvent:**   go around   undeviating   nonconfrontational

5. **concord:**   disagreement   peace   harmony

Your Words, Your World

Genealogy—Have you ever asked your grandparents what your mom and dad were like as kids? Have you ever asked them about the generation that immigrated to the United States? At the next family dinner, look into that **genealogy** of yours.

Flippant—We all appreciate being around funny people. Saying someone is funny can mean many things, though. There are those who like to laugh along with others, and then there are those who use humor in a less constructive way. If someone is *sarcastic*, *mocking*, or *superficial*, is she trying to make others feel better or worse? Being funny is fun for all, but being **flippant** . . . not necessarily so.

PART TWO

affectation n. (ah feck TAY shun)—pretension; false display
*When Robert came home with a Southern drawl after one month of working in Atlanta, everyone knew it was an **affectation**.*

amity n. (aah muh TEE)—friendship
*Correspondence over the years contributed to a lasting **amity** between the colleagues.*

assimilation v. (ah sim ih LAY shun)—act of blending in, becoming similar
*Language classes were offered to help new immigrants with their **assimilation** into the American culture.*

brusque adj. (bruhsk)—rough and abrupt in manner
*Vivian's **brusque** treatment of the bank customers quickly cost her the position of teller.*

callous adj. (CAHL us)—thick-skinned, insensitive
*Bud's **callous** personality allowed him to not only survive, but to thrive in the high-pressure office.*

chagrin n. (shuh GRIN)—shame, embarrassment, humiliation
*With much **chagrin**, Lenny told his parents that he hadn't been hired for the job.*

civility n. (sih VILL ih tee)—courtesy, politeness
*The new train conductor treated the commuters with such **civility** that he quickly became their favorite.*

ingratiate v. (ihn GRAY shee ayt)—to gain favor with another by deliberate effort, to seek to please somebody so as to gain an advantage
*Helen **ingratiated** herself with her fellow interns by volunteering for some of the less-desirable tasks.*

levity n. (LEH vih tee)—an inappropriate lack of seriousness, overly casual
*Trey's joke added needed **levity** to the otherwise serious meeting.*

objective adj. (ob JEHK tihv)—impartial, uninfluenced by emotion
*Hector knew he had to try and be **objective** when his daughter asked whether or not she should go away to college.*

onus n. (OH nuhs)—a burden, an obligation
*Antonia was beginning to hate the **onus** of having to answer the phone for her boss at work.*

MEMORY TIP

When you and your family or group of friends is dealing with a problem, just think: "The **onus** is *on us.*" An **onus** is a *burden* and burdens should be shared.

---

panegyric n. (paan uh JEER ihk)—elaborate praise; formal hymn of praise
*The director's **panegyric** letter to the donor kept the charitable donations coming.*

persistence n. (puhr SIS tuns)—the act, state, or quality of not giving up
*Jamie's **persistence** at getting the petition signed impressed everyone on the team.*

pertinent adj. (PUHR tih nent)—applicable, appropriate
*Greg felt his complaints were **pertinent** and did not hesitate to mention them at his first staff meeting.*

Practice 2

DIRECTIONS: Consider the two word choices in the parentheses, and circle the one that best fits in the context of the sentence.

6. A parent phoned the school to complain that Mr. Kroenig was too (**callous** OR **prominent**) in his written feedback on student essays.

7. With the hopes of creating an atmosphere of politeness, Mrs. Young's students voted to make (**concave** OR **civility**) the class theme for the year.

8. Nobody took Frankie's music reviews seriously because she always wrote (**panegyric** OR **affluent**) articles that never contained a harsh word.

9. Marny won the Coach's Award because of her (**persistence** OR **amity**) in recovering from knee surgery and returning to the basketball court.

10. Greg tended to be too wordy and Miss Dickens reminded him to just include the (**pertinent** OR **onus**) information in his research paper.

Your Words, Your World

Affectation—To have an **affectation** is to have a *quirk* or *mannerism*. Picture a soap opera actress who uses her hands dramatically when she speaks. This is an **affectation**. Although **affectation** is a noun, it is synonymous with *posing* (and is usually used in a critical manner). Posing in a pretentious way is not a new thing. The word **affectation** has its roots in the Latin *affectatio*.

Brusque—Derived from the British *broosk* and the Italian *brusco*, **brusque** is to be *rude*; to be *curt* or *short* with someone. Have you ever been handled *briskly* by someone? You wanted a job and the manager pushed you out of the door after a 30-second interview? If you can remember a time when someone was abrupt and brushed you off, then you know what it means to be **brusque**.

Chagrin—Do your cheeks turn red when you feel embarrassed? Do you drop your gaze to the floor? Shuffle your feet? Dig your hands down deep into your pockets? Picture just one of these things and you will remember what it means to feel the *mortification* that is **chagrin**.

Levity—The Latin *levitas* means light, a physical state used today to describe the way some people can keep a situation from becoming too serious. As a matter of fact, to *levitate* is to raise something up. By bringing **levity** to a situation, you are raising it from something plain—or worse, uncomfortable or confrontational—to something *enjoyable*.

PART THREE

conformity n. (kon FORM ih tee)—similarity in form or character
*Bruce made it his business to act in **conformity** with the rules and traditions of the law firm.*

disheveled adj. (di SHEHV uld)—marked by disorder, untidy
*The employment counselor suggested Bruce do something about his **disheveled** appearance before the interview.*

emulate v. (EHM yoo layt)—to strive to equal or excel, to imitate
*For better and for worse, eager employees often **emulate** their superiors.*

feign v. (fayn)—to pretend, to give a false appearance of
*James **feigned** enjoyment during the golf outing, to give his boss a good impression.*

gauche adj. (gohsh)—lacking social refinement
*When Eddie snapped his fingers for the waiter, Mr. Swanson quickly told him to stop acting so **gauche**.*

indecorous adj. (in DEHK uh rus)—improper, lacking good taste
*Gloria was shocked at the **indecorous** behavior at the company holiday party.*

indiscretion n. (in dis KRESH un)—lack of prudence, mistake
*Jerry's **indiscretion** at the convention cost his company the new account.*

insolence n. (IN su lehns)—rudeness, impertinence
*Mark's boss refused to promote him because his **insolence** was so insulting.*

opportune adj. (ah puhr TOON)—appropriate, fitting
*Her investment in microchips, just before the technological revolution of the 1990s, was **opportune**.*

patrician adj. (puh TRIH shuhn)—aristocratic
*Though she really couldn't afford an expensive lifestyle, Cleo had **patrician** tastes.*

plebian adj. (plee BEE uhn)—crude or coarse; characteristic of commoners
*Although Anders & Co was a top-notch accounting firm, its office parties were often **plebeian** to the point that security had to be called.*

prepossessing adj. (pree puh ZEH sing)—attractive, engaging
*Terry's **prepossessing** appearance made him the most eligible bachelor in the office.*

propriety n. (pro PRIY ih tee)—correct behavior; appropriateness
*At the company lunch, **propriety** demanded that the employees all wait for the CEO to taste his soup first.*

provincial adj. (pruh VIHN shuhl)—limited in outlook, narrow, unsophisticated
*Having grown up in the city, Anita had to adjust to the **provincial** attitudes of her country cousins.*

requite v. (rih KWIYT)—to return or repay
*Ben knew that Melinda had forwarded the email with his inappropriate joke to personnel and planned to **requite** her backstabbing ways.*

sybarite n. (SIH buh riyt)—a person devoted to pleasure and luxury
*A confirmed **sybarite**, Judge Noonan only held court two days a week; the other days he played golf or went sailing.*

versatile adj. (vuhr suh TIYL)—adaptable, all-purpose
*By being **versatile** around the office, Lila hoped never to lose her job.*

Practice 3

DIRECTIONS: Fill in the blanks, using five of the ten words provided below.

conformity	feign	gauche	indiscretion
patrician	opportune	versatility	provincial
emulate	plebian		

11. Despite his uncle's generous job offer, Vincent just couldn't _____ interest in a mortuary career.

12. The private school demanded _____ in its teachers, so Wally decided to accept the job teaching in the city where he had more freedom to be original.

13. Grace proved her _____ by making well-received changes to the newsletter's layout, writing, and photography.

14. Carla would have gone to the party with Bo, but his suggestion of renting a horse-drawn carriage to get there was way too _____ for her.

15. No one in Larry's family minded when he decided to _____ Bill Gates's love of computer programming.

Your Words, Your World

Gauche—Nobody wants to eat with a **gauche** dinner guest. Would you invite somebody **gauche** out to dinner or to your house for dinner? What would you do if you were on a blind date and your date turned out to be *vulgar* and *rude*? To further cement this image in your mind, think of the most **gauche** person you know. And the next time you see this *tasteless* person, remember to thank him or her for helping you remember a word.

Indecorous—*Impolite*? *Rude*? *Inappropriate*? Nobody likes these characteristics in a date or customer, but oftentimes, these traits make for the most memorable characters. Who is your favorite *rude* dude? How about an *impolite* woman? Think about books you've read and some of the movies and TV shows you've watched.

PRACTICE ANSWERS AND EXPLANATIONS

Practice 1

1. **Abeyance** means suspension or postponement, both opposites of *proceed*. *Wait* and *anticipate* are virtually synonymous with one another, as well as with **abeyance**.

2. **Auspicious** means *promising* or having favorable prospects. Therefore, its opposite is *pessimistic,* which means having a negative outlook. *Fortunate* is another positive word that is similar to **auspicious**.

3. **Bombastic** means *pretentious,* which is the opposite of *modest,* which means shy or diffident. If something is *ignitable* it is flammable, which is unrelated to **bombastic**.

4. To **circumvent** is to *go around,* which is the opposite of being *undeviating* (not departing from one's course). If someone is *nonconfrontational,* he or she also might **circumvent** a situation to get out of it.

5. If two things are in **concord**, they are in *harmony,* which is also similar to *peace.* The opposite of peace and harmony is *disagreement.*

Practice 2

6. Nobody wants to be criticized, and if a teacher is **callous** (heartless and abrupt), the student will not feel very good about his or her work, let alone that teacher. *Prominent* means famous and does not apply to Mr. Kroenig's feedback.

7. *Concave* is curved inward while **civility** is a form of being polite and fair. So **civility** it is for Mrs. Young's class!

8. Apparently, Frankie was a fan of music, but not of being objective. Her **panegyric**, or elaborate praise, did little to inform her readers, thus she was losing those readers.

9. Marny didn't get herself back on the basketball court through friendship and peace—*amity* just doesn't fit. No, it was through hard work, through sweat and tears, through **persistence**, that she was able to recover from knee surgery and win the Coach's Award.

10. Greg needed to know what was important and relevant to the topic of his paper. He needed to just write about the **pertinent** information. This may have been his burden, or his *onus,* as he sat down to write, but the answer is clearly **pertinent**.

Practice 3

11. To **feign** is to pretend and Vincent just couldn't put on a show for his uncle.

12. **Conformity** means to follow a preestablished pattern; to stick to the norm. If Wally saw teaching as an art, he probably wanted to make sure he could use his own style and not have to follow some sort of code of **conformity**.

13. Way to go, Grace! Being able to edit writing, layout, and photography: now that's **versatility**!

14. If Bo was hoping to impress Carla with his money he failed. To be **patrician** is to be aristocratic and it sounds like Carla just wasn't into that.

15. To **emulate** is to imitate, and Larry's family must have hoped that he would emulate Bill Gates's earnings, as well.

CHAPTER 3 QUIZ

Take your time, not only with the questions, but when reading the answer explanations that follow. Set a goal for yourself—80% (16 correct answers) is recommended—and if you don't reach that goal, go back and read through the chapter again. Good luck!

DIRECTIONS: For questions 1–10, circle T for True or F for False. For questions 11–20, circle the synonym.

1. **T F** **adept**—unskilled

2. **T F** **digress**—to deviate from the point

3. **T F** **incisive**—perceptive

4. **T F** **callous**—thick-skinned

5. **T F** **ingratiate**—to offend on purpose

6. **T F** **persistence**—refusing to give up

7. **T F** **provincial**—limited in outlook; unsophisticated

8. **T F** **affectation**—a pretentious habit

9. **T F** **conventional**—atypical

10. **T F** **levity**—a lack of seriousness

11. **indiscretion**:	careless	discrete	introverted
12. **onus**:	burden	desirable	undesirable
13. **versatile**:	unchanged	adaptable	high quality
14. **objective**:	solid	partial	impartial
15. **prepossessing**:	unattractive	ownership	attractive
16. **commensurate**:	commiserate	proportional	promise
17. **flippant**:	respectful	acrobatic	lighthearted
18. **amity**:	friendship	conformity	bombastic
19. **emulate**:	criticize	divert	imitate
20. **propriety**:	polite behavior	impolite behavior	real estate

CHAPTER 3 QUIZ ANSWERS AND EXPLANATIONS

1. **False.** **Adept** means skilled, not unskilled.

2. **True.** To **digress** is to deviate from the point.

3. **True.** To be **incisive** is to be perceptive.

4. **True.** **Callous** is thick-skinned.

5. **False.** To **ingratiate** is to please so it is not to offend, and certainly not to offend on purpose.

6. **True.** When someone has **persistence**, he or she refuses to give up.

7. **True.** **Provincial** is unsophisticated and limited in outlook and perspective.

8. **True.** An **affectation** is a pretentious habit.

9. **False.** **Conventional** is the opposite of atypical, as it means usual and predictable.

10. **True.** **Levity** is a lack of seriousness.

11. **Indiscretion** is *careless,* and the opposite of *discrete.* Introverts are rarely indiscrete.

12. An **onus** is a *burden* or responsibility and neither *desirable* nor *undesirable.*

13. **Versatile** is *adaptable* and has nothing to do with *high quality. Unchanged* is an antonym.

14. **Objective** is *impartial* and not *partial.* The final choice, *solid,* is irrelevant.

15. **Prepossessing** is *attractive. Ownership* of something may be attractive, but it isn't an acceptable definition, nor is *unattractive.*

16. **Commensurate** is *proportional* and although *promise* sounds similar to *proportional,* and *commiserate* (to express pity for) sounds similar to **commensurate**, neither choice is correct.

CHAPTER 3 QUIZ ANSWERS AND EXPLANATIONS *(cont'd)*

17. To be **flippant** is to be disrespectfully *lighthearted,* so *respectful* is an antonym. And don't be fooled by the choice of *acrobatic* (flexible), as it is a distracter based on the flip in **flippant**.

18. **Amity** is a positive word meaning *friendship. Bombastic* (pompous) is a negative word and *conformity* (sticking to the norm) is irrelevant.

19. **Emulate** is the highest form of flattery, as it is to *imitate.* To *criticize* is the opposite and to *divert* is to redirect, which is unrelated.

20. **Propriety** means decorum, or *polite behavior.* Impropriety is *impolite behavior,* so it qualifies as an antonym, while *real estate* is a distracter based on the word *property.*

CHAPTER 4

Business Headlines

*Words for your banker, broker, and even
the bully who wants your lunch money*

BUILDING BLOCK QUIZ

By answering the 12 questions below, you will get a sense of how closely you'll have to study this chapter in order to master the vocabulary you'll find in the professional world, in business classes, and when reading the financial pages. If you choose incorrect answers for the final two questions, you'll want to go back to chapter 3 for some review.

DIRECTIONS: After reading the four choices, circle the one that you think most accurately defines the word.

1. Quentin tended to _____ when he told stories, but no one minded the exaggeration as his wild tales were so funny.

   (A) antagonize   (B) denigrate

   (C) aggrandize   (D) aggravate

2. When Sal _____ the book club funds to pay for the homecoming dance band, the librarian was not happy.

   (A) appropriated   (B) described

   (C) defended   (D) improper

3. By not telling anyone about the kids breaking into the vending machine, Jackson was also _____ of the crime.

   (A) concave   (B) culpable

   (C) interested   (D) innocent

4. Reading Theresa's report card, Mr. and Mrs. Hammill were pleased to see several references to how _____ their daughter was.

   (A) retired   (B) indolent

   (C) industrious   (D) conflagration

5. During the holidays, the Future Business Leaders of America club collected canned goods for the _____.

   (A) penurious   (B) legible

   (C) controlled   (D) prosperous

6. The CEO of a local bank came to speak to the class, but everyone quickly lost interest in what the _____ man had to say.

   (A) turgid   (B) diluvial

   (C) aggrandize   (D) algorithms

7. In receiving over $30,000 in scholarship money, Talia finally _____ the rewards of all her hard work.

   (A) dispersed   (B) reaped

   (C) contested   (D) bereaved

8. Working summers at the bank, Leroy used to _____ every little detail, hoping to one day open a bank of his own.

   (A) cleanse   (B) produce

   (C) potable   (D) scrutinize

9. Although Paulo was voted Most _____ in the high school yearbook, he went on to be an honest insurance salesman and chairman of the city's Ethics in Business Committee.

   (A) Fast   (B) Slow

   (C) Wily   (D) Banal

10. Although Jennell could not _____ her sister's athletic successes, she excelled in the classroom and received an academic scholarship.

    (A) replicate   (B) create

    (C) renegotiate   (D) adjudicate

11. To impress women, Tomas often _____ having thousands of shares of Google stock.

    (A) fixed   (B) feigned

    (C) permanent   (D) fainted

12. Since childhood, Gretchen had wanted to live in a(n) _____ neighborhood with huge lawns and swimming pools.

    (A) forgetful   (B) reverence

    (C) remembrance   (D) affluent

BUILDING BLOCK ANSWERS AND EXPLANATIONS

1. C. To **aggrandize** is to exaggerate and although one may **aggrandize** while *antagonizing* (provoking) or *denigrating* (belittling) another person, those answers are not synonymous. *Aggravate* means to bother. It sounds like **aggrandize** and rhymes with exaggerate, but has nothing to do with the answer (even if those who exaggerate do aggravate you!).

2. A. **Appropriated** is to have allocated or distributed. Sal took every last penny from the book club and spent it on the homecoming dance band. He did not *describe* anything and he did not *defend* anything. And although his actions were *improper* in the eyes of the librarian, this adjective does not work here, where a verb is needed.

3. B. **Culpable** is guilty, so *innocent* is an antonym and *interested* is an unrelated word. *Concave* means curved inward, so it has nothing to do with being guilty (or with stealing snacks!).

BUILDING BLOCK ANSWERS AND EXPLANATIONS *(cont'd)*

4. C. Industrious is productive and hardworking, and although *retired* people can certainly be **industrious**, productive is the best choice for what Theresa's parents would read on her report card. To be *indolent* is to be lazy, thus an antonym of **industrious**. A *conflagration* is a destructive fire and completely unrelated.

5. A. Penurious means poor. *Legible* and *controlled* are irrelevant. *Prosperous* may sound a little like **penurious**, but it actually means the opposite: well-off.

6. A. Turgid is synonymous with pretentious, pompous, and affected. *Diluvial* has to do with flood debris, and to *aggrandize* is to exaggerate (which may or may not be a trait of the **turgid**, but is a verb, so does not fit as a possible answer). *Algorithms* have to do with math and the word does not fit in with the rest of the sentence. (If you got this one wrong, you might want to return to chapter 2 for some review.)

7. B. To **reap** is to collect. *Contested* means competed and *dispersed* means distributed, so both are unrelated. The *bereaved* are in mourning, which has nothing to do with **reap** . . . unless you want to stretch and make a connection to the Grim Reaper.

8. D. To **scrutinize** is to examine very closely, so Leroy carefully studied every detail that summer so as to learn how banking works. He may have even *cleansed* the bank in hopes of getting ahead, but the definition just doesn't fit here. The same can be said of *produce*, as he certainly didn't produce every detail of the bank. *Potable* is out of the question, as it is an adjective that describes drinkable water.

9. C. Wily is cunning, and neither *fast*, *slow*, nor *banal* (commonplace) work in the context of the sentence, especially given the contrast of Paulo's subsequent accomplishments.

10. A. To **replicate** is to duplicate. *Adjudicate* (to settle a dispute) and *renegotiate* (to revise) are verbs that might sound like possibilities, but their definitions rule them out. *Create* means to make something original, and is almost an antonym of **replicate**, so it does not work, either.

BUILDING BLOCK ANSWERS AND EXPLANATIONS *(cont'd)*

11. B. Feigned means lied or pretended. *Fixed* would mean he had repaired, and *fainted* would mean he had passed out, so both of those are incorrect. *Permanent* is an adjective that does not fit in the context of the sentence, either. If you answered this question incorrectly, you might want to go back to chapter 3 for some review.

12. D. To be **affluent** is to be wealthy and can describe people and places. None of the other answers, from *forgetful* (absentminded) to *reverence* (respect and admiration) to *remembrance* (commemoration), describes a neighborhood someone would want to live in. If you answered this question incorrectly, you might want to go back to chapter 3 for some review.

PART ONE

accrue v. (ah CROO)—to accumulate, grow by addition
*Timmy's aunt gave him a savings bond that would **accrue** in a bank account over the years to help pay for college.*

aggrandize v. (ah gran DIYZ)—to make larger than what really is; to exaggerate
*The parents were extremely upset to learn that the principal had **aggrandized** the test scores to make the school look good.*

> **MEMORY TIP**
>
> You will find the word *grand* right smack in the middle of **aggrandize**. And to **aggrandize** is to *exaggerate* or make seem bigger and better than is really the case. When trying to remember what **aggrandize** means, look to the word in the middle.

ancillary adj. (ayn sil AHR ee)—accessory; subordinate; helping
*Absorbing the bottling business as an **ancillary** was part of a larger plan for the young cola company.*

appropriate v. (uh PROH pree ayt)—to assign to a particular purpose, allocate
*As class treasurer, Clark suggested they **appropriate** $2,000 for the school's library and spend less on the trip.*

arrears n. (uh REERZ)—unpaid, overdue debts or bills; neglected obligations
*After the expensive lawsuit, Dominic's accounts were in **arrears**.*

beget v. (bee GEHT)—to produce, especially as an effect or outgrowth; to bring about
*Principal Browning was sure that his charitable acts would **beget** charitable acts by the students.*

bilk v. (bihlk)—to cheat, defraud
*Though the lawyer seemed honest, Enrique feared he would try to **bilk** him out of all his money.*

cache n. (kaash)—a hiding place; stockpile
*Everyone believed that the assistant principal had a **cache** of leftover class funds hidden in a Swiss bank account.*

clientele n. (kly ehn TEL)—body of customers or patrons
*The Chili Dog was proud to count the high school students among its **clientele**.*

cohesion n. (ko HEE zhun)—act or state of sticking together; close union
*Charlie felt a sense of of **cohesion** as he and his sister begged for a family vacation to Disney World.*

collaborator n. (koh lahb ehr AY tohr)—someone who helps on a task
*Lucy had no qualms about working with a **collaborator**, just so long as the project was finished on time.*

compensate v. (kohm pehn SAYT)—to repay or reimburse
*The moving company **compensated** Tom for the furniture it had broken.*

cull v. (kuhl)—to select, weed out
*As the Future Business Leaders considered student proposals, they used errors in spelling and grammar to **cull** the pile of paperwork to a more manageable size.*

culpable adj. (KUHL puh bull)—guilty, responsible for wrong
*The class treasurer was found **culpable** in the scheme to steal from the prom funds.*

deficit n. (DEH fih sit)—shortfall, debit, disadvantage
*With the nation nursing a staggering **deficit**, the Philanthropy Club had a hard time choosing a charity to support.*

Practice 1

DIRECTIONS: Consider the definition and then circle T for True or F for False.

1. **T F**   **ancillary**—an accessory

2. **T F**   **bilk**—to cheat

3. **T F**   **cache**—a collection of goods that is valueless

4. **T F**   **cull**—to distribute

5. **T F**   **culpable**—to be upset

Your Words, Your World

Accrue—What's more fun, **accruing** money from each paycheck so you can get that car you want, or taking on a second job to pay off credit card debt? To **accrue** is to *amass*, *increase*, *accumulate*, and *grow*.

Appropriate—*Budgeting* is a skill beyond compare. To be able to *allocate* money in the right way is one of life's challenges. When you get your hands on some money, do you spend it right away or do you **appropriate** it for bills or for big purchases somewhere down the road?

Beget—Will you **beget** positive changes in your life or negative changes? Breaking bad habits is one of the hardest things to do, but the second you start, you will *produce*, *cause*, and *bring about* positive results. Just to become aware of your spending habits is a step in the effort to **beget** financial stability.

Compensate—Just as you are **compensated** for whatever work you do, all of the folks you do business with expect to be *paid* for their goods and services. Have you appropriated enough money to *cover* your expenses? Have you accrued enough cash for both bills and fun? When answering these questions for yourself, don't aggrandize!

PART TWO

disclose v. (dihs CLOHZ)—to make known, expose to view
The journalist was kept in jail for four hours because she would not disclose the source of her article.

discourse n. (DIHS kohrs)—verbal exchange, conversation
Mr. Hemmings knew that he might convince Colby to apply to college if they engaged in a calm discourse, one-on-one.

discretion n. (dihs KREH shin)—ability to judge on one's own
Sales at Starburst coffeehouses quickly grew, aided in part by the fact that store managers could choose the day's special at their own discretion.

divulge v. (diy VULJ)—to make known
Pat was fired for divulging the company's secrets to its competitor.

industrious adj. (ihn DUHS tree uhs)—hardworking, diligent
Growing up with an industrious father, Ron couldn't help but have a good work ethic.

liability n. (liy uh BIHL uh tee)—handicap, something holding one back
When Team Blue complained that Darren was a liability, Mrs. Sweetney subtracted a point, reminding them that good teammates are never critical of one another.

patronize v. (PAY truh niyz)—to adopt an air of condescension toward; to buy from.
Mrs. Berger patronized the honors students with smiley-face stickers and pats on the head.

peculate v. (PEHK yoo layt)—to embezzle
No one in the front office could believe it when the superintendent was accused of peculating transportation funds so that he could pad his retirement fund.

pecuniary adj. (pih KYOO nee ehr ee)—relating to money
As an economics teacher, Ms. Jackson hoped her students would make wise pecuniary decisions for the rest of their lives.

penurious adj. (puh NOOR ee us)—poverty-stricken; destitute
*The **penurious** people in Scrooge's neighborhood could not believe his Christmas spirit.*

pragmatic adj. (prag MAH tihk)—practical; moved by facts rather than abstract ideals
*Because he prided himself on his **pragmatic** ways of thinking, Paul chose not to take the philosophy class with his friends.*

prohibitive adj. (proh HIHB ih tiv)—excessive; too expensive
*Gutierrez fought for lower prices on produce nationwide, saying that the cost was **prohibitive** to the impoverished and a contributor to their poor health.*

propel v. (proh PEHL)—to cause to move forward
*Mr. Sanders promised the board that the research and development would **propel** the company into the next century.*

prophetic adj. (proh FEH tik)—foretelling events by divine means
*The secretary's early warnings proved **prophetic**, as the security guard was fired for using school computers to shop online.*

Practice 2

DIRECTIONS: Read the three choices and then circle the *antonym*.

6.	**discourse:**	discussion	study	uncommunicative
7.	**inauspicious:**	poor	favorable	infamous
8.	**pecuniary:**	barter	financial	stingy
9.	**penurious:**	wealthy	poor	middle class
10.	**prohibitive:**	disallowed	affordable	restricting

Your Words, Your World

Divulge—In **divulge** we find the Latin *divulgare, di* meaning apart and *vulgare* meaning to make public. Imagine, if you will, a large crowd of people standing before a stage with a podium. And guess who is standing behind the podium? That's right: you. And you're about to **divulge** something very important. Something very secretive. Your hand reaches for the microphone and . . . what do you say?

Peculate—Remember those handcuffs? Well, you can picture them once more, but this time they don't represent a responsibility. You really have been arrested. Everybody told you not to embezzle that money. But you did. You **peculated** other people's life savings, so now you must pay; pay back the money and pay your debt to society.

PART THREE

proximity n. (prok SIM ih tee)—nearness
*Shovanda worked in close **proximity** to her crush, Dan, at her after-school job at Pizza World.*

proxy n. (PRAHK see)—a person authorized to act for someone else
*Janet acted as **proxy** for Diana at the debate when Diana lost her voice.*

quid pro quo n. (kwid proh KWOH)—something done or given in return for another thing
*After working four Saturdays in a row, Kyle reminded Bob of their **quid pro quo** agreement and moved into the corner office.*

reap v. (reep)—to obtain a return, often a harvest
*While the grasshopper starved in the winter, the ant **reaped** the benefits of his hard labor.*

remiss adj. (ree MIS)—negligent or careless about a job
*After reviewing the class checkbook, Mrs. Edgars informed Jon that he had been **remiss** as class treasurer and should resign.*

remuneration n. (rih MYOO nuh ray shuhn)—payment for goods or services or to recompense for losses
*Oliver expected **remuneration** for his business travel expenses and was surprised when his boss returned his receipts and said no.*

replicate v. (REP lih kayt)—to duplicate, repeat
*Wendy knew that, in order to **replicate** the grades she earned in the second quarter, she'd have to get at least a 90 percent on the test.*

requisition v. (re kwi ZIH shun)—to demand the use of
*Monty **requisitioned** access to the executive bathroom and was pleased when the boss personally handed him a key.*

retroactive adj. (reh troh AHK tiv)—applying to an earlier time
*Mrs. Linden announced that all of the high school kids who stayed on at the restaurant would receive raises **retroactive** to their date of hiring.*

scapegoat n. (SKAYP goht)—someone blamed for every problem
*Devon always told his mother that he was the teacher's **scapegoat**, but she knew better.*

scrutinize v. (SKROOH tihn iyz)—to observe carefully
*Outside consultants were hired to **scrutinize** the company's finances, but doubled the company's debt with their expensive billing.*

status quo n. (stah tus KWOH)—the state of affairs at a particular, usually current, time
*The **status quo** was good enough for Nancy, so she never pushed for a raise—and, outside of cost-of-living increases, never got one.*

> **MEMORY TIP**
>
> **Status quo** is a Latin phrase that is used in the business world but also as a common phrase. It means "state in which" or, more specifically, "the state of affairs at the current time."

subterfuge n. (SUB ter fyooj)—deceptive strategy
*Everyone knew that Zana had climbed the company ladder by use of **subterfuge**, but nobody was ever able to prove it.*

toady n. (TOH dee)—one who flatters in the hope of gaining favors
*Whenever Ray was being a **toady** with Ms. Hollingsworth, somebody in class would say, "Ribbit! Ribbit!"*

usury n. (YOO zuh ree)—the practice of lending money at exorbitant rates
*Wesley was accused of **usury** when the customer discovered that he was charging 40 percent interest to cash a check.*

wily adj. (WIY lee)—clever; deceptive
*Susan was **wily**, but couldn't get out of doing her day of community service, a requirement of every student in Mr. Mayall's class.*

Practice 3

DIRECTIONS: Consider the two word choices in the parentheses, and circle the one that best fits in the context of the sentence.

11. Max wouldn't take cash from his neighbor; instead he preferred a barter system that was (**quid pro quo** OR **status quo**).

12. The first thing Bernice learned in her ethics class at business school was that corporate (**subterfuge** OR **proximity**) is unacceptable.

13. The English professor reminded her students to (**subterfuge** OR **scrutinize**) their bibliographies so as to ensure that all sources were cited.

14. Will had learned from experience that sports-betting bookies practiced (**usury** OR **wily**).

15. It was no surprise to learn that Ernie was a (**wily** OR **scapegoat**) businessman, as he had always made money selling baseball cards and Blow-Pops on the playground when no teachers were looking.

Your Words, Your World

Requisition—How did you come to own this book? Was it a gift? Or did you **requisition** it, demanding that a parent, aunt, uncle, or grandparent purchase it for you? Did you use a guilt trip to get this book? What form of **requisition** do you use most often?

Retroactive—Have you ever received **retroactive** remuneration for a job done in the past? Have you ever requisitioned funds, **retroactive** to a previous time? **Retro** means *prior to* or back in the *past* while **active** actually means *applied to*. Think of something you did a few weeks ago. If it was around the house, you might want to bring this back up again when you want something (like the car for the night). If you did this chore or favor for a friend or coworker, you might want to remind him or her before asking a favor of your own.

PRACTICE ANSWERS AND EXPLANATIONS

Practice 1

1. **True.** Something **ancillary** is an accessory.

2. **True.** To **bilk** is to cheat.

3. **False.** A **cache** is a stockpile, usually of something valuable.

4. **False.** To **cull** is to select, a near-antonym of distribute.

5. **False.** To be **culpable** is to be guilty.

Practice 2

6. **Discourse** is a form of communication, so *uncommunicative* is a perfect antonym. *Discussion* is a synonym and *study* is unrelated.

7. **Inauspicious** indicates unfavorable or *poor* conditions, so *favorable* is the antonym. *Infamous* contains the same root, but means having a bad reputation.

8. Anything **pecuniary** relates to money, while to *barter* is to trade goods, making it the antonym. *Financial* also relates to money, and *stingy* is synonymous with cheap.

9. **Penurious** is to be *poor*, so *wealthy* is the best antonym. *Middle class* is very different from *poor*, but *wealthy* is at the exact opposite end of the spectrum.

10. **Prohibitive** is to be too expensive, so *affordable* is the antonym. *Restricting* and *disallowed* are both negative words similar to **prohibitive**.

Practice 3

11. **Quid pro quo** is the best choice, as it means "something for something." *Status quo* indicates the state of current affairs, so doesn't fit.

12. Deceptive ploys fall into the **subterfuge** category, and the students were being warned about the negatives of being deceptive. No need to teach about *proximity*, or closeness.

PRACTICE ANSWERS AND EXPLANATIONS *(cont'd)*

13. *Subterfuge* just doesn't fit in the context of this sentence. The professor is giving a warning about plagiarism and wants to make sure that every detail is **scrutinized**—examined and reexamined—in particular, the list of the books, articles, and websites that the students used in putting together their papers.

14. Usury is a situation in which those in debt find themselves paying an extremely high interest rate. Although someone who practices **usury** might be cunning, *wily* is an adjective that does not work in the context of the sentence.

15. Ernie was **wily**—he was so cunning that he always got away with business practices that border on the illegal. There is no *scapegoat*, or someone being falsely blamed, here.

CHAPTER 4 QUIZ

Take your time, not only with the questions, but in reading the answer explanations that follow. Set a goal for yourself—80% (16 correct answers) is recommended—and if you don't reach that goal, go back and read through the chapter again. Good luck!

DIRECTIONS: For questions 1–10, circle T for True or F for False. For questions 11–20, circle the synonym.

1. **T F**   **retroactive**—back to an earlier time

2. **T F**   **usury**—using someone as a consultant

3. **T F**   **subterfuge**—under the surface

4. **T F**   **remiss**—doing a job carelessly

5. **T F**   **prophetic**—psychic and visionary

6. **T F**   **pragmatic**—practical

7. **T F**   **discourse**—verbal exchange

8. **T F**   **status quo**—the usual

9. **T F**   **industrious**—easygoing

10. **T F**   **proxy**—an authorized representative

11. **a helper:**	clientele	collaborator	culpable
12. **overdue debts:**	arrears	accrue	bilk
13. **to accumulate:**	cull	usury	accrue
14. **to exaggerate:**	cache	culpable	aggrandize
15. **patrons:**	collaborators	liabilities	clientele
16. **a responsibility:**	accrue	usury	liability
17. **additional:**	ancillary	inaccessible	summary
18. **reveal:**	conceal	divulge	unknown
19. **flatterer:**	critic	froggy	toady
20. **deceptive:**	prophetic	candid	wily

CHAPTER 4 QUIZ ANSWERS AND EXPLANATIONS

1. **True.** **Retroactive** refers back to an earlier time.

2. **False.** **Usury** is actually lending money at an extremely high rate, not the hiring of a consultant.

3. **False.** **Subterfuge** can be thought of as a deception that is "under the surface," but that definition is not close enough for the answer to be true. **Subterfuge** is a noun.

4. **True.** **Remiss** is, indeed, doing a job carelessly. Do not be **remiss** in your vocabulary work!

5. **True.** To be **prophetic** is to anticipate the future; it is to be visionary and psychic.

6. **True.** To be **pragmatic** is to be practical.

7. **True.** **Discourse** is discussion, dialogue, verbal exchange—all of the above.

8. **True.** The **status quo** is the state in which things usually are. It is normal.

9. **False.** To be **industrious** is to be very productive, not to be easy-going.

10. **True.** A **proxy** is an authorized representative, often named in legal or medical situations.

11. A helper is a **collaborator**. *Clientele* receive the help, and *culpable* means guilty.

12. Overdue debts are **arrears**. To *bilk* is to cheat and to *accrue* is to gather.

13. To accumulate is to **accrue**. *Usury* is the practice of loaning money at an extremely high rate of interest. To *cull* means to select.

14. To exaggerate is to **aggrandize**. To be *culpable* is to be guilty, while a *cache* is a hiding place of sorts. Neither fits the definition.

CHAPTER 4 QUIZ ANSWERS AND EXPLANATIONS *(cont'd)*

15. Patrons are a business's **clientele**. They can be *liabilities* and they may even be *collaborators*, but to be a patron is to be among the **clientele**.

16. A responsibility is a **liability**. *Usury* and *accrue* do not fit, grammatically or in terms of meaning.

17. An **ancillary** is a supplementary (additional) thing, most often an added-on document. *Inaccessible* (unable to get through) and *summary* (a review) are unrelated.

18. To **divulge** is to reveal. *Conceal* (hide) and *unknown* are virtual antonyms.

19. A **toady** is a flatterer. A *critic* is the opposite, while *froggy* is a silly answer.

20. To be **wily** is to be deceptive. To be *candid* is to be honest, which is almost an antonym. To be *prophetic* is to be a visionary.

CHAPTER 5

Political Headlines

*Words most likely heard on the news
regarding politics and world events*

BUILDING BLOCK QUIZ

By answering the 12 questions below, you will get a sense of how closely you'll have to study this chapter in order to master the vocabulary of politics.

DIRECTIONS: Fill in the blanks, using the most appropriate of the four multiple-choice answers. The correct answer will always fit into the sentence grammatically.

1. When Billy tried to _____ the remote control, his sister reminded him that she'd let him watch football the day before.

    (A) arrogate   (B) accede

    (C) autonomous   (D) vacillate

2. The senator was the perfect choice to delay the passing of the tax bill since his _____ usually lasted for hours on end.

    (A) abdicates   (B) arrogates

    (C) filibusters   (D) harangues

3. Margaret's favorite part of social studies was learning about the U.S. Constitution and her _____ rights.

    (A) inviolable   (B) discord

    (C) intransigent   (D) oligarchy

4. What Troy hated most about being student body president was feeling compelled to _____ between concentrating on student concerns and the concerns of the principal.

   (A) arrogate   (B) accede

   (C) abeyance   (D) vacillate

5. The press conference was a total _____: the air-conditioning blew warm air, the lights flickered off twice, and the microphones did not work.

   (A) pandemic   (B) dogmatic

   (C) debacle   (D) austere

6. As a freshman, Joan had been such a(n) _____ class president, refusing to change her stance on many issues, that the staff was shocked to learn she'd been reelected.

   (A) oligarchy   (B) inviolable

   (C) stratify   (D) intransigent

7. No one thought that a(n) _____ could rule the Middle Eastern country for much longer.

   (A) inviolable   (B) oligarchy

   (C) filibuster   (D) harangue

8. From coast to coast, the lack of flu shots was a concern of _____ proportions.

   (A) pandemic   (B) turgid

   (C) paean   (D) propel

9. History teaches that dictators tend to be _____ and cruel to their people.

   (A) cartographer   (B) misnomer

   (C) aerate   (D) dogmatic

10. The letter informed Hillary that because of five unpaid tickets, her license was in a state of _____ until further notice.

    (A) abeyance   (B) potable

    (C) accede   (D) diluvial

11. The teenagers felt frustrated and _____ when the town adopted a 9 P.M. curfew for everyone age 18 and younger.

    (A) prominenced   (B) propelled

    (C) patronized   (D) debacled

12. Ms. Jenkins liked to _____ her students' research papers to make sure they hadn't been plagiarized from the Internet.

    (A) pandemic   (B) vacillate

    (C) feign   (D) scrutinize

BUILDING BLOCK ANSWERS AND EXPLANATIONS

1. A. To **arrogate** is to claim as your own without right; one example is claiming the remote control when you already had a turn. To *accede* is to agree, *autonomous* is independent, and to *vacillate* is to waver back and forth.

2. C. The senator was known for his **filibusters**, or prolonged speeches, which are often used in politics as delay tactics. *Abdicates* (renounces) and *arrogates* (to claim without right) are verbs. *Harangues* are angry lectures or speeches. While this is a potential choice, **filibusters** makes more sense in the context of delaying a bill.

3. A. **Inviolable** rights are sacred rights, and Margaret likes to know that she has such unbreakable rights. *Discord*, which is disagreement, and *oligarchy*, which is rule by a group, are nouns that do not fit within the context of the sentence. *Intransigent* is an adjective synonymous with stubborn, which cannot be used to describe rights.

BUILDING BLOCK ANSWERS AND EXPLANATIONS *(cont'd)*

4. D. Troy was trying to make everyone happy, thus the feeling of wavering (or **vacillating**) back and forth between staff and students. To *arrogate* is to claim without right and to *accede* is to agree, both of which do not work in the context of the sentence. *Abeyance* is the temporary suppression of something, but that answer must be suppressed in this case because it is incorrect. **Vacillate** perfectly describes Troy's situation.

5. C. A **debacle** is a total mess or disaster, as this press conference was. Since the conference took place in one room, it couldn't possibly be *pandemic* (over a widespread area). The situation also can't be considered *austere* (strict or severe), even though it sounds like it was less than pleasant. *Dogmatic* is synonymous with *austere*, so it is ruled out as well.

6. D. To be **intransigent** is to be stubborn, so the fact that such an inflexible person could get reelected was surprising. An *oligarchy* is rule by a group, so it does not apply to Joan's situation or style. *Inviolable* is unbreakable and sacred, so it is an inappropriate choice. To *stratify* is to break into layers for further study, so it is also irrelevant.

7. B. An **oligarchy** is a group that rules. A *filibuster* does not work as it is a long speech. To *harangue* is to lecture and *inviolable* is unbreakable.

8. A. **Pandemic** is over a widespread area, as in an epidemic: in this case, the flu. The other three choices are unrelated: *turgid* (pompous), *paean* (an artistic tribute), and *propel* (to drive forward).

9. D. By nature, a leader who takes control—usually through military power—is **dogmatic**, meaning inflexible and strict. These leaders are not cruel mapmakers (*cartographer*), they are not cruelly misnamed (*misnomer*), and they do not have anything to do with cruel ventilation (*aerate*).

10. A. **Abeyance** is a noun meaning a state of temporary suspension. *Diluvial* and *potable* relate to water and are irrelevant. To *accede* is to agree and for Hillary, there was nothing agreeable about this situation!

11. C. When a group feels **patronized**, it feels it has been talked down to and treated unfairly. *Propelled* is in the right neighborhood, as the teens may be pushed into action, but that's just too much of a stretch to be correct. In turn, *prominenced* and *debacled* aren't real words. If you answered this question incorrectly, you might want to go back to chapter 4 for some review.

BUILDING BLOCK ANSWERS AND EXPLANATIONS *(cont'd)*

12. D. Ms. Jenkins **scrutinized** those research papers, meaning she searched them carefully for language and style that didn't seem like it would come from one of her students. *Pandemic* (something occurring over a widespread area) does not apply or fit grammatically and to *vacillate* is to waver. To *feign* is to fake, which is relevant but incorrect—Ms. Jenkins did not fake her students' research papers. If you answered this question incorrectly, you might want to go back to chapter 4 for some review.

PART ONE

abdicate v. (aab dih KAYT)—to give up a position, right, or power
*Facing impeachment, Nixon decided to **abdicate** the presidency and resigned.*

abrogate v. (AAB ruh gayt)—to annul; to abolish by authoritative action
*Students, staff, and parents were all upset when Principal Redford decided to **abrogate** the student council's controversial decision.*

accede v. (aak SEED)—to express approval, to agree to
*Harry hinted to the political party that he would **accede** if asked to run for mayor.*

accentuate v. (aak SEN choo ayt)—to stress or emphasize; intensify
*It's natural for a politician to **accentuate** positive aspects of a situation in a campaign speech, while speaking little about the negative.*

actuate v. (AAK choo ayt) to put into motion, to activate; to motivate or influence to activity
*Mara's speech **actuated** the crowd of usually apathetic students, and they marched toward the governor's mansion.*

ameliorate v. (ah MEEL yor ayt)—to make better, improve
*Crime statistics in the city were **ameliorated** under the last mayor.*

arrogate v. (AA ruh gayt)—to claim without justification; to claim for oneself without right
*With Soviet support, Castro **arrogated** the personal property of the wealthy and turned Cuba into a communist country.*

autonomous adj. (aw TOHN uh muss)—separate, independent
*The history teacher told the class that the goal of America's founding fathers was to make the colonies **autonomous** from England.*

FLASHBACK

In the first chapter, you learned that the word root **auto** means *self*. As long as you can remember this, you will remember that to be **autonomous** is to be *independent*. It is to be able to rely on your*self*, to answer only to your*self*, and to be responsible for your*self*.

---

belligerent adj. (buh LIJ ehr ent)—hostile, tending to fight; Latin for "to wage war"
*When the class clown became **belligerent**, Mrs. Ivans finally decided it was time for a parent-teacher conference.*

beneficent adj. (buh NEHF ih sihnt)—pertaining to an act of kindness
*Anonymously, somebody made a **beneficent** donation of $50,000 to the Boy Scouts.*

caucus n. (KAW kuhs)—smaller group within an organization; a meeting of such a group
*Gus was proud to be a part of the student **caucus** asked to help the police combat teen drinking and driving.*

collusion n. (kuh LOO zhen)—collaboration, complicity, conspiracy
*When they learned that Coach Woodson was in **collusion** with the opposing coach to get his quarterback the county record, the Booster Club refused to hold a banquet for him.*

concordant adj. (kon KOR dint)—harmonious, agreeing
*Bruce told his mother how her advice had helped him and the **concordant** words brought a smile to her lips.*

convoluted adj. (KON vuh loo tid)—twisted, complicated, involved
*Joel lost the election because his speech was too **convoluted** for anyone to understand.*

Practice 1

DIRECTIONS: Consider the two word choices in the parentheses, and circle the one that best fits in the context of the sentence.

1. The mayor and superintendent were in (**a caucus** OR **collusion**) to lie about their citywide test scores just to keep real-estate values high.

2. Dean Harris had a hard time following Christy's (**abdicated** OR **convoluted**) story about why she was late and simply gave her a detention.

3. In their graduation card, Jack's parents described watching him with pride as he became so much more (**convoluted** OR **autonomous**) between his freshman and senior years.

4. The (**concordant** OR **caucus**) of concerned parents convinced the school to cancel the prom, much to the disappointment of everyone at school.

Your Words, Your World

Actuate—When was the last time you **actuated**, or *instigated*, a plan of action? And how did you do it? How did you *motivate* everyone to follow suit? Did you convince one other person first? If you can't recall a time you played *leader*, how about second-in-command?

Ameliorate—To **ameliorate** is to *upgrade*. When you've got a little extra cash in your pocket, how do you *upgrade*? At the diner, do you get a milk-shake instead of a soda and ask for melted cheese and gravy on your fries? When shopping, do you splurge a little? Have you ever flown first class on an airplane? This is yet another form of *upgrading*.

Accentuate—Have you ever heard the phrase "Accentuate the positive"? When you **accentuate**, you *highlight*; you *emphasize*. For example, do you always look at life as if your glass were half full or as if it were half empty? If you see your glass as half full, then you are **accentuating** the positive.

PART TWO

demagogue n. (DEH muh gahg)—a leader, rabble-rouser, usually appealing to emotion or prejudice
Taking on the role of demagogue, Will almost won the election for student council president as a write-in candidate.

disavow v. (dis uh VOW)—to refuse to acknowledge
When his son announced he'd be running against him as a Democrat, Senator Dowd disavowed him, refusing to even shake his hand.

discord n. (DIS kord)—lack of agreement; inharmonious combination
The discord at the environmental summit was quickly reported to the press.

FLASHBACK

In the examples **disavow** and **discord**, it is clear that the word root **dis** means *apart* or *away from*. **Disavow** is often used to describe someone who is physically or politically moving *away from* someone else, and **discord** is a description of two people or parties that are *apart*.

---

dogmatic adj. (dawg MAA tik)—rigidly fixed in opinion, opinionated
The students thought Principal White was unfairly dogmatic, but the parents loved her.

equitable adj. (eh KWI tuh buhl)—fair; just and impartial
Everyone appreciated that Governor Brown had at least tried to find an equitable solution to the problem.

filibuster n. (FIL ih buh stuhr)—the use of obstructionist tactics, especially prolonged speechmaking, in order to delay something
Terry's filibuster included everything from intimidating security guards to protesting unfair policies, but the assistant principal couldn't be distracted from handing down the suspension.

galvanize v. (GAAL vuh niyz)—to shock; to arouse awareness
The shutting down of a third homeless shelter galvanized the activist group into action.

harangue v. (huh RAANG)—to give a long speech
*Maria and her friends **harangued** the school board to the point that it finally agreed to allow seniors to drive to school.*

imperious adj. (ihm PEER ee uhs)—commanding, domineering; urgent
*Though King Edgar had been a kind leader, his daughter was **imperious** and demanding during her rule.*

intransigent adj. (ihn TRAANZ uh jihnt)—uncompromising, refusing to abandon an extreme position
*Superintendent Townsend's **intransigent** stance on Saturday detentions actually led to a decrease in behavior problems at the high school.*

malfeasance n. (maal FEE zuhns)—wrongdoing or misconduct, especially by a public official
*The president's **malfeasance** made it difficult for teachers to decide what was appropriate during discussions of current events.*

mandate n. (MAN dayt)—a command or instruction; Latin for "to put into one's hand"
*The **mandate** of the new SAT exam left teachers and students scrambling to prepare for a test none of them had ever seen before.*

maxim n. (MAK suhm)—fundamental principle
*The students were taught the **maxim**, "Do unto others as you would have them do unto you."*

mediate v. (MEE dee yayt)—to resolve a dispute between two other parties
*The training of students to **mediate** disagreements between other students became popular during the 1990s.*

megalomania n. (mehg uh loh MAY nee uh)—obsession with great or grandiose performance
*The student council jokingly accused its advisor of **megalomania** when she suggested a "royal wedding" theme for the prom.*

Practice 2

DIRECTIONS: Read the four choices, and circle the word that does not fit with the other three (which are synonymous with the vocabulary word in bold).

5. **disavow:**   renounce   deny   reject   pledge

6. **galvanize:**   shock   restrain   stimulate   rouse

7. **harangue:**   scold   praise   lecture   criticize

8. **mandate:**   permission   consent   refusal   authorization

Your Words, Your World

Equitable—Think of the most *reasonable, fair, objective* person you know; someone with an *unbiased, impartial* outlook on the world. Has this person ever acted greedily (like a demagogue)? Has he ever pretended to care about others while really only looking out for his own interests? If you consider him to be **equitable**, then chances are he hasn't. To remember this word, you can think of this person.

Mediate—The Latin *mediatus* describes the act of *resolving* a problem between two people. This is also the definition for **mediation**. To **mediate** is to *intervene* in a positive manner. *Mediare*, also Latin, means "to divide in the middle." So, to remember the definition of **mediate**, picture a babysitter placing a line of tape right down the middle of a bedroom. On one side is one brother and on the other side, the other brother. They've been fighting and in the effort to **mediate** a peaceable solution, this babysitter is getting them separated.

PART THREE

paradigm n. (PAAR uh diym)—an outstandingly clear or typical example
*Mr. Bloomfield used the great difference in payrolls of professional baseball teams as a **paradigm** of the capitalist system.*

paramount adj. (PAAR uh mownt)—supreme, dominant, primary
*Since many voters still didn't know who he was, Harrison knew it was of **paramount** importance to get face time on the news before election day.*

parity n. (PAAR ih tee)—equality
*In discussing feminism, Mrs. Lutskaya agreed that life had improved for women but pointed out that there were still many **parity** issues to be dealt with.*

polarize v. (POH luhr iyz)—to tend toward opposite extremes
*Gay marriage **polarized** many voters in the 2004 election.*

polyglot n. (PAH lee gloht)—a speaker of many languages
*Ling's extensive travels have helped her to become a true **polyglot**.*

precept n. (PREE sept)—principle; law
*The justices of the Supreme Court do their best to abide by the **precepts** of the United States Constitution.*

prudent adj. (PROO dihnt)—careful, cautious
*Considering how close the election was, the mayor was **prudent** about not making too many changes right away.*

puissant adj. (PYOO sihnt)—powerful
*Pat Johnson was a **puissant** student leader, not because of her good grades but because of her athletic ability and achievement.*

reconciliation n. (reh con sil ee AY shun)—the act of agreement after a quarrel, the resolution of a dispute
*The juniors attempted **reconciliation** with the seniors by returning their homecoming float and personally delivering to them ten large pizzas.*

succumb v. (suh KUHM)—to give in to stronger power; yield
*The principal decided to **succumb** to the students' request as a means of rewarding their activism.*

vacillate v. (vah sil AYT)—to waver, show indecision
*Governor Wiggins cost himself countless votes when he **vacillated** on the health care question during the debate.*

vacuous adj. (vah kyoo UHS)—empty, void; lacking intelligence, purposeless
*The congresswoman's **vacuous** speech angered the voters, who were tired of hearing her empty promises.*

Practice 3

DIRECTIONS: Consider the definition and then circle T for True or F for False.

9. **T F**   **paradigm**—a poorly explained example

10. **T F**   **parity**—equality

11. **T F**   **polyglot**—someone who can speak several languages

12. **T F**   **succumb**—to stand your ground

Your Words, Your World

succumb—Whereas having a friend who will **succumb** to your requests is a good thing, if a politician **succumbs** too easily to pressure, that can't be good—not for his career and certainly not for the people who voted him into office.

reconciliation—Whereas the tendency to succumb is sometimes good and sometimes bad, any kind of **reconciliation** is good. Whether between friends or politicians, the ability to *mend* relationships and return to happier times is always a positive. When friends argue, they must be able to come to a *resolution*. The same thing can be said of politicians. If anything is to be accomplished, first there must be a cease-fire and then there must be *compromise*.

PART FOUR

cede v. (SEED)—to surrender possession of something
*Argentina **ceded** the Falkland Islands to Britain after a brief war.*

compatriot n. (KOHM pay tree oht)—fellow countryman
*Halfway across the world, Jeff felt most comfortable in the company of his **compatriots**.*

emissary n. (EHM ih ser ee)—an agent sent as a representative
*After cutting class, Paul sent Heather as his **emissary**, armed with a note of apology.*

hegemony n. (heh jeh MOH nee)—the domination of one state or group over its allies
In the traditional flag football game, the senior girls claimed hegemony over the junior girls.

impotent adj. (IMP uh tent)—powerless, ineffective, lacking strength
Senator Cliff was impotent to prevent the media from learning of his daughter's arrest.

indomitable adj. (in DOM ih tu buhl)—fearless, unconquerable
Sam was the most indomitable goalkeeper in the county, until the underdogs from Jefferson High scored three goals off of her.

inviolable adj. (in VY uh lu buhl)—safe from violation or assault
The relieved refugees felt inviolable as UN troops stood guard over the camp.

unanimity n. (YOO nahn ih mih tee)—state of total agreement or unity
The unanimity of the council members on this issue was surprising—they rarely agreed on anything.

Practice 4

DIRECTIONS: In completing the sentences, use four of the seven words below. Use each of the words just once.

indomitable	cede	impotent	hegemony
emissary	inviolable	precept	

13. Benjamin Franklin spent many years living and working in Paris, as a(n) _____ of the United States government.

14. The United Nations usually gets involved when one country tries to exercise _____ over another.

15. A "lame duck" president who doesn't have to face another election is often _____ to pass legislation.

16. Every politician knows that the people have certain rights and laws that they consider _____, and therefore can never be altered.

Your Words, Your World

cede—In recent weeks, have you had the confidence to *yield*, to *surrender*, to **cede**? Well, good for you. Do you think that most politicians are willing to admit defeat, back off on an issue, or let an argument go? That seems doubtful. It's as if the word **cede** weren't in their vocabulary.

unanimity—Who in your family do you share absolute **unanimity** with? Who is the one person you *agree* with most often? Maybe within political parties there can be *harmony*, *union*, and *unity*. However, these qualities are rare in politics in general.

PRACTICE ANSWERS AND EXPLANATIONS

Practice 1

1. To be in **collusion** is to be in a state of collaboration, which perfectly describes the mayor and superintendent. A *caucus* is a small group within a group, so it is not relevant to the topic.

2. If something is **convoluted**, it is twisted and complicated. To *abdicate* is to give up power, which does not describe a story.

3. To be **autonomous** is to be independent. To be *convoluted* is to be twisted, as in distorting the truth, which does not work in the context of the sentence.

4. To be *concordant* is to be harmonious and although those parents were in agreement, *concordant* is not the best word to describe them. A **caucus** is a group or committee and the goal of this group had been to cancel the prom, a mission they accomplished.

Practice 2

5. To **disavow** is not to *pledge*, but rather to *renounce*, *deny*, and *reject*.

6. To **galvanize** is not to *restrain*, but rather to *shock*, *stimulate*, and *rouse*.

7. To **harangue** is not to *praise*, but to *scold*, *lecture*, and *criticize*.

8. A **mandate** is not a *refusal*, but rather *permission*, *consent*, and *authorization*.

PRACTICE ANSWERS AND EXPLANATIONS *(cont'd)*

Practice 3

9. False. A **paradigm** is not a poorly explained example, but a model that is held up as an example.

10. True. Parity is equality.

11. True. A **polyglot** is someone who can speak several languages.

12. False. To **succumb** is to give in, the opposite of standing your ground.

Practice 4

13. An **emissary** is like an ambassador; it is somebody who lives in another country in order to represent his or her homeland.

14. Hegemony is when one country tries to dominate another country. Most often, this attempt at supremacy comes through the use of force.

15. If a president is powerless to pass legislation, then he or she is **impotent**.

16. Inviolable laws and rights are unbreakable and virtually sacred. The Bill of Rights is a set of **inviolable** rules established to protect individual rights.

CHAPTER 5 QUIZ

Take your time, not only with the questions, but in reading the answer explanations that follow. Set a goal for yourself—80% (16 correct answers) is recommended—and if you don't reach that goal, go back and read through the chapter again. Good luck!

DIRECTIONS: For questions 1–11, circle T for True or F for False.
For questions 12–20, circle the synonym.

1. **T F** **impotent**—to be powerless

2. **T F** **prudent**—lacking care

3. **T F** **precept**—a principle or law

4. **T F** **polarize**—opposite extremes

5. **T F** **capitulate**—to overcome

6. **T F** **mediate**—to leave a dispute unresolved

7. **T F** **mandate**—authorization

8. **T F** **imperious**—submissive

9. **T F** **unanimity**—disagreement

10. **T F** **collusion**—adversarial

11. **T F** **indomitable**—afraid

12. **discord:**	harmony	disagreement	accord
13. **disavow:**	deny	acknowledge	accept
14. **ameliorate:**	improve	devolve	amenable
15. **abrogate:**	delegate	cancel	succumb
16. **paramount:**	trivial	mountainous	supreme
17. **accentuate:**	gloss over	emphasize	arrogate
18. **galvanize:**	shock	placate	appease
19. **autonomous:**	dependent	equitable	independent
20. **emissary:**	enemy	demagogue	delegate

CHAPTER 5 QUIZ ANSWERS AND EXPLANATIONS

1. **True.** To be **impotent** is to be powerless.

2. **False.** **Prudent** is not lacking care, it is to proceed with care.

3. **True.** A **precept** is a law or principle.

4. **True.** **Polarize** has do with positions—usually political opinions—that are at opposite extremes.

5. **False.** To **capitulate** is to surrender, not to overcome.

6. **False.** To **mediate** is to resolve an issue and not to leave it unresolved.

7. **True.** A **mandate** is an authorization.

8. **False.** To be **imperious** is to be domineering, not to be submissive.

9. **False.** **Unanimity** is a state of agreement, so disagreement is an antonym.

10. **False.** **Collusion** is to be in a state of collaboration, so to be adversarial is the exact opposite.

11. **False.** To be **indomitable** is to be fearless and unconquerable, so afraid is an antonym.

12. **Discord** is to be in *disagreement*, not to be in *harmony* or in *accord*.

13. To **disavow** is to *deny* and not to *acknowledge* or *accept*.

14. **Ameliorate** is to *improve* and not to be *amenable*; *devolve* means to pass on by succession or to degenerate and is not synonymous with **ameliorate**.

15. **Abrogate** is to *cancel* and not to *succumb* or *delegate*.

16. **Paramount** is not synonymous with *trivial* (unimportant) or *mountainous*. The closest definition is *supreme*.

17. To **accentuate** is not to *gloss over* (ignore); nor is it to *arrogate* (claim without justification), although both are verbs. To *emphasize* is actually to *accentuate*.

CHAPTER 5 QUIZ ANSWERS AND EXPLANATIONS *(cont'd)*

18. To **galvanize** is to *shock* into action. While *placate* and *appease* are synonymous with one another, they are antonyms of **galvanize**. They involve calming people down and making them happy and comfortable.

19. To be **autonomous** is to be *independent*. To be *dependant* is to rely on others and to be *equitable* is to be reasonable and fair; not necessarily a way **autonomous** people, especially leaders, have to act.

20. An **emissary** is a *delegate* or representative. *Enemy* is nearly an antonym, while *demagogues* (troublemaking popular leaders) are rarely representative of anybody or anything other than themselves.

CHAPTER 6

Arts and Leisure

Using these words is an art form unto itself

BUILDING BLOCK QUIZ

By answering the ten questions below, you will get a sense of how closely you'll have to study this chapter in order to master the vocabulary of the world of arts and leisure.

DIRECTIONS: Fill in the blanks, using the most appropriate of the four multiple-choice answers. The correct answer will always fit into the sentence grammatically.

1. Harvey's wearing Dartmouth football shorts _____ the fact that he never went to Dartmouth, let alone played football there.

   (A) versatile   (B) vilified
   (C) belied   (D) elaborated

2. The _____ film festival cost the student council over $3,000 and hardly seemed worth the expensive decorations and refreshments.

   (A) licentious   (B) vernacular
   (C) paean   (D) lavish

3. Vargas was not the first to go into politics after a successful career as a(n) _____, in this case as a published author.

   (A) artisan   (B) ornate
   (C) paean   (D) interlude

4. Melody, who'd always had an eye for fine detail, quickly became famous for her _____ stained glass.

    (A) versatile   (B) proxy

    (C) allusive   (D) ornate

5. Upon moving out to Brooklyn, Gabe made sure to engage everyone he met in conversation, so as to learn the local _____.

    (A) vernacular   (B) lavish

    (C) censure   (D) hackneyed

6. Surprisingly, when the film was _____ by the president, donations poured in to the director and he was able to distribute the film nationally.

    (A) belied   (B) censured

    (C) ancillary   (D) proxied

7. The loft was perfect in that it was _____ enough to host everything from painting lessons to dancing lessons to yoga!

    (A) vilify   (B) ornate

    (C) versatile   (D) lavish

8. Giovanni welcomed the brief _____ during his book tour, allowing him to catch up on emails and work on his new novel.

    (A) constant   (B) proxy

    (C) licentious   (D) interlude

9. Some saw Annette's paintings as beautiful portrayals of the human body, while others called them _____.

    (A) interlude   (B) vernacular

    (C) licentious   (D) nonchalant

10. The _____ was intended to be a tribute to Robert Frost, but ended up celebrating some other poets who were fantastic in their own right.

    (A) paean (B) ornate

    (C) artisan (D) gourmand

BUILDING BLOCK ANSWERS AND EXPLANATIONS

1. C. To **belie** is to misrepresent. *Vilified* (spoke badly about) and *elaborated* (explained) are grammatically correct, but do not make sense. *Versatile* means multitalented and does not make sense in context.

2. D. **Lavish** means extravagant, as indicated by the $3,000. A *paean* is an artistic tribute. *Licentious* (immoral) is an adjective, but does not work as well as **lavish**. *Vernacular* means common language and doesn't make sense.

3. A. An **artisan** is an expert in the creative arts, including everything from tile work to writing. *Ornate* (intricate) and *paean* (an artistic tribute) are both related to the arts, but they don't fit in the blank. *Interlude* is irrelevant, as it means a break or brief interval.

4. D. **Ornate** means elaborate. *Allusive* (always making indirect references), *versatile* (capable of doing many things), and *proxy* (substitute) do not make sense in context.

5. A. **Vernacular** is a common dialect; in this case, the way people in Brooklyn speak. *Lavish* is extravagant, so that answer can be ruled out. *Censure* is finding fault and this is not what Gabe was doing. Finally, *hackneyed* is clichéd, and although some may call any accent or **vernacular** clichéd, the word is an adjective and does not work in context.

6. B. *Proxy* and *ancillary* both indicate substitutions, so they are irrelevant. To **censure** is to criticize and this is what the president did. To *belie* is to disprove or contradict, which is close, but not as acceptable as **censure**.

7. C. *Ornate* and *lavish* are synonymous (detailed and extravagant), so they rule each other out. To *vilify* is to belittle, and the blank must be filled with a positive word like **versatile**, which means adaptable.

BUILDING BLOCK ANSWERS AND EXPLANATIONS *(cont'd)*

8. D. An **interlude** is an interval and is the best choice. *Constant* is an antonym, *proxy* is a substitute, and *licentious* is immoral, so none of these works in context.

9. C. **Licentious** is immoral and fits in with the contrast of the sentence. *Vernacular* (current language) and *nonchalant* (casual) may seem to be decent choices, but they fall short of the criticism of **licentious**. *Interlude* (interval) does not make sense in context.

10. A. A **paean** is a tribute and in this case, a tribute to Robert Frost. *Ornate* (intricate) and *artisan* (a creative person) are topical but don't fit. *Gourmand* is a glutton or gourmet and has nothing to do with poetry.

PART ONE

abnegate v. (ahb nuh GAYT)—to deny; renounce
*Citing artistic freedom, Arnold decide to **abnegate** the honors project and submit his poem rather than the required research paper.*

allusive adj. (ah LOO siv)—making many indirect references
*Although Gabrielle's presentation dealt with the 2000 election, it was more **allusive** than factual and she received a C–.*

apotheosis n. (ah poh thee OH sis)—glorification; glorified ideal
*As a kid growing up in the '80s, Miguel thought that Michael Jackson was the **apotheosis** of cool.*

belie v. (bee LIY)—to misrepresent; expose as false
*The low grade **belied** all of the time Matt had spent studying for the test, so Ms. Vasquez promised to help him better structure his time.*

endure v. (en DOOR)—carry on despite hardships
*Peg **endured** the flu and gave a tremendous solo during the piano recital.*

ensemble n. (on SOM buhl)—group of parts that contribute to a whole single effect
*Louis's string **ensemble** was hired to play at the Garrison wedding and soon had gigs every weekend.*

exorbitant adj. (eg ZOR bih tant)—extravagant, greater than reasonable
*The artist charged **exorbitant** prices for his paintings, but gave one to the high school for free since he so appreciated the training he'd received there.*

garish adj. (GAHR ish)—gaudy, glaring
*Sandra thought the costumes too **garish** for the low-key school play.*

grandiose adj. (GRAN dee ohs)—magnificent and imposing; exaggerated and pretentious
*The architect agreed that the high school should have a **grandiose** façade so that the students would feel important every time they entered the building.*

matriarch n. (MAY tree ark)—woman who rules a family or clan
*Deborah Stone had been principal for over 20 years, running the school as a **matriarch** with the students' best interests at heart.*

mimic v. (MIM ihk)—copy, imitate
*Henrietta asked the principal if the way Lea **mimicked** her movements could be considered bullying.*

nonchalant adj. (non shuh LAHNT)—calm, casual, seemingly unexcited
*Rick was very **nonchalant** when he won the art scholarship, but inside his heart was bursting with joy!*

Practice 1

The key to memorization is testing yourself in as many different formats as possible. Here's one exercise that will help reinforce the words you learned in this section.

DIRECTIONS: Read the three possible synonyms, then circle the word you think best defines the word in bold.

1. **abnegate**:	portray	deny	celebrate
2. **exorbitant**:	reasonable	content	extravagant
3. **grandiose**:	modest	magnificent	humble
4. **mimic**:	imitate	rhapsody	compliment
5. **nonchalant**:	nonsense	casual	nonplussed

Your Words, Your World

apotheosis—Rather than visualizing your hero, think of someone who has been *glorified* to a degree that really annoys you. Who is the one person everybody always speaks so highly of and who you just don't think deserves the praise? *Theos* is Greek for *God* (think theology), and not many people out there deserve to be elevated to god status.

ensemble—French for *together*, an **ensemble** is a group of people working toward a *common* goal. Think, for example, of your favorite *band*. Four or five folks—maybe even a whole orchestra!—gathered on a stage or in a studio, making the kind of music you absolutely love. It doesn't matter if it's hard rock, hip-hop, choral, gospel, or international. What matters is this: when a group of people can get *together* and produce something enjoyable, it is to be appreciated. Imagine your favorite **ensemble** and you'll be all set.

PART TWO

ablution v. (ahb LOO shun)—act of cleansing
*Taking off her makeup was the last step in Minnie's nightly **ablutions**.*

aesthetic adj. (aas THEH tik)—pertaining to beauty or art
*The museum curator, with her fine **aesthetic** sense, created an exhibit that crowds lined up for hours to see.*

artisan n. (ar tih SAN)—craftsperson; expert
*Not surprisingly, the local **artisans** were among the most popular guests at the Career Fair.*

novel adj. (NOH vuhl)—new and not resembling anything formerly known
*Piercing any part of the body other than the earlobes was **novel** in the 1950s, but now it is quite common.*

opulence n. (AH pyoo lehns)—wealth
*Mr. Livingston knew that being a teacher meant he'd never have a life of **opulence**, but told his students that it was rewarding nonetheless.*

ornate adj. (ohr NAYT)—elaborately ornamented
*The **ornate** stained glass looked wonderful above the entrance to the auditorium.*

ostentatious adj. (ah sten TAY shuhs)—showy
*Many people found the movie star's abundant gold and diamond jewelry to be beyond **ostentatious**—it was downright obnoxious!*

pretense n. (PRE tens)—false appearance or action
*The three students snuck into the art gallery's grand opening under the **pretense** that they were caterers.*

promulgate v. (PROM ul gayt)—to make known publicly
*The publicist **promulgated** the news of the rock star's "secret" wedding through one of his anonymous sources.*

repose n. (ree POHZ)—relaxation, leisure
*A week after wrapping up the film, the director found **repose** in the Caribbean with his wife and kids.*

sinecure n. (SIN ih kyoor)—a well-paying job or office that requires little or no work
*After using his connections to get a **sinecure** in marketing, Adam was able to use his free time to write poetry.*

solitary adj. (SOL ih ter ee)—alone; remote, secluded
*Melody found that the only way she could finish her novel was by retreating to a **solitary** cabin in the woods.*

> **MEMORY TIP**
>
> Have you ever played the card game Solitaire? If not, it is a way to play cards when there is no one around to play with. Picture someone at a table, all alone, with the cards spread out before him. This will help you to memorize **solitary**, which is a word to describe any *solo* activity or endeavor.

stoic adj. (STOH ihk)—indifferent to or unaffected by emotions
*His friends couldn't believe that a **stoic** man like Alonzo was capable of writing such emotionally charged plays.*

sully v. (SUH lee)—to tarnish, taint
*Voluntarily doing community service around town helped Gary to restore his **sullied** reputation.*

vernacular n. (vuhr NAA kyoo luhr)—everyday language used by ordinary people; specialized language of a profession
*Francine tried to capture the **vernacular** of her new high school, but after a few weeks decided to just speak like herself.*

Practice 2

DIRECTIONS: Read the three choices, then circle the *antonym* of the word in bold.

6. **novel:**   new   hackneyed   original

7. **sully:**   tainted   muddied   clean

8. **ablution:**   cleansing   sullied   purified

9. **promulgate:**   conceal   disseminate   broadcast

10. **stoic:**   impervious   emotional   impassive

Your Words, Your World

Aesthetic—One of the joys in life is finding what is **aesthetically** appealing to you. Actually, the joy is making sure that this thing—music, paintings, drawings, flowers, candles, whatever—is readily available throughout your day. Whether in a locker, dorm room, or cubicle at work, often having something **aesthetically** pleasing at hand can make a bad day good.

Ornate—You may use it to criticize something that is overly complicated, but most often, **ornate**, or *elaborately decorated*, is a compliment. Beautiful tile work in a mansion, layers of stringed instruments in an orchestra, 3-D scenes from a video game, all of these can be **ornate**! A synonym of *lavish* and *opulent*, **ornate** is a vocab word that makes one feel artistic just using it.

Ostentatious—So you want to criticize something *overly complicated* and *showy*, but don't want to use *ornate* or *opulence* in a negative sense? Well, there's always **ostentatious**. *Loud, obnoxious, pretentious*, and *flamboyant* are all synonyms for **ostentatious**.

PART THREE

callow adj. (CAL oh)—immature, lacking sophistication
*Because the **callow** students ruined the first act of* Hamlet *for everybody else, there was a standing ovation when security escorted them from the theater.*

caustic adj. (KAW stihk)—biting, sarcastic; able to burn
*Walt gained his reputation as a **caustic** comedian because of his cutting commentary.*

defamatory adj. (dih FAAM uh tohr ee)—injurious to the reputation
*The famous actress decided to sue the tabloid for making **defamatory** statements about her romantic relationships.*

fodder n. (FOH duhr)—raw materials (as for artistic creation); readily abundant ideas or images
*Mrs. Lorens asked her students to try to make a real social statement when choosing the **fodder** for their collages.*

interlude n. (IN ter lood)—an intervening period of time
*Willy was happy to get up and stretch his legs during the opera's **interlude**.*

iridescent adj. (ir ih DEH sihnt)—showing many colors
*The photography students quickly snapped as many pictures as they could before the **iridescent** butterfly flew away.*

libertine n. (LIH buhr teen)—a freethinker, usually used disparagingly; one without moral restraint
*Ursula lost her position as art critic for the school paper when a minister complained that having a **libertine** on staff was immoral.*

> **MEMORY TIP**
>
> Can you see the *liberty* in **libertine**? That *liberty* equals *freedom*, and somebody who is classified as a **libertine** feels tremendous *freedom* when he or she speaks. This kind of person often gets criticized for taking too many *liberties*.

licentious adj. (lih SEHN shuhs)—immoral; unrestrained by society
*In an open letter, Kelly asked the town's older citizens to stop accusing her generation of **licentious** behavior and realize that the world had changed.*

melee n. (MAY lay)—tumultuous free-for-all
*The red carpet became slippery in the rain, causing a sloppy **melee** at the Oscars.*

mellifluous adj. (mehl IH floo uhs)—having a smooth, rich flow
*Betsy was such a talented flutist that her **mellifluous** playing transported the audience to another world.*

mundane adj. (muhn DAYN)—ordinary, commonplace
*The plot of the detective story was completely **mundane**, and the book even ended with the line, "The butler did it."*

nostalgic adj. (nah STAHL jik)—longing for things of the past
*After his ten-year high school reunion, Brad became **nostalgic** for the good old days.*

paean n. (PEE uhn)—a tribute, a song or expression of praise
*Marcus told the reporter that the painting was a **paean** to his late wife.*

pariah n. (puh RIY uh)—an outcast
*When Anna used racial slurs in her campaign speech, she immediately became a **pariah** among her fellow students.*

rhapsody n. (RAHP suh dee)—emotional literary or musical work
*In defending the music to his father, Marvin said that the name "rap" was based on **rhapsody** because the songs were so emotional.*

vicariously adv. (viy KAAR ee uhs lee)—felt or undergone as if one were taking part in the experience or feelings of another
*Elena loved to read because she lived **vicariously** through the characters in her books.*

vilify v. (vihl ih FIE)—to slander, defame
*Since gossip columnists make money from **vilifying** celebrities, they're often held in low regard.*

whimsical adj. (wihm sih KUHL)—playful or fanciful idea
*The ballet was **whimsical**, delighting the children with its colorful costumes and upbeat music.*

Practice 3

DIRECTIONS: Fill in the blanks, using five of the ten words provided below.

defamatory	callow	melee	mellifluous
libertines	licentious	fodder	iridescent
paean	rhapsody		

11. Although the film was R-rated and deemed _____ by many, it led all movies in ticket sales for the weekend.

12. Gail earned critical acclaim for her _____ paintings of tropical fish.

13. Paula was fond of artists who were _____; they had subtly rebelled against current culture and then subtly reshaped it.

14. In 1913, on the streets of Paris, a _____ followed the first-ever performance of Stravinsky's *Rite of Spring*.

15. Going to the opera put Melanie in a state of pure _____.

Your Words, Your World

Defamatory—To **defame** is to *injure* someone's *reputation* or in a sense, to take from that person's fame. This is literally the Latin root of the word as *fama* means fame and *dis* means take. Who knew that today's popular phrase for **defamation**, *dissed*, came from Latin? Think of the last time you saw someone get dissed (disrespected). Or maybe you yourself got dissed. Thinking of the verb *dissed* should help you to remember the definition for **defamatory**.

Mellifluous—*Smooth* and *honeyed* phrases are considered **mellifluous**—and doesn't the word sound like what it describes? Rather than picturing an image as you've done in other exercises, this time use your ears rather than your inner eye. *Mel* is Latin for honey while *fluere* means to flow. Words that are **mellifluous** *flow* in a *rich, smooth* way.

Paean—Who would you pay *tribute* to if you were given the chance? Who would you most like to sit down and say thank you to? Imagine this actor or actress, this singer, this writer, this doctor, this family member, this dancer, this painter, this philanthropist, or this politician. Choose one person and imagine being able to not only create but deliver a **paean** to him or her. In ancient Greece, a *paian* was a hymn of praise for any of the gods, but especially for Apollo, god of the arts. Who is your Apollo?

PRACTICE ANSWERS AND EXPLANATIONS

Practice 1

1. To **abnegate** is to *deny*, not to *portray* or *celebrate*.

2. Something **exorbitant** is *extravagant*. It is not *content* and it is far from *reasonable*.

3. Something that is **grandiose** is *magnificent*, and an antonym to something *modest* and *humble*.

4. To **mimic** is to *imitate* and usually not in a *complimentary* way. *Rhapsody* is a state of ecstasy and does not fit.

5. **Nonchalant** is *casual*. *Nonsense* and *nonplussed* (confused) may share the root of **non**, but they are both nonanswers!

Practice 2

6. **Novel** is something *new* and *original*, thus *hackneyed* (old and clichéd) is the antonym.

7. To **sully** can be to *taint* or *muddy* something, so the antonym is *clean*.

8. **Ablution** can be the act of *cleansing* or *purifying*, so *sullied* (something tainted or muddied) is the antonym.

9. To **promulgate** is to *disseminate* or *broadcast*. So to *conceal* (hide) is the antonym.

10. **Stoic** is *impervious* and *impassive*. To be *emotional* (demonstrative and dramatic) is the antonym.

PRACTICE ANSWERS AND EXPLANATIONS *(cont'd)*

Practice 3

11. To be **licentious** is to be immoral and depraved; that's just the thing many people seem to enjoy in a movie.

12. Fish do look **iridescent** in real life, so that must have been Gail's goal.

13. Libertines are freethinkers thought of as immoral by certain segments of society.

14. There really was a **melee**, as people rioted in the streets.

15. Rhapsody is so often used to describe music—and the reaction to that music—that at one point it even described a type of music (such as Gershwin's *Rhapsody in Blue*).

CHAPTER 6 QUIZ

Take your time, not only with the questions, but in reading the answer explanations that follow. Set a goal for yourself—80% (16 correct answers) is recommended—and if you don't reach that goal, go back and read through the chapter again. Good luck!

DIRECTIONS: For questions 1–10, circle T for True or F for False.
For questions 11–20, circle the synonym.

1. **T F** **mundane**—extraordinary
2. **T F** **licentious**—moral
3. **T F** **stoic**—unaffected by emotions
4. **T F** **solitary**—alone
5. **T F** **promulgate**—to announce
6. **T F** **aesthetic**—artistic
7. **T F** **grandiose**—extravagant
8. **T F** **mimic**—imitate
9. **T F** **nonchalant**—cowardly
10. **T F** **novel**—traditional

11. **exorbitant**:   extravagant   celestial   plain
12. **endure**:   estimate   persevere   consider
13. **abnegate**:   deny   allude   contemplate
14. **ablution**:   sully   cleanse   curse
15. **ostentatious**:   gaudy   plain   earthy
16. **iridescent**:   plain   earthy   colorful
17. **pigment**:   dye   density   dark
18. **sully**:   clean   endure   tarnish
19. **callow**:   immature   sophisticated   iridescent
20. **pariah**:   hero   fish   outcast

CHAPTER 6 QUIZ ANSWERS AND EXPLANATIONS

1. **False.** **Mundane** is ordinary, not strange or unusual.

2. **False.** **Licentious** is immoral, not honest or ethical.

3. **True.** To be **stoic** is to be unaffected by emotions.

4. **True.** **Solitary** is to be alone.

5. **True.** To **promulgate** is to announce.

6. **True.** Something **aesthetic** is something artistic and appealing.

7. **True.** **Grandiose** is extravagant, in an ostentatious way.

8. **True.** To **mimic** is to imitate.

9. **False.** To be **nonchalant** is to be casual, while cowardly is to be scared and not courageous.

10. **False.** **Novel** is not something traditional. It is something new and interesting.

11. **Exorbitant** is *extravagant,* and not *celestial* or *plain.*

12. To **endure** is to *persevere*; it has nothing to do with *estimate* and *consider.*

13. **Abnegate** is to *deny*, but not to *allude* or *contemplate.*

14. **Ablution** is not to *sully* or *curse.* It is to *cleanse*, usually in a religious sense.

15. **Ostentatious** is synonymous with *gaudy* and the opposite of *plain* and *earthy.*

16. **Iridescent** is not *plain* and *earthy*, but *colorful.*

17. **Pigment** is more associated with *dye* than *density* or *dark.*

18. To **sully** is to *tarnish* or dishonor. To *clean* is an antonym, and to *endure* (survive) is irrelevant.

CHAPTER 6 QUIZ ANSWERS AND EXPLANATIONS *(cont'd)*

19. **Callow** is *immature* and usually describes a person. *Sophisticated* is the opposite: worldly and mature. *Iridescent* (shimmering) is an adjective for describing objects and does not fit either.

20. A **pariah** is an *outcast,* so *hero* is incorrect. And although **pariah** may sound like piranha, *fish* is incorrect.

CHAPTER 7

Literature

Words to help in your reading,
your book club, and in English class

BUILDING BLOCK QUIZ

By answering the questions below, you will get a sense of how closely you should study this chapter in order to master the vocabulary you need to speak knowledgeably about books, magazines, and the menu options on your new DVD!

DIRECTIONS: Fill in the blanks, using the most appropriate of the four multiple-choice answers. The correct answer will always fit into the sentence grammatically.

1. Some English teachers like Hemingway's books, while others think he benefits from undeserving _____.

   (A) archipelagos   (B) adulation

   (C) scrupulous   (D) naïve

2. Mrs. Lowenstein argued that Shakespeare and Dickens are not _____ because Dickens wrote stories about the poor while Shakespeare wrote plays about the powerful.

   (A) debunk   (B) abridge

   (C) analogous   (D) accolade

3. All of the students appreciated Ms. Hollingsworth's _____ when it came to discussing grades.

   (A) candor   (B) denizen
   (C) epitaph   (D) egregious

4. The low-rent apartment building was inhabited by 12 artists, and each _____ was committed to the idea of supporting the creativity of the others.

   (A) illegible   (B) humane
   (C) dentistry   (D) denizen

5. Lenny was planning to _____ his big plot twist in the first chapter of his novel.

   (A) lexicon   (B) missive
   (C) foreshadow   (D) quandary

6. Jenna liked to _____ desire in her stories without being obvious about it.

   (A) pseudonym   (B) imply
   (C) tutelage   (D) vignette

7. As their first bookmaking project, the students had to construct a(n) _____ of the school's most popular words.

   (A) elegy   (B) lexicon
   (C) rhetoric   (D) profound

8. Elena was presented with a tough _____, as she had to choose between writing for the school paper and the school literary magazine.

   (A) quandary   (B) prediction
   (C) figurative   (D) irony

9. Under the _____ of the professors at The Word Institute, Gary's poems went from greeting-card rhymes to true art.

   (A) censure   (B) cosmopolitan

   (C) tutelage   (D) denizen

10. Wendell wanted his short stories to be _____, but was constantly disappointed by how simplistic they seemed.

    (A) illegible   (B) epilogue

    (C) pigment   (D) profound

BUILDING BLOCK ANSWERS AND EXPLANATIONS

1. B. As **adulation** is undeserved praise, this is the answer. *Archipelagos* are strings of islands, so this word does not fit. *Scrupulous* (careful) and *naïve* (immature and innocent) are adjectives, and the sentence requires a noun.

2. C. **Analogous** means comparable, and as Mrs. Lowenstein was arguing against comparing Dickens and Shakespeare too closely, this is the correct answer. An *accolade* is a form of praise and does not fit. *Debunk* (expose) and *abridge* (shorten) are out, based on their definitions and the fact that they are verbs.

3. A. People always appreciate the truth, especially when presented in a tactful manner, so the answer is **candor** (honesty of expression). *Denizen* (an inhabitant or resident) and *egregious* (obvious) do not fit grammatically. As an *epitaph* is something written on a gravestone, that couldn't be right (or one would hope not!).

4. D. Another word for inhabitants, or residents, is **denizen**. *Dentistry* is just a silly answer that sounds like **denizen**, while *illegible* means unreadable (as in poor handwriting), and *humane* means caring. *Humane* is an adjective, so it is grammatically incorrect.

5. C. To **foreshadow** is to provide a hint or clue, so this is the answer. *Lexicon* (dictionary) and *missive* (note or letter) are both nouns indicating a form of communication, while a *quandary* is a problem.

BUILDING BLOCK ANSWERS AND EXPLANATIONS *(cont'd)*

6. B. The verb **imply** (suggest) is the correct answer, as Jenna attempted to be subtle with her art. A *pseudonym* (fake name) and a *vignette* (short piece of literature) are inappropriate, as is *tutelage* (support or guidance).

7. B. A **lexicon** is a dictionary, so this is the best choice. An *elegy* is a poem or song at a funeral, so it is not the best choice. *Rhetoric* is the art of speaking or writing effectively, and *profound* is an adjective meaning deep or meaningful.

8. A. Elena had a problem, which is synonymous with **quandary**. *Prediction* is a trick answer as it sounds like predicament (which is also synonymous with problem and **quandary**). *Figurative* (symbolic language) and *irony* (insincere satire) are both nouns, but they don't describe a problem or choice.

9. C. **Tutelage** (guidance) is the right answer, while *censure* (to criticize) is not. *Cosmopolitan* means sophisticated and worldly, and *denizen* means citizen or resident, so neither of these choices works.

10. D. Whereas Wendell wanted to be **profound** (deep, meaningful), he felt his writing was coming closer to *illegible* (unreadable from sloppiness and not poor writing). An *epilogue* is a section of writing that comes at the end, and *pigment* is a color or dye.

PART ONE

abridge v. (ah BRIJ)—to condense, shorten
*Mrs. Gonzalez assigned an **abridged** version of* Tristram Shandy *to her class, as the original was very long.*

accolade n. (AH ko lade)—praise, distinction
*After Sarah won the national spelling bee, **accolades** were heaped upon her.*

adage n. (ah DAJ)—old saying or proverb
*Benjamin Franklin's "A penny saved is a penny earned" is a popular **adage**.*

adulation n. (AAH juh la shuhn)—excessive flattery or admiration
The adulation Leslie showed for her professor's novel seemed insincere.

allegory n. (AL la gory)—symbolic representation
The story of Rip Van Winkle is an allegory for the way life changed after the Industrial Revolution.

alliteration n. (ah lit er A shun)—repetition of the beginning sounds of words
Mrs. Graves told Becky she'd never be a real poet if she continued to rely on alliteration.

MEMORY TIP

Analytically analogous . . . Pretty practical presentation . . . Having the same first letters in each group of words is the basis for **alliteration**.

---

analogous adj. (uh NAL oh guhs)—comparable, parallel
"In terms of creating characters," Professor White told his class, "the writer is analogous to God, and this is a great responsibility."

antagonist n. (an TAG on ist)—foe, opponent, adversary
Quintasia based her paper around the theory that every great story has a strong antagonist.

antecedent adj. (an tea SEE dent)—coming before in place or time
Dr. Baylor challenged the class to uncover the antecedents to Dean's erratic behavior in On the Road.

antidote n. (an tuh DOTE)—a remedy, an agent used to counteract
Jessica was of the opinion that books were the antidote to ignorance.

assertion n. (uh SIR shun)—declaration, usually without proof
"Hillary's assertion that Shakespeare was a woman is totally false!" Gail argued.

astute adj. (ah STOOT)—having good judgment
Judy Blume is an astute writer of books for children and teens.

bard n. (bard)—lyrical poet
*Shakespeare is one of the most famous **bards** in English literature.*

bibliophile n. (bib lee uh FIL)—book lover
*Mr. Vicks was a self-proclaimed **bibliophile** and everybody's choice for school librarian.*

candor n. (KAN der)—honesty of expression
*The **candor** of Mike's writing impressed Mr. Wright and earned him a B+.*

Practice 1

DIRECTIONS: In completing the sentences, use five of the eight words below. Use each of the words just once.

antagonist	assertion	astute	allegory
adage	antecedent	alliteration	abridge

1. Mr. Kweller always said that a good book must include a main character and his or her _____.

2. Due to budget cuts, the editors had to _____ the yearbook.

3. "If the shoe fits, wear it," is a well-known _____.

4. Danny's research paper argued that *Huckleberry Finn* was the _____ to all great American novels of the 20th century.

5. Dr. Hart warned the students against too much _____ and too little research in their persuasive essays.

Your Words, Your World

Antecedent—What was it that *came before* this memorization activity? Throughout the book, the **antecedent** to the list of words that the chapter is based on is a Building Block Quiz. In turn, the **antecedent** to these Your Words, Your World activities is a Practice. What's the **antecedent** to a baseball game? That's right, it's "The Star-Spangled Banner." The **antecedent** to a wedding is an engagement, and the **antecedent** to an engagement is a proposal. In fact, almost everything has an **antecedent**.

Analogous—**Analogous** is similar to the word *similar*, isn't it? And isn't **analogous** like the word *like*: as in a Coke is like a Pepsi? And don't you think that **analogous** is comparable to the word *comparable*? Indeed, it is. They all are. As with siblings who look somewhat alike, **analogous** is related to the word . . . *related*.

PART TWO

cogent adj. (KOH juhnt)—logically forceful; compelling, convincing
*Felix's **cogent** defense of Stephen King gained credit when King won the National Book Award for Distinguished Contribution to American Letters.*

colloquial adj. (kuh LOH kwee uhl)—characteristic of informal speech
Mrs. Halloway's class enjoyed The Outsiders, *in part because it was written in a **colloquial** style.*

debunk v. (dee BUNK)—to expose the falseness of
*Dr. Louis was such a good professor because he invited students to **debunk** his theories.*

egregious adj. (i GREE jiss)—conspicuously bad
*The textbook contained several **egregious** errors, including "gramer" instead of "grammar."*

epilogue n. (EH puh log)—concluding section of a literary work
*In the **epilogue** of his novel, Mike described how the characters carried on with their lives after surviving the hurricane.*

epitaph n. (EH pih taf)—engraving on a tombstone; literary piece for a dead person
*Upon George Washington's death, Henry Lee uttered the fitting **epitaph**: "First in war, first in peace, and first in the hearts of his countrymen."*

eponymous adj. (ih PAHN uh muhs)—giving one's name to a place, book, restaurant, etc.
*Macbeth is the **eponymous** protagonist of Shakespeare's play.*

figurative adj. (FIG yur uh tiv)—metaphorical, symbolic
*"You're driving me up the wall," is a **figurative** saying and not meant to be taken literally!*

foreshadow v. (for SHAH dow)—to indicate beforehand
*In Lynn's memoir, her mother's visit to the asylum **foreshadowed** her mother's descent into madness.*

MEMORY TIP

When the sun is behind you, what comes before you? Your shadow. And this is how you can remember the word **foreshadow**. Break it down into parts: *fore* indicates something that is up front or that comes before, while *shadow* is not a thing itself, but a representation of the thing. In a mystery novel, that representation might be a look at a murder weapon long before the reader learns about the murder itself.

---

humane adj. (HYOO mayn)—merciful, kindly
*Writers love to create **humane** characters, as they usually win the hearts of readers.*

illegible adj. (ih LEJ ih bul)—unreadable, indecipherable
*Robert's handwriting was so utterly **illegible** that his teacher jokingly suggested he become a doctor.*

Practice 2

DIRECTIONS: Match the word (left column) with its definition (right column).

6. **cogent**	informal words
7. **colloquial**	convincing
8. **humane**	clearly bad
9. **egregious**	a thing named after oneself
10. **eponymous**	kind

Your Words, Your World

Epitaph—Often people will ask that a *quote* or *short statement* be engraved on their gravestone. When words other than the name, birth date, and other such facts are included, they are considered an **epitaph**. If you can imagine the lettering, carved with care into the granite or marble, you will be able to remember that an **epitaph** is a written tribute.

Epilogue—An **epilogue** appears *at the end of a story*. **Epilogues** are often used to *sum up a story* by showing what becomes of an important character. Perhaps the main character was in her teens throughout the story, but the **epilogue** lets the reader know what she was like as an old woman.

PART THREE

insinuate v. (in SIN yoo ayt)—to suggest, say indirectly, imply
*Brenda **insinuated** that the character's name, JC, was a reference to Jesus Christ.*

irony n. (IY ur nee)—incongruity between expectations and actualities
*Mr. Vonblonk often reminded his students that **irony**, even more than plot twists, makes a story more interesting.*

lexicon n. (LEHK sih kahn)—a dictionary; a stock of terms pertaining to a particular subject or vocabulary
*Terms like "Gen X" and "catch-22" have entered the American **lexicon** through books.*

naïve adj. (niy EEV)—lacking experience and understanding; French for "natural"
*Nandi was **naïve** about the self-serving motives of the character.*

paradox n. (PAR uh doks)—contradiction, incongruity; dilemma, puzzle
*The class discussed the **paradox** of the traditional Christian idea of God's being both one and three entities.*

paragon n. (PAAR uh gon)—a model of excellence or perfection; an exemplar
*As far as novelists go, Philip Roth is a **paragon** of caring about every word.*

profound adj. (pro FOWND)—deep, meaningful; far-reaching
*The entire school listened carefully to the **profound** ideas of Toni Morrison.*

> **MEMORY TIP**
>
> Learning a new concept that has a real impact on you and your life is basically the same as finding something, like $20 or a message in a bottle from a long-lost friend. In trying to remember what **profound** means, break the word in two: *pro found*. You found out something deep and meaningful. To make it even easier, consider the fact that the word root **pro** means *much* or *a lot*. You sure did learn a lot!

prosaic adj. (proh SAY ihk)—relating to prose (as opposed to poetry); dull, ordinary
*Simon's **prosaic** writing took away from the effectiveness of his story.*

protagonist n. (pro TAG uh nist)—main character in a play or story; hero
*Charles Dickens created some of the world's more memorable **protagonists**.*

protégé n. (PRO tuh zhay)—one receiving personal direction and care from a mentor
*Although David was once a **protégé** of Tobias Wolf's, he'd quit the writing program and developed his own style of writing.*

pseudonym n. (SOO duh nihm)—a fictitious name, used particularly by writers to conceal identity
*George Eliot was the **pseudonym** that Marian Evans used when she published her classic novel* Middlemarch.

quandary n. (KWAN du ree)—predicament, dilemma
*John recognized his **quandary** as both editors informed him of their due dates, which fell on the same day!*

redundancy n. (ri DUN din see)—unnecessary repetition
*Jamie deleted a few paragraphs to cut down on the **redundancy** in his fourth chapter.*

rhetoric n. (REH tuhr ihk)—the art of speaking or writing effectively; skill in the effective use of speech
*Unfortunately, Lester's talent for **rhetoric** didn't carry over into his writing.*

scrupulous adj. (SKROOP yuh luhs)—acting in strict regard for what is considered proper; punctiliously exact
*Miller was known as the most **scrupulous** writer in his class, and the valedictorian asked him for help with her speech.*

tutelage n. (TOOT uh lihj)—guardianship, guidance
*Under the **tutelage** of Professor McSweeney, Michelle was able to flesh out the problem haunting her main character.*

Practice 3

DIRECTIONS: Consider the definition and then circle T for True or F for False.

11. **T F**   **irony**—flat and smooth

12. **T F**   **naïve**—lacking experience

13. **T F**   **paradox**—religious

14. **T F**   **protagonist**—the main character

15. **T F**   **scrupulous**—thorough

Your Words, Your World

Tutelage and **Protégé**—While **tutelage** is what the teacher or coach provides, the student who is learning is the **protégé**. You have obviously played the role of **protégé**. Just think of the teacher you have admired most, or the person who had the most influence on you and on where you think you might head in life. You surely benefited under his or her **tutelage**. Take a moment to think, now, about whether or not *you* have ever had a **protégé**. . . .

Prosaic and **Profound**—Whereas **prosaic** is defined as writing that is boring and ordinary, a story that is **profound** has deep meaning. It is interesting, it evokes emotion, and it leaves an impression on you when you're done reading it. When you open a book or begin reading a magazine article, you, like everyone else, hope that the writer has put together something **profound**. Nobody ever hopes to read something **prosaic**.

PRACTICE ANSWERS AND EXPLANATIONS

Practice 1

1. An **antagonist** is a foe, and Mr. Kweller felt that each book should have a main character and somebody who causes him or her problems.

2. To **abridge** is to shorten and because they lacked funding, the editors had to condense the yearbook.

3. An **adage** is often metaphoric for a common observation. It's usually a familiar saying.

4. Danny is not alone in believing that Mark Twain's novel is an **antecedent** to many other books, as they followed his use of the journey as a theme.

5. An **assertion** is a declaration lacking in proof. Research provides proof!

Practice 2

6. When something is **cogent** it is convincing, as in a **cogent** argument or theory.

7. When somebody says something that is considered **colloquial**, it is slang or a statement consisting of informal words.

8. To be **humane** is to be compassionate and kind.

9. When a statement, object, or action is **egregious** it is clearly bad. An oft-used term is "an **egregious** error."

10. When a band names an album after the band's name—for example, Metallica's album *Metallica*—the album is considered **eponymous**. When a restaurant, store, or even a child is named after the owner or parent (in other words, a thing named after oneself) then it is **eponymous**.

Practice 3

11. False. Irony is satire and insincerity—contrasting expectations and actualities—and not flat and smooth like ironing!

PRACTICE ANSWERS AND EXPLANATIONS *(cont'd)*

12.   True. To be **naïve** is to be lacking in experience and understanding.

13.   False. A **paradox** is an inconsistency or contradiction and not religious.

14.   True. The **protagonist** is the main character in a story and is often considered the hero.

15.   True. To be **scrupulous** is to act in regard for what is proper. It is to be conscientious and meticulous.

CHAPTER 7 QUIZ

Take your time, not only with the questions, but in reading the answer explanations that follow. Set a goal for yourself—80% (16 correct answers) is recommended—and if you don't reach that goal, go back and read through the chapter again. Good luck!

DIRECTIONS: For questions 1–11, circle T for True or F for False.
For questions 12–20, circle the synonym.

1. **T F   adulation**—unnecessary criticism
2. **T F   allegory**—in total
3. **T F   analogous**—an opponent
4. **T F   antidote**—a remedy
5. **T F   assertion**—to withdraw
6. **T F   bibliophile**—a book lover
7. **T F   cogent**—illogical
8. **T F   denizen**—an inhabitant
9. **T F   figurative**—not literal, but symbolic
10. **T F   profound**—boring
11. **T F   prosaic**—deep, meaningful

12. **insinuate:**	to state	to suggest	to specify
13. **protagonist:**	main character	antagonist	villain
14. **paragon:**	exemplar	imperfect	Paraguay
15. **naïve:**	knowledgeable	inexperienced	sophisticated
16. **paradox:**	contradiction	consistency	reliability
17. **lexicon:**	dictionary	encyclopedia	Qur'an
18. **pseudonym:**	false name	Bob	vignette
19. **quandary:**	solution	diorama	dilemma
20. **rhetoric:**	missive	lexicon	public speaking

CHAPTER 7 QUIZ ANSWERS AND EXPLANATIONS

1. **False.** **Adulation** is excessive, over-the-top flattery and not unnecessary criticism.

2. **False.** An **allegory** is a symbolic story. The definition is not in total.

3. **False.** To be **analogous** is to be comparable, or similar, and not to be an opponent.

4. **True.** An **antidote** is a remedy. Sometimes, this takes the form of medicine, while other times it might mean a decision to ease people's minds or a solution to solve a problem.

5. **False.** An **assertion** is not to withdraw. It is actually more the opposite: a statement or declaration usually made without any proof.

6. **True.** A **bibliophile** is a book lover.

7. **False.** To be **cogent** is to be convincing in a logical way, the opposite of illogical.

8. **True.** A **denizen** is an inhabitant or resident.

9. **True.** When something is presented in a **figurative** manner, it is symbolic or metaphoric. The use of rain is often a **figurative**, or symbolic, representation of a character's sadness.

10. **False.** When a book is **profound** it is meaningful and deep and not uninteresting. It is not boring, either.

11. **False.** **Prosaic** is an adjective which describes writing that is dull. Not only is it simplistic, it does not have a lasting impact on the reader.

12. To **insinuate** is *to suggest*. It is *to hint* and not *to state* or *specify*.

13. The **protagonist** is the main character in the story. Although she or he may be a *villain*, *main character* is the much more obvious answer. In addition, *antagonist* and *villain* are synonymous, or at least closely associated, as they both represent the protagonist's foe.

14. A **paragon** is a model of perfection or an *exemplar*. If a model is *imperfect* it is not a **paragon**. And although there may be **paragons** in Paraguay, *Paraguay* is the name of a country.

CHAPTER 7 QUIZ ANSWERS AND EXPLANATIONS *(cont'd)*

15. To be **naïve** is to be *inexperienced.* It is not to be *knowledgeable,* nor *sophisticated.*

16. Another word for a *contradiction* is a **paradox. Paradox** is synonymous with inconsistency, so *consistency* is out, as is *reliability.*

17. Another word for a *dictionary* is a **lexicon.** An *encyclopedia* is a reference book, but is not a dictionary. Nor is the religious text of Islam, the *Qur'an.*

18. *Bob* is not a *false name.* A **pseudonym,** however, is. A *vignette* is a short story.

19. Another word for *dilemma,* or problem, is **quandary.** So *solution* is actually an antonym. *Diorama* doesn't work either, as it is a miniaturized scene, often seen in museums.

20. **Rhetoric** is the skill of *public speaking* or writing. A *missive* (note or letter) and a *lexicon* (dictionary) are incorrect.

CHAPTER 8

The Law

Words that will help you understand
everything from CSI *to your parking ticket*

BUILDING BLOCK QUIZ

By answering the 12 questions below, you will get a sense of how closely you should study this chapter in order to master all of that vocabu*law*ry! And if you choose incorrect answers for the final two questions, you'll want to go back to chapter 7 for some review.

DIRECTIONS: Fill in the blanks, using the most appropriate of the four multiple-choice answers. The correct answer will always fit into the sentence grammatically.

1. When international news carried the story of the thief who had his hand amputated for stealing, many said it was a(n) _____ punishment.

   (A) attest   (B) apposite

   (C) opposite   (D) arbitrary

2. When Jim Klonberg released his legal thriller, he _____ that the details of the plot were taken from a recent celebrity court case.

   (A) averred   (B) arraigned

   (C) absconded   (D) paradoxed

3. All of Allen's photographs were ruined when the security guards subjected him to a random search and _____ at the airport.

   (A) candor   (B) substantiation

   (C) conviction   (D) confiscation

4. Meghan was _____ in her pursuit of justice as a public defense attorney, especially when the death penalty was involved.

   (A) hazardous   (B) castigated

   (C) dogged   (D) denizen

5. When Mr. Applebaum was told that there would be a(n) _____ involving his various bank accounts, he broke down in tears and admitted his guilt.

   (A) epochal   (B) inquest

   (C) negligible   (D) quandary

6. As soon as the police officer explained to Grandma Brown what _____ meant, she knew that Frankie had slipped back into stealing cars and racing them.

   (A) recidivism   (B) meticulous

   (C) tutelage   (D) deft

7. As the deal _____, instead of jail time the running back would serve two hundred hours of community service at area high schools.

   (A) stipulated   (B) exculpated

   (C) confiscated   (D) impugned

8. Terry was relieved to learn that his story had been _____ by the cashier who saw a man slip the CD in his bag.

   (A) purloined   (B) proscribed

   (C) nullified   (D) substantiated

9. If the civil suit were to be won, Jan had to find at least one doctor to _____ that the man had experienced back problems before the accident.

    (A) censure (B) attest

    (C) de facto (D) gravity

10. Warren finally agreed: the following day he would _____ control of the case to the junior partner and resign.

    (A) concede (B) corroborate

    (C) abscond (D) profound

11. In studying freedom of speech, students are always interested in debating _____ like banning flag burning and barring hate groups like the Ku Klux Klan from marching.

    (A) paradoxes (B) prosaics

    (C) protagonists (D) disputants

12. When the Supreme Court turned down the case, they said it would be a(n) _____ , as Congress had already passed a law dealing with the voting age.

    (A) astute (B) reprieve

    (C) redundancy (D) adage

BUILDING BLOCK ANSWERS AND EXPLANATIONS

1. B. As **apposite** means strikingly appropriate, it is the correct choice. *Attest* (testify) is a verb. *Arbitrary* (subjective) is also wrong. *Opposite* sounds like **apposite**, but it is also incorrect.

2. A. **Averred** means to vow or claim to be true. To *arraign* is to accuse, and to *abscond* is to escape, so neither is appropriate. *Paradox* (contradiction) is a word, but *paradoxed* isn't.

3. D. A **confiscation** takes place when something is taken away from someone, like Allen. *Substantiation* is when an accusation is proven, and a *conviction* is when you are found guilty, neither of which applies (hopefully!) to Allen. *Candor* is honesty and is an incorrect choice.

BUILDING BLOCK ANSWERS AND EXPLANATIONS *(cont'd)*

4. C. To be determined is to be **dogged** and Meghan was **dogged** in defending her low-income clients. *Hazardous* is dangerous, *castigated* is punished, and a *denizen* is a resident, so none of those fits as well as **dogged**.

5. B. An **inquest** is an investigation and in this case, the **inquest** was sure to turn up something, so Mr. Applebaum gave up. If something is *epochal*, it is a tremendously important moment in history. If something is *negligible*, it is not important, so that is incorrect. A *quandary* is a problem and although that's not the answer, Mr. Applebaum did have problems.

6. A. **Recidivism** occurs when someone falls back into a pattern of behavior, usually criminal. To be *meticulous* is to be very careful and to be *deft* is to be highly skilled. *Tutelage* is incorrect, too, as it means studying under a mentor.

7. A. To make a part of a deal is to **stipulate** and in this case, community service hours were **stipulated**. *Exculpated* (cleared of blame), *confiscated* (legally taken), and *impugned* (questioned) are all relevant, but not right.

8. D. Terry's story was **substantiated**, or verified, so he was proven innocent. *Purloined* means stolen and *proscribed* means forbidden, so those are incorrect. *Nullified* is close, as perhaps the charges against Terry were nullified, but **substantiated** is more appropriate.

9. B. Jan needed someone to **attest**, or testify, so that her client isn't blamed for the man's bad back. To *censure* is to criticize, *de facto* is "from the fact" in Latin, and *gravity* describes a situation's seriousness. None of these fits as well as **attest**.

10. A. Warren was going to give in, or **concede**. Since he was resigning, he could not *corroborate* (support) the case. He may *abscond* (run away), but that only fits into the theme of the sentence and not the blank. *Profound* (thoughtful) is an inappropriate choice.

11. A. **Paradoxes** are interesting situations involving inconsistencies and contradictions, so this is the best answer. *Prosaics* is not a word, although *prosaic* means dull writing. *Protagonists* (main characters) and *disputants* (those involved in a disagreement) are close, but not close enough. If you answered this question incorrectly, you might want to go back to chapter 7 for some review.

BUILDING BLOCK ANSWERS AND EXPLANATIONS *(cont'd)*

12. C. A **redundancy** is an unnecessary repetition. In this case, the Supreme Court did not feel it necessary to revisit the voting age. If someone is *astute*, he or she is smart. If someone receives a *reprieve*, he or she is pardoned. And an *adage* is an old saying. To repeat . . . **redundancy** wins! If you answered this question incorrectly, you might want to go back to chapter 7 for some review.

PART ONE

abet v. (uh BEHT)—to aid; to act as an accomplice
*While Dale was convicted, Malcolm was also sent to jail for aiding and **abetting** his friend.*

abscond v. (aab SKAHND)—to leave quickly in secret
*During the night, Sean **absconded** with all of his mother's money.*

absolve v. (ahb SAHLV)—to forgive, free from blame
*Although Sean's mother **absolved** him, his father did not.*

adjudicate v. (uh JOOD ih kayt)—to hear and settle a matter; to act as a judge
*Principal Wykowski **adjudicated** the disagreement between the two students.*

annul v. (ah NULL)—to cancel, nullify, declare void, or make legally invalid
*The couple asked the court to **annul** their marriage, as they both felt it was a big mistake.*

MEMORY TIP

We all know what it means when someone says, "The deal is **null** and void." It's off is what it means. And as **nul** appears at the end of **annul**, use this phrase to trigger your memory. To **annul** is to *cancel* or *nullify* something—something like a deal.

---

apposite adj. (AAP puh ziht)—strikingly appropriate or well adapted
*Barry's **apposite** approach with the jury meant a life sentence instead of the death penalty.*

arbitration n. (ar bih TRAY shun)—process where a dispute is settled by an outside party
*The NHL and the Players' Association tried using **arbitration** to settle the strike, but to no avail.*

arraign v. (ah RAYN)—call to court to answer an indictment
*Jesse was **arraigned** yesterday, but failed to show up in court.*

aver v. (ah VER)—to declare to be true, affirm
*The witness **averred** that Eddie had, in fact, been holding the gun.*

> **FLASHBACK**
>
> In Latin, ver*itas* means *true*. And as a word root, **ver** also means *true*. So it only makes sense that **aver** means *to tell the truth*.

castigate v. (kas ti GAYT)—to punish, chastise, criticize severely
*Authorities in Singapore harshly **castigate** people convicted of crimes that would be considered minor in the U.S.*

concede v. (kon SEED)—to yield, admit
*Ralph **conceded** that the case would be nearly impossible to win, but vowed to try nonetheless.*

confiscation n. (kon fis KAY shun)—seizure by authorities
*The **confiscation** of Bethany's cell phone was the administration's first step in stopping students from calling one another in school.*

corroborate v. (ke ROB uh rayt)—to confirm, verify
*Fingerprints **corroborated** Theo's testimony that he saw the defendant holding the bag.*

Practice 1

DIRECTIONS: Consider the two word choices in the parentheses, and circle the one that best fits in the context of the sentence.

1. Judge Tinsely overruled the objection, allowing the witness to (**abscond** OR **aver**) the defendant's presence at the party that night.

2. Karl was nervous when his case went to (**confiscation** OR **arbitration**) as he had no idea if the mediator would be sympathetic or not.

3. Penny hoped that her history of charity work would be enough to (**annul** OR **attest**) to her innocence.

4. Jerry couldn't believe that Michael, his partner in the restaurant for over ten years, would (**adjudicate** OR **abscond**) with the cash, the cappuccino machine, and even the CDs from the jukebox.

5. Everyone agreed that one hundred hours of community service was the (**apposite** OR **absolve**) punishment for the one hundred flowers Hank had ridden through on his bike.

Your Words, Your World

Castigate—To **castigate** is to *punish,* and two images might help you to remember this definition. There is the old rule about a guilty person not casting the first stone. The casting, or throwing of the stone, was intended as a *punishment.* Second is the image of a gate swinging shut as the prisoner enters the prison. Think of *cast* and *gate,* and you should remember the idea of punishment.

Adjudicate—*Adjudicare* is Latin for *to judge.* One way to remember a word is to think about its origins. Let the letters **jud** serve as a reminder as well. Look at those letters and think of **jud**ge. The definition of **adjudicate** is to hear and settle a matter. This is the main responsibility of judges, from the ancient days of Rome right up to today.

PART TWO

de facto adj. (dee FAK toh)—officially recognized, but not necessarily legally established; Latin for "from the fact"
*Alexi was the **de facto** head of the Russian mob in town.*

dogged adj. (DAW guhd)—stubbornly persevering
*Detective Conrad's **dogged** investigation helped catch the stalker.*

epochal adj. (EHP uh kuhl)—momentous, highly significant
*The Supreme Court's **epochal** decision will no doubt affect generations to come.*

exculpate v. (EK skul payt)—to clear of blame or fault, vindicate
*In a system based on "innocent till proven guilty," no defense attorney should ever have to **exculpate** a client, but of course they make that their goal.*

expedite v. (EK spe diyt)—to speed up the progress of
*The right to a speedy trial is why Judge West tries to **expedite** the judicial process.*

extirpate v. (EHK stuhr payt)—to root out, eradicate, literally or figuratively; to destroy wholly
*Lawrence became a cop so as to **extirpate** crime in his beloved city.*

FLASHBACK

In Chapter 1, Word Roots, you learned that **ex** means *out* or *out of*. To **extirpate** is to *root something out* and destroy it. The *rooting out* is derived from the **ex**. In **exculpate**, the **ex** represents getting someone *out of trouble*. And in **expedite**, you could say that the **ex** stands for getting something like a package or message *out in a hurry*. Whatever helps you to get the definition *out* of your memory bank when you need it!

---

gravity adj. (GRAH vih tee)—importance, seriousness
*Phyllis, not grasping the **gravity** of the situation, strode into the police station with a smile on her face.*

impugn v. (im PYOON)—to call into question, attack verbally
*Harry was quite upset when the detective **impugned** his explanation.*

incriminate v. (in KRIM uh nayt)—accuse of a crime, implicate
*Although being found with a dead body is usually very **incriminating**, Peg's alibi was airtight.*

inquest n. (IHN kwehst)—an investigation, an inquiry
*Chief Masterson ordered an internal **inquest** as a means of cleaning up the police department's image.*

meticulous adj. (meh TIK yoo luss)—extremely careful, painstaking
*Carmine was a **meticulous** private investigator, and he charged a lot for his services.*

negligible adj. (NEG lih ju bul)—not worth considering
*The Freihoffs decided to move to Madison because the crime rate was so low as to be **negligible**.*

Practice 2

DIRECTIONS: After reading the three choices, circle the one that you think is the *antonym*.

6.	**de facto**:	untrue	proven	fact
7.	**dogged**:	stubborn	quitter	persevering
8.	**exculpate**:	to pardon	to acquit	to prosecute
9.	**expedite**:	to speed up	to hinder	to advance
10.	**impugn**:	to censure	to charge	to acquit

Your Words, Your World

Meticulous—When a person is **meticulous**, she takes great *care*, using *caution* in everything that she does. And this doesn't just apply to hazardous situations. Her desk, handbag, car, bedroom, and life, are *well organized*. Are you **meticulous**? If not, can you think of someone who is? Imagine that person's face, and you'll be reminded of what this word means.

Epochal—An **epochal** situation may include the hazardous and it may be filled with gravity, but the key to this definition is *historical*. When something is **epochal**, it marks a new and important era in history. Possible examples include a world war or a global disease of epidemic proportions. What **epochal** events have happened during your lifetime?

PART THREE

nolo contendere n. (nah loh kahn TEN duh ree)—no contest; Latin for "I do not wish to contend"
Studying his bar exam flashcards, Mike used "no" to remind himself that nolo contendere means no contest.

perjure v. (PIR joor)—to tell a lie under oath
Benson perjured himself to protect his son, forgetting what he'd said earlier and claiming he'd been with him on the night in question.

precedent n. (PRESS uh dent)—earlier example of a similar situation
Denise was proud when she finally unearthed the precedent-setting case she'd been assigned to find.

procure v. (pro KYOOR)—to acquire, obtain; to get
The evidence was inadmissible, as Officer Jefferson had not procured it legally.

proscribe v. (proh SKRIEB)—to condemn or forbid as harmful or unlawful
During Prohibition, alcohol was proscribed in the U.S.

purloin v. (PUHR loyn)—to steal
Dupay purloined the photograph and brought it to the police department immediately.

recidivism n. (rih SIHD uh vih zihm)—a tendency to relapse into a previous behavior, especially criminal behavior
According the statistics, the recidivism rate for high school dropouts is tremendous.

refute v. (re FYOOT)—to contradict, discredit
Ned refuted the charge against his client by highlighting his positive traits with a lot of character witnesses.

reprieve n. (re PREEV)—postponement of a punishment; relief from danger
Stevens earned a brief reprieve as the governor considered the case one last time.

sedition n. (seh DIH shuhn)—behavior that promotes rebellion or civil disorder against the state
Lee was arrested for sedition after handing out Karl Marx's Communist Manifesto.

sequester v. (suh KWEH stuhr)—to set apart, seclude
When juries are sequestered, it can take days, even weeks, to come up with a verdict.

statute n. (STA choot)—law, edict
According to the new town statutes, it is illegal to throw chewed bubblegum onto the street.

stipulate v. (STIHP yuh layt)—to specify as a condition or requirement of an agreement or offer
As part of the plea bargain, the defense stipulated that a public apology would not be required.

substantiate v. (sub STAN she ayt)—to verify, confirm, provide supporting evidence
The ice cream cone in the garbage can substantiated Jill's alibi.

surrogate n. (SUR uh git)—a substitute; one filling in for someone else
The boy was assigned a surrogate by the state and given a court date.

verbatim adv. (ver BA tum)—word for word
A court stenographer's job is to record everything said in court, verbatim.

Practice 3

DIRECTIONS: Fill in the blanks, using five of the eight words provided below.

proscribed	verbatim	precedent	surrogate
recidivism	refute	stipulated	statute

11. When the _____ concerning seat belts went into effect, police officers issued hundreds of tickets to enforce the new law.

12. The stenographer's fingers flew over the keys as she recorded the trial _____.

13. As both his parents were deceased, Heather often acted as Taylor's _____, especially in matters at school that required signatures.

14. The principal used Mick's 66% average as a _____ in deciding that he had cheated in order to score a 98% on the test.

15. Dr. Warner _____ that if Danielle were allowed to return, she had to promise to never again bring drugs to school.

Your Words, Your World

Refute—What's the hardest you have ever had to work to *right* a wrong? Can you remember a time when you really had to put forth great effort to *discredit* someone who'd tried to discredit you? A *rebuttal* is a more official form of **refutation**; for example, in a court case or in a debate. If someone has ever accused you of perjury, purloining, or even procuring, chances are you tried to **refute** that charge.

Substantiate—Have you ever been accused of something, and the only way to *prove your innocence* was by **substantiating** your story? It is an awful feeling to be threatened in this way, but at least there is an *opportunity to refute the story*. Think of how you (or if not you, a friend) **substantiated** the story. What facts did you present? Who *validated* your story for you? Were your parents convinced? The principal? The police?!?!

PRACTICE ANSWERS AND EXPLANATIONS

Practice 1

1. To **aver** is to declare to be true, and this was what Judge Tinsely wanted to hear. To *abscond* is to leave quickly.

2. This is not a case of *confiscation*, even though something may be taken from Karl after his **arbitration** hearing. **Arbitration** is a process in which a dispute is settled by an outside party (arbiter).

3. Penny was hoping her charitable ways would verify, or **attest** to, her innocence. To *annul* is to cancel, so this is definitely not what she was hoping for.

4. To **abscond** is to leave quickly and in secret, which is what Michael did. To *adjudicate* is to give a ruling or decision and this is incorrect.

5. A punishment that is **apposite** is appropriate and fitting. There is no such thing as an *absolve* (pardon or forgive) punishment as *absolve* is a verb and not an adjective.

Practice 2

6. **De facto** is Latin for "from the fact" and so untrue is not true!

7. To be **dogged** is to be determined or stubbornly persevering. To be **dogged** is not to be a quitter.

8. To **exculpate** is to clear someone of fault or blame. It is to vindicate and not to prosecute.

9. To **expedite** is to speed up the progress of something. To hinder is its antonym.

10. To **impugn** is to call someone into question. At worst, it is to accuse. At best, it is to hold that person responsible for his or her actions. To acquit is the antonym.

PRACTICE ANSWERS AND EXPLANATIONS *(cont'd)*

Practice 3

11. A **statute** is a law and in this case, the law involves wearing a seat belt.

12. **Verbatim** translates from Latin as "word for word." The stenographer, even if she was using shorthand, was recording every word from the trial.

13. A **surrogate** is a substitute and often, children who do not have family to look out for them are assigned a legal surrogate. Makes you appreciate mom and/or dad a little bit more, doesn't it?

14. A **precedent** is an earlier example of a similar situation. Lawyers will use **precedent**-setting cases to try and convince a judge, and in the case of Mick's grade, an educator used past behavior as a **precedent** in making a tough decision.

15. To **stipulate** is to order or specify in detail. In Danielle's situation, the **stipulation** was a trade-off: a return to school for a promise.

CHAPTER 8 QUIZ

Take your time, not only with the questions, but in reading the answer explanations that follow. Set a goal for yourself—80% (16 correct answers) is recommended—and if you don't reach that goal, go back and read through the chapter again. Good luck!

DIRECTIONS: For questions 1–10, circle T for True or F for False.
For questions 11–20, circle the synonym.

1. **T F** **abet**—to aid

2. **T F** **arraign**—to declare innocent

3. **T F** **procure**—to acquire

4. **T F** **incriminate**—to plead innocent

5. **T F** **abscond**—to obtain

6. **T F** **castigate**—to punish

7. **T F** **annul**—to proceed

8. **T F** **arbitrary**—consistent

9. **T F** **nullify**—to cancel

10. **T F** **corroborate**—to verify

11. **surrogate**:	substitute	substantiate	statute
12. **refute**:	contradict	rebate	proscribe
13. **exculpate**:	arraign	vindicate	verify
14. **substantiate**:	verify	substitute	subject
15. **meticulous**:	verbatim	thorough	abscond
16. **proscribe**:	forbid	permit	purloin
17. **negligible**:	stipulate	unimportant	vital
18. **sequester**:	seclude	inquest	hazardous
19. **arbitration**:	a hearing	dispute	arbitrary
20. **stipulate**:	de facto	gravity	requirement

CHAPTER 8 QUIZ ANSWERS AND EXPLANATIONS

1. **True.** To **abet** is to aid.

2. **False.** To **arraign** is to formally charge with a crime. It is not to be acquitted (declared innocent).

3. **True.** To **procure** is to acquire, obtain, or get.

4. **False.** When someone is implicated in a crime he or she is **incriminated**. It is not to plead innocent, although that might be what this person does.

5. **False.** To **abscond** is to leave quickly, often in secret, and not to obtain something.

6. **True.** To **castigate** is to punish.

7. **False.** To **annul** is to cancel and not to proceed, which is an antonym.

8. **False.** If something is done in an **arbitrary** fashion, it is done haphazardly. It is done purely on a whim and not in a manner consistent with anything that has been done before.

9. **True.** To **nullify** is to make legally invalid.

10. **True.** When somebody **corroborates** a story, he or she confirms or verifies it.

11. A **surrogate** is a *substitute* and not a *statute* (law) or to *substantiate* (verify).

12. To **refute** a point (or a criminal charge) is to *contradict* it. It is not to *proscribe* (ban or bar) the point, nor is it to *rebate* (get a refund for) it.

13. To **exculpate** is to *vindicate* or clear of fault. To *arraign* is to charge, while to *verify* is to confirm.

14. To **substantiate** a story is to *verify* it. To *substitute* is to replace and to *subject* is to expose, so those are both incorrect.

15. To be very *thorough* and careful is to be **meticulous**. *Verbatim* (word for word) and *abscond* (to leave) are both out.

CHAPTER 8 QUIZ ANSWERS AND EXPLANATIONS *(cont'd)*

16. To **proscribe** is to *forbid*. To *permit* is the opposite, while to *purloin* is to steal. Stealing may be forbidden, but it is still an incorrect choice.

17. When something is **negligible** it isn't worth considering. It is *unimportant* and so could not be *vital*. To *stipulate* is to make a demand, which may or may not be worth considering. Either way, stipulate is incorrect.

18. To **sequester** is to *seclude*, or separate, as often happens to an important jury. An *inquest* is an investigation and something *hazardous* is dangerous.

19. To go to **arbitration**, or *a hearing*, is to have your argument heard by a third party. Although a *dispute* is being settled, this is incorrect, as is *arbitrary* (random or inconsistent).

20. To include a *requirement* is to **stipulate** that something has to be done or included to get a deal done. *De facto* (from the fact) and *gravity* (importance) are not correct.

Etiquette, Culture, and Religion

Build your vocabulary for everything from manners to culture and religion

BUILDING BLOCK QUIZ

By answering the ten questions below, you will get a sense of how closely you should study this chapter in order to master the vocabulary you need to speak knowledgeably about etiquette, culture, and religion.

DIRECTIONS: Fill in the blanks, using the most appropriate of the four multiple-choice answers. The correct answer will always fit into the sentence grammatically.

1. Sam told his friends that he wasn't sure how he felt about organized religion and that he was either an atheist or a(n) _____.

   (A) archipelago   (B) agnostic
   (C) cherubic   (D) arcane

2. Rashaad promised his mother he would _____ for all of his mistakes, starting with an apology to the principal.

   (A) adverse   (B) condone
   (C) espouse   (D) atone

3. Father Joseph's sermon was about the _____ of the government in making the Girl Scouts pay taxes on their cookie sales.

   (A) benign   (B) avarice

   (C) anoint   (D) substantiate

4. The rabbi could tell how _____ the little girl was, so he advised her parents to talk with her about right and wrong, rather than punishing her.

   (A) contrite   (B) humane

   (C) adverse   (D) clairvoyant

5. For Muslims, praying five times a day is a source of _____, giving them the strength to be true to their faith.

   (A) tenet   (B) dissident

   (C) fortitude   (D) malediction

6. As a part of her newspaper editorial, the minister thanked the congregants for their _____ donations to the tsunami relief fund.

   (A) munificent   (B) avarice

   (C) contrite   (D) blasphemous

7. The leaders of the commune said that organic farming was one of its _____, along with holistic medicine and home schooling.

   (A) impenitents   (B) tenets

   (C) rhetorics   (D) incantations

8. The chief of police allowed the Hare Krishnas to walk the streets, singing their songs and beating their drums, even though some townspeople called their behavior _____.

   (A) verbatim   (B) adulterate

   (C) ethos   (D) blasphemous

9. When the girls started their Secret Society of the Tree House, they made up a whole list of _____ rituals and passwords.

    (A) credo   (B) arcane

    (C) zealot   (D) perfidious

10. After surviving the _____ conditions of war, Wilt became a regular attendee at church.

    (A) adverse   (B) agnostic

    (C) sanctimonious   (D) prostrate

BUILDING BLOCK ANSWERS AND EXPLANATIONS

1. B. An atheist doesn't believe in God, while an **agnostic** simply questions God's existence. An *archipelago* is a string of islands, *cherubic* is to look angelic, and *arcane* is mysterious, so those choices are all incorrect.

2. D. To **atone** is to make amends for a mistake, or for many mistakes in Rashaad's case. To *condone* (overlook) and to *espouse* (support) are almost antonyms. *Adverse* means unfavorable, but it is an adjective and this sentence needs a verb.

3. B. **Avarice** is greed and Father Joseph felt the government was being stingy. *Benign* is kind, so that definitely isn't right. To *anoint* is to bless, and to *substantiate* is to verify.

4. A. To be **contrite** is to be deeply sorrowful, and obviously, the girl feels regretful. Although *clairvoyant* (psychic) fits grammatically as an adjective, its meaning does not fit. *Humane* (caring) and *adverse* (unfavorable conditions) are both incorrect.

5. C. The praying is a source of strength, or **fortitude**. A *tenet* is a principle, so that is close, but not close enough. A *dissident* is a rebel, and a *malediction* is a curse, so those are obviously wrong.

6. A. **Munificent** is an adjective used to describe generous deeds. *Avarice* (greed) and *blasphemous* (sacrilegious) are basically antonyms. To be *contrite* is to be full of remorse, so that is not the best option.

BUILDING BLOCK ANSWERS AND EXPLANATIONS *(cont'd)*

7. B. A **tenet** is a principle or belief; in this case, organic farming was one of the keystone beliefs of the commune. *Impenitent* is to not be remorseful, and *rhetoric* is public speaking, neither of which is ever written in the plural form (with an *s* at the end). *Incantations* are songs or prayers, so this is incorrect.

8. D. The complainers saw the behavior as profane, irreverent, and **blasphemous**, but the police chief disagreed. Of the other three choices, *verbatim* means word-for-word, *adulterate* (a verb, while an adjective is called for here) means to contaminate, and *ethos* (a noun) is a group philosophy.

9. B. The girls were trying to be mysterious, so they came up with a bunch of **arcane** (secretive) rituals and passwords. A *credo* is a set of beliefs, a *zealot* is a passionate (or fanatical) believer, and *perfidious* means disloyal, so none of those is appropriate.

10. A. The choice is **adverse**, as war is full of traumatically difficult situations. An *agnostic* doubts God's existence, but Wilt's faith deepened due to the war. To be *sanctimonious* is to make a pretense of being devout, and to be *prostrate* is to lie facedown in a submissive position.

PART ONE

abjure v. (aab JOOR)—to renounce under oath; to abandon forever; to abstain from
*Although he had been a Catholic all his life, Paul **abjured** his religious beliefs and became a Buddhist.*

adulterate v. (ah DULL ter ayt)—to corrupt or make impure
*Father Gowen wrote a convincing sermon about television's ability to **adulterate** unsupervised children.*

adverse adj. (ad VERHS)—unfavorable, unlucky; harmful
*In **adverse** conditions, many people turn to religious leaders for solace.*

agnostic n. (aag NAHS tik)—one who doubts that God exists
*Upon telling his parents that he was an **agnostic**, Matt was surprised at their lack of anger.*

anoint v. (ah NOYNT)—to apply oil to someone or something especially as a sacred rite
*The ceremony required Kelly to **anoint** her daughter's head with oil.*

apostate n. (uh PAHS tayt)—one who renounces a religious faith
*King Charles XII declared himself an **apostate** so that he could marry out of his faith.*

arcane adj. (ahr KAYN)—secret, obscure; known only to a few
*Walter decided to do a research paper on the **arcane** rituals of the world's lesser-known religions.*

atone v. (ah TON)—to make amends for a wrong
*Rabbi Schultz was pleased to hear that the three boys wanted to **atone** for their wrongdoings.*

avarice n. (AH var iss)—greed
*Rebecca told her brother, "You'd be hard-pressed to find a faith that doesn't warn against **avarice**."*

baleful adj. (BAYL ful)—harmful, with evil intentions
*Mishka worried that her son was turning **baleful** as a result of the divorce.*

benign adj. (buh NIYN)—kindly, gentle, or harmless
*Sully was relieved to learn that the reverend was **benign** and not cruel or judgmental in the least.*

blasphemous adj. (BLAS fuh muhs)—cursing, profane, irreverent
*Jack had a long conversation with his daughters about avoiding **blasphemous** behavior and was pleased that they seemed to understand.*

canonize v. (KAN on iyz)—to declare a person a saint; raise to highest honors
*Everyone in the city was excited to learn that the nun from St. Francis would be **canonized** in Rome.*

clairvoyant adj., n. (klayr VOY nt)—exceptionally insightful, able to foresee the future; a person with those abilities
*Having tried organized religion, Nancy turned to a **clairvoyant** for guidance.*

Practice 1

DIRECTIONS: Match the word (left column) with its definition (right column).

1. **arcane**:   obscure

2. **baleful**:   one who doubts God's existence

3. **anoint**:   to apply oil in a sacred rite

4. **blasphemous**:   unfavorable

5. **agnostic**:   to be irreverent

Your Words, Your World

Benign—Has anyone ever called you **benign**? If so, did you know you were being complimented? To be called *gentle* and *kind* may not be what you're aiming for (especially if you're a teenage boy or a business executive), but it's nice to hear, nonetheless.

Canonize—Maybe you've surpassed *benign* and gone straight to **canonization**! If so, this means that somebody has noticed your good deeds and *declared you a saint*. Of course, chances are they are just being figurative, but it is a great *accolade* nonetheless. Does *benign* describe you? Should you be *praised*, if not **canonized**?

PART TWO

condone v. (kon DOHN)—to pardon or forgive; overlook, justify, or excuse a fault
*Despite being Muslim, Shef could not **condone** the suicide bombings in Israel.*

consecrate v. (KON si krayt)—to declare sacred; dedicate to a goal
*Father Mike **consecrated** the rings, and Ben and Wendy were married!*

contrite adj. (kon TRYT)—deeply sorrowful and repentant for a wrong
*Ted seemed **contrite**, but his family was slow to forgive him, as he had apologized for his drunk driving many times before.*

credo n. (KREE doh)—system of principles or beliefs
*Taylor knew that if she chose a virtuous **credo** to live by, she could be spiritual without necessarily being religious.*

dissident adj., n. (DIHS ih duhnt)—disagreeing with an established religious or political system; the person who disagrees in this way
*Everyone suspected Gene cared more about being a **dissident** than about the actual issues.*

espouse v. (ih SPOWZ)—to take up and support as a cause
*Because of his religious beliefs, Karl could not **espouse** the family-planning curriculum at the high school.*

ethos n. (EE thohs)—beliefs or character of a group
*In accordance with the **ethos** of the Quakers, Lowell did not have to serve in the military.*

expound v. (ehk SPOWND)—to explain or describe in detail
*To the point of being distasteful, the minister liked to **expound** the sins that haunt mankind.*

exultant adj. (eg ZUHL tent)—triumphant
*The Dalai Llama was **exultant** in his own peaceful way.*

fidelity n. (fih DEL ih tee)—loyalty, faithfulness
*During their marriage counseling sessions, the priest constantly reminded Frank and Heather of the importance of **fidelity**.*

heretical adj. (huh REH tih kuhl)—departing from accepted beliefs or standards, oppositional
*Throughout history, the actions of many spiritual leaders have been called **heretical**.*

impenitent adj. (im PEN ih tent)—not remorseful
*David was so **impenitent** that his outraged father put the boy in the back of the car and drove straight to the synagogue.*

incantation n. (in kan TAY shun)—a verbal spell
*Speaking in tongues is a form of **incantation**.*

Practice 2

DIRECTIONS: Consider the definition and then circle T for True or F for False.

6. **T F** **impenitent**—remorseful

7. **T F** **heretical**—deeply religious

8. **T F** **credo**—system of beliefs

9. **T F** **ethos**—to glorify

10. **T F** **consecrate**—to declare sacred

Your Words, Your World

Incantation—In Spanish, *cantar* means to sing. Imagine the sound of singing coming from a church, synagogue, mosque, or any other sort of spiritual gathering. An **incantation** is a *chant, prayer,* or *song.*

Dissident—History is full of people who have **dissed** religions, and if you can picture one of them, Martin Luther, making a **dent** while posting his "95 Theses" on the door of the Castle Church, you will be able to remember that a **dissident** is *one who disagrees with an established religion or system.*

PART THREE

intrapersonal adj. (in trah PER sah nul)—occurring within one person's mind or self
*As Jane matured, her **intrapersonal** strengths grew.*

FLASHBACK

In Chapter 1, Word Roots, you learned that **intra** means *within.* Not to be confused with **inter** (*between*), **intra** has a personal, individual aspect to it. As in **intrapersonal**, which means *occurring within one's mind,* when a word includes the root **intra** it refers to a private occurrence.

---

mea culpa n. (me ah KUL puh)—my fault; Latin for "my fault"
*Meghan's mother always blamed herself for everything, muttering **mea culpas** constantly.*

medium n. (MEE dee um)—psychic
*Carla was so upset about the death of her grandmother that she decided to use a **medium** to contact her and say a proper good-bye.*

munificent adj. (myoo NIF ih sint)—generous
*After the Wilsons made their **munificent** donation, the church finally was able to build a rectory.*

omniscient adj. (ahm NISH ent)—having knowledge of all things
*Marty questioned whether it was rational to believe in an **omniscient** God.*

orthodox adj. (OR thu doks)—adhering to what is customary or traditional
*Robert wanted to continue going to church, but knew he needed a congregation that was a little less **orthodox**.*

penitent adj. (PEH nih tehnt)—expressing sorrow for sins or offenses, repentant
*Manson's eyes were more crazed than **penitent**, and everybody was relieved to hear that he'd been convicted.*

perfidious adj. (pir FID ee uss)—faithless, disloyal, untrustworthy
*Martha was upset to learn that her daughter was **perfidious**, and she longed to get the girl some spiritual counseling.*

repentant adj. (re PEN tant)—apologetic, remorseful, guilty
*After stealing from the collection plate, Ralph was so **repentant** that he offered to do everything from lawn work to carpentry for the church.*

sanctimonious adj. (SAANGK tih MOH nee uhs)—hypocritically devout; acting morally superior to another
*Father Chris's **sanctimonious** tone drove many parishioners away.*

secular adj. (SEH kyoo luhr)—not specifically pertaining to religion, relating to the world
*In addition to the Bible, Reverend Sheila had a copy of the Qur'an, Friday's New York Times, and several **secular** novels by her bed.*

serendipity n. (se ren DIP ih tee)—habit of making fortunate discoveries by chance
*Rosemary would tell anyone willing to listen that her **serendipity** was a sure sign of God's presence.*

stringent adj. (STRIHN juhnt)—imposing severe, rigorous standards
*The class debated whether the Pilgrims' **stringent** ways were a help or a hindrance in the New World.*

talisman n. (TAL iss man)—magic object that offers supernatural protection
*Greg counted on the little bobblehead **talisman** on the dashboard to keep his old Toyota running.*

Practice 3

DIRECTIONS: Read the three possible synonyms, then circle the word you think best defines the word in bold.

11.	**repentant**:	refusing	apologetic	sanctimonious
12.	**intrapersonal**:	introspective	interactive	international
13.	**orthodox**:	paradox	traditional	serendipity
14.	**secular**:	worldly	separate	religious
15.	**munificent**:	municipal	medium	generous

Your Words, Your World

Serendipity—**Serendipity** is good fortune. When something nice happens by chance to you, it is **serendipitous**. Have you ever had a great week? Perhaps a want ad for the perfect job landed in your lap, a check arrived from a long-lost relative, or you randomly found a friend from childhood while surfing the Internet.

Stringent—But luck changes . . . sometimes serendipity disappears and you have to face a **stringent** new teacher or manager. His *severe rules* and his *rigorous standards* bring everyone down. Can you think of someone you know who is **stringent**?

PRACTICE ANSWERS AND EXPLANATIONS

Practice 1

1. If something is **arcane** it is obscure, or vague.

2. If something, or someone, is **baleful** it is menacing and harmful.

3. To **anoint** is to apply oil in a sacred rite or ceremony.

4. If someone is acting in a **blasphemous** manner, that person is being irreverent and, more specifically, sacrilegious.

5. An **agnostic** is one who doubts the existence of God.

Practice 2

6. **False. Impenitent** is the opposite of remorseful.

7. **False.** To be **heretical**, one must depart from accepted beliefs. **Heretical** does not mean deeply religious.

8. **True.** A **credo** is the system of beliefs of a person or group.

9. **False.** An **ethos** is the beliefs or character of a group. It is not to glorify.

10. **True.** To **consecrate** is to declare sacred.

Practice 3

11. To be **repentant** is to be penitent and *apologetic*. *Refusing* is incorrect as is *sanctimonious* (self-righteous).

12. When something is **intrapersonal**, usually it means that the person is being *introspective*. She or he is thinking about things and working them out. *Interactive* involves doing things with other people, while *international* involves other countries.

13. If something (or someone), is **orthodox**, it is not a *paradox*. It is *traditional* and conformist. *Serendipity* refers to the chance occurrence of good fortune.

PRACTICE ANSWERS AND EXPLANATIONS *(cont'd)*

14.   When something (or someone) is considered **secular**, it is *worldly* and not religious or spiritual. For example, the U.S. government is supposed to be **secular**, through the doctrine of "separation of church and state." But neither *separate* nor *religious* is the right answer.

15.   The adjective **munificent** is used to describe a *generous* act or person. *Municipal* is a distracter based on a similar prefix, and a *medium* is a psychic or clairvoyant.

CHAPTER 9 QUIZ

Take your time, not only with the questions, but in reading the answer explanations that follow. Set a goal for yourself—80% (16 correct answers) is recommended—and if you don't reach that goal, go back and read through the chapter again. Good luck!

DIRECTIONS: For questions 1–10, circle T for True or F for False. For questions 11–20, circle the synonym.

1. **T F** **medium**—psychic
2. **T F** **anoint**—to apply oil as a sacred rite
3. **T F** **expound**—to describe in detail
4. **T F** **atone**—noise
5. **T F** **repentant**—remorseful
6. **T F** **baleful**—full of love
7. **T F** **incantation**—a hymn, chant, or prayer
8. **T F** **benign**—obscure
9. **T F** **blasphemous**—reverent
10. **T F** **consecrate**—to declare sacred

11. **contrite**:	gleeful	contrasting	repentant
12. **credo**:	system of beliefs	statement of disbelief	nonbeliever
13. **penitent**:	repentant	offensive	facedown
14. **fidelity**:	unfaithful	stringent	loyalty
15. **arcane**:	secret	well known	prehistoric
16. **malediction**:	foolish notion	lexicon	curse
17. **munificent**:	glorious	affable	generous
18. **abjure**:	to reject	to accept	to be official
19. **orthodox**:	traditional	clean	adverse
20. **perfidious**:	faithless	loyal	trusting

CHAPTER 9 QUIZ ANSWERS AND EXPLANATIONS

1. **True.** A **medium** is a psychic.

2. **True.** To **anoint** is to apply oil, especially as a part of a religious ceremony.

3. **True.** To **expound** is to explain or describe in detail.

4. **False.** To **atone** is to make amends for a wrong and has nothing to do with sound!

5. **True.** To be **repentant** is to be apologetic and remorseful. It is to admit guilt and ask for forgiveness.

6. **False.** To be **baleful** is not to be full of love and joy. It is the opposite: to have evil intentions and to be harmful.

7. **True.** An **incantation** is a hymn, chant, or prayer. Remember the Spanish *cantar* (to sing or chant)?

8. **False.** To be **benign** is to be kindly and gentle. It is not to be obscure.

9. **False.** To be **blasphemous** is to be disrespectful and irreverent, not reverent.

10. **True.** To **consecrate** is to declare sacred.

11. To be **contrite** is to be *repentant* for a wrong. It is the opposite of *gleeful* and has nothing to do with *contrasting*.

12. A **credo** is a *system of beliefs*. It isn't a *statement of disbelief*, nor is it a person who is a *nonbeliever*.

13. To be **penitent** is to be *repentant*. It is to express sorrow for your misdeeds. To be prostrate is to lie *facedown* on the ground, and one might be **penitent** after committing an *offensive* act.

14. To have **fidelity** is to have *loyalty*: to be faithful. So *unfaithful* doesn't fit. *Stringent*, which means strict, may seem close, but isn't close enough.

CHAPTER 9 QUIZ ANSWERS AND EXPLANATIONS *(cont'd)*

15. If something is **arcane**, it is *secret* or obscure (thus ruling out *well known*). The choice of *prehistoric* is irrelevant.

16. A **malediction** is a *curse* and not a *foolish notion*, although you might find the notion of curses to be foolish. A *lexicon* is a dictionary.

17. To be **munificent** is to be *generous*. And although generosity can be *glorious* and *affable* (pleasant), those are incorrect choices.

18. To **abjure** is to officially *reject* something or to renounce under oath. It is not to be *official* or to *accept*.

19. **Orthodox** means *traditional*. It has nothing to do with being *clean*. *Adverse* refers to unfavorable conditions.

20. To be **perfidious** is to be *faithless*. It is not to be *loyal*, nor is it to be *trusting*.

CHAPTER 10

The Five Senses

*Descriptive words
for a world worth describing*

BUILDING BLOCK QUIZ

By answering the ten questions below, you will get a sense of how closely you should study this chapter in order to master the vocabulary you need to speak knowledgeably about the sights, sounds, smells, touches, and tastes of the world around you.

DIRECTIONS: Fill in the blanks, using the most appropriate of the four multiple-choice answers. The correct answer will always fit into the sentence grammatically.

1. The point of the science experiment was to show that light without water would cause the plants to _____.

   (A) parch   (B) onerous

   (C) delectable   (D) munificent

2. As the odor in the science lab might have indicated a(n) _____ situation, Mr. Bryant should have evacuated the building and alerted the principal.

   (A) incandescent   (B) stringent

   (C) deleterious   (D) vapid

3. The _____ from the landfill smelled so strongly that homeowners in the area didn't want to open their windows.

    (A) effervescence   (B) effluvia

    (C) effort   (D) efficacious

4. When Mrs. Bailey told Jenna about her failing grade in front of the whole class, she lived up to her reputation as the most _____ teacher in the school.

    (A) nocturnal   (B) communicable

    (C) agile   (D) nefarious

5. Professor Traylor refused to move the April 1st deadline, despite complaints that the assignment was long and _____.

    (A) onerous   (B) calculated

    (C) ersatz   (D) palpable

6. Charlie was excited about his Home Economics project, but the brownies came out thin and _____.

    (A) raucous   (B) vapid

    (C) reprehensible   (D) resolute

7. The Children's Museum was full of _____ items that kids could easily touch and understand.

    (A) venerable   (B) nefarious

    (C) palpable   (D) jagged

8. Dean Jobey had no patience for the _____ behavior of the school's troublemakers.

    (A) wanton   (B) mature

    (C) destitute   (D) blanch

9. Gail's _____ efforts were inspiring and soon everyone at the church was raising money for the hurricane victims.

(A) stringent (B) heckler

(C) olfactory (D) resolute

10. Before the divorce, Teddy's house was full of _____, so he spent many nights with his grandmother.

(A) visceral (B) acrimony

(C) astringent (D) askance

BUILDING BLOCK ANSWERS AND EXPLANATIONS

1. A. To **parch** is to dry out and shrivel. *Onerous* (burdensome), *delectable* (delicious), and *munificent* (generous) do not apply here.

2. C. Deleterious is the best answer as it means harmful or destructive. *Incandescent* (shining brightly) and *vapid* (tame and uninspiring) are incorrect and although *stringent* (severe) might work here, it does not fit as well as **deleterious**.

3. B. Effluvia is the odor given off by waste. *Effervescence* is fizz or sparkle, and *efficacious* means effective. *Effort* means exertion or attempt. You'll notice the wrong answers all sound like the correct answer—don't let that confuse you.

4. D. To be **nefarious** is to be wicked or vicious and Mrs. Bailey was just that. To be *nocturnal* is to live at night, to be *communicable* is to be infectious, and to be *agile* is to be flexible and athletic.

5. A. Although Professor Traylor disagreed, the class thought that the assignment was **onerous**, or burdensome, much more so than being *calculated* (planned out), *ersatz* (fake), or *palpable* (obvious).

6. B. Unfortunately, Charlie's brownies were **vapid**, or dull and tasteless. They were not *raucous* (harsh sounding), nor were they *resolute* (determined). And although you could argue that they were *reprehensible* (worthy of public scorn), **vapid** is still the best choice.

BUILDING BLOCK ANSWERS AND EXPLANATIONS *(cont'd)*

7. C. Palpable has two definitions and both work here: touchable and understandable. *Venerable* (respected), *nefarious* (wicked), and *jagged* (sharp) are all incorrect.

8. A. Wanton behavior is reckless. **Wanton** students are undisciplined and apparently unappreciated by the dean! Although *destitute* may sound right, it means impoverished. To *blanch* is to become pale, and the students' behavior was the opposite of *mature*.

9. D. It was Gail's firm determination that earned everyone's respect, so **resolute** is the answer. *Stringent* could work in the sentence, but it seems less likely that strict, rigid efforts would gather a following. *Heckler* (obnoxious critic) and *olfactory* (relating to the sense of smell) are incorrect.

10. B. Acrimony describes bitterness and hostility, so it's no wonder Teddy didn't want to be around. *Visceral* describes an instinctive feeling or reaction, while *astringent* describes something harsh or severe (close, but not quite right here). Note that both of those are adjectives and the sentence requires a noun. *Askance* is an adverb that means doubtfully or suspiciously.

PART ONE

acrid adj. (AHK rid)—harsh, bitter
*The **acrid** smell of the vinegar drove Janet from the kitchen.*

acrimony n. (AK ri MOH nee)—bitterness, animosity
*The game ended in **acrimony** after the pitcher hit three successive batters.*

> **MEMORY TIP**
>
> **Acrid** rhymes with acid, so when you see words that begin with *acri*, like **acrid** and **acrimony**, think of the harsh, bitter taste of acid.

agile adj. (AH jil), (ah JIYL)—well coordinated, nimble
*Ned was **agile** enough to talk on the phone, peel a banana, and nudge the cat away from the dog's food, all at the same time.*

askance adv. (uh SKAANS)—with disapproval; with a skeptical sideways glance
*Freida looked **askance** at her son's awful report card.*

avuncular adj. (ah VUHNG kyuh luhr)—like an uncle in behavior, especially in kindness and warmth
*Coach Williams's **avuncular** style made him well liked.*

blanch v. (BLAHNCH)—to pale; take the color out of
*Ward's face turned red, but quickly **blanched** as the hot sauce worked its way down to his stomach.*

cadence n. (KAYD ns)—rhythmic flow; marching beat
*All of the reviews complimented P Nice's original style, the **cadence** he used when he rapped.*

clamor n. (KLAH mor)—noisy outcry
*The **clamor** of band practice was so bad that Principal Howell personally raised money for soundproof walls.*

communicable adj. (ka MUN ihk ka bul)—transmittable
*Universal protection includes rubber gloves to help caregivers avoid **communicable** diseases.*

declaim v. (dih KLAYM)—to speak loudly and vehemently
*Grandpa Myers always **declaims** at Thanksgiving grace, using it as an opportunity to criticize everyone from liberals to foreigners to his neighbors.*

deleterious adj. (de le TEER ee us)—harmful, destructive, detrimental
*In order to protect Mother Earth, environmentalists are constantly lobbying to outlaw **deleterious** substances.*

destitution n. (des tih TOO shun)—complete poverty
*The **destitution** that prevailed during the Great Depression left many Americans without the means even to buy bread.*

Practice 1

DIRECTIONS: In completing the sentences, use five of the eight words below. Use each of the words just once.

cadence	askance	declaimed	acrid
deranged	avuncular	blanched	deleterious

1. Julia always enjoyed the measured _____ of marching bands, so halftime was her favorite part of every football game.

2. Miss Mayall looked _____ at the boys who were chewing gum.

3. It wasn't until he'd been sent to the emergency room that Jerry realized how _____ alcohol was to his body.

4. Coach Dennis's _____ style might not have won the team many games, but his players really liked playing for him.

5. The candidates for class president _____ their positions at a schoolwide assembly.

Your Words, Your World

Destitution—This word is used to describe the condition of not just some-one on *welfare*, but a person living in complete *poverty*. Have you ever seen a homeless person? If you've never seen a *homeless* person, think of the *starving* children who live in places like Ethiopia.

Communicable—Have you ever been confused by this word, thinking that it has something to do with *communications* and *cable*? Instead of text or images, **communicable** refers to the *transmission of diseases*. A disease that is **communicable** is one that people can pass to one another.

Acrimony—Is there a friend or family member whom you love dearly, but *fight* with constantly? You could almost say that **acrimony** is the opposite of matrimony: rather than a happy "marriage," **acrimony** describes *bitter-ness* and *animosity*. Hopefully, none of your friendships are **acrimonious** and *hostile*.

PART TWO

discern v. (dih SUHRN)—to perceive something obscure
It is easy to discern the difference between real butter and margarine.

effluvia n. (ih FLOO vee uh)—waste; odorous fumes given off by waste
The effluvia coming off the river was so bad that Jen and Harrison considered moving.

ersatz adj. (uhr SAHTZ)—being an artificial and inferior imitation
The ersatz strawberry shortcake tasted more like plastic than real cake.

incandescent adj. (ihn kahn DEHS uhnt)—shining brightly
The incandescent glow of the moon forced Tate to pull down her shade.

incongruous adj. (in KONG roo us)—inappropriate, incompatible
Tracy found the explanation to be incongruous because she already knew the facts.

insidious adj. (in SIHD ee uhs)—subtly harmful, beguiling, alluring
Professor Coleman's reputation was destroyed by the insidious rumors that spread like wildfire through the campus.

jeopardize v. (JEH pehr diyz)—endanger, expose to injury
The frostbite jeopardized three of Erin's fingers.

nefarious adj. (nih FAHR ee uhs)—intensely wicked or vicious
Nefarious deeds were the Wicked Witch's trademark.

olfactory adj. (ohl FAAK tuh ree)—relating to the sense of smell
After years of coffee and cigarettes, BJ's olfactory abilities were gone.

palpable adj. (PAHLP uh buhl)—capable of being touched or felt; easily perceived
The students were excited to learn that heartbeats and pulses are both palpable.

parch adj. (PARCH)—dry up, shrivel
The pile of mail, not to mention the parched plants, indicated to Renee that her house sitter hadn't once entered the house.

raucous adj. (RAW kus)—harsh sounding; boisterous
The middle school cafeteria was a raucous place at lunchtime.

Practice 2

DIRECTIONS: After reading the three choices, circle the one that you think is the *antonym*.

6. **discern:**   perceive   overlook   describe

7. **effluvia:**   fragrant   odoriferous   air pollution

8. **ersatz:**   artificial   fascinating   genuine

9. **incongruous:**   contemptuous   incompatible   fitting

10. **jeopardize:**   protect   endanger   expose

Your Words, Your World

Olfactory—What are your favorite *smells*: chocolate-chip cookies fresh out of the oven, a bouquet of flowers, a baby's hair, perfume or cologne? Take one of these or one of your own, and think of it when you think of **olfactory**.

Palpable—Almost as easy as picturing your prized possessions is remembering how they *feel* in your *hands*. Think of one of those. Whether it's the *feel* of *hard* metal, *polished* wood, *soft* cotton, or a *rubbery* toy, as long as you associate *physical contact* with the word **palpable**, you'll be able to define it.

Parch—If you've ever played a sport in hundred-degree weather, hiked through a desert, or drank caffeine all day without having a glass of water, then you know what it means to be **parched**. When your body is crying out for water, you are *dehydrated* or at least close to it.

PART THREE

reprehensible adj. (rehp ree HEHN suh buhl)—blameworthy, disreputable
Lenny was disliked around the neighborhood for his reprehensible behavior.

resplendent adj. (ree SPLEHN dehnt)—splendid, brilliant, dazzling
As a bride, Marian looked resplendent in her long train and gentle veil.

> **MEMORY TIP**
>
> Whenever you see the prefix **re-** some sort of emphasis is being placed on the word's meaning. Take **reprehensible**, for example: there is an emphasis being put on someone's *bad behavior*. If a person is **resolute**, she or he is *firmly determined*. And if something can be described as **resplendent**, it is *dazzling*.

squalid adj. (SKWA lihd)—filthy and degraded as the result of neglect or poverty
Karl hated his family's squalid living conditions and resolved to move out of the apartment building as soon as possible.

tactile adj. (TAAK tihl)—producing a sensation of touch
As opposed to reading and taking tests, it is easier for many people to learn new subject matter through tactile activities.

turpitude n. (TUHR pi tood)—inherent vileness, foulness, depravity
Lord of the Flies provides insight into the turpitude of life without societal constraints.

venerable adj. (VEN erh ah bul)—respected because of age
Noelle often sought the advice of her venerable grandfather.

vestige n. (VES tij)—trace, remnant
Three years after the accident, vestiges still marked the crossroads.

visceral adj. (VIHS urh uhl)—instinctive, not intellectual; deep, emotional
When Joseph's twin was wounded in the war, he had a visceral reaction, suddenly crying out at the dinner table.

vociferous adj. (voh SIH fuhr uhs)—loud, noisy
There is still debate about whether or not Khrushchev banged his shoe on the table in vociferous protest at the UN.

unobtrusive adj. (uhn ob TROO siv)—modest, unassuming
The countess demanded that her servants be unobtrusive and that they carry out their duties quietly and efficiently.

wanton adj. (WAHN tuhn)—undisciplined, unrestrained; reckless
The townspeople were outraged by the wanton disrespect shown by the graffiti on the town hall.

Practice 3

DIRECTIONS: Consider the two word choices in the parentheses, and circle the one that best fits in the context of the sentence.

11. The sound in the gym during Battle of the Bands was so (**visceral** OR **vociferous**) that half of the teachers left early.

12. Due to his (**reprehensible** OR **reputable**) behavior, Clyde was given a three-day suspension.

13. Principal Brown called the local paper to complain that a harsh criticism like (**vapid** OR **vestige**) did not belong in a review of a school play.

14. Regina's parents were (**resolute** OR **ersatz**) about her punishment, and so she could not go to the homecoming game.

15. Without knowing about the long, slow death of Gerry's grandfather, his teachers mistakenly complained that he was (**tactile** OR **wanton**).

Your Words, Your World

Sophomoric—This word should probably be "freshmanic," as most students know. If someone you know is behaving in a **sophomoric** manner, he or she is being *immature* and *unsophisticated*. And actually, one of **sophomoric**'s synonyms is *collegiate*, so the word has less to do with tenth graders and more to do with young adults who are a bit *too confident* in their *uninformed opinions*.

Tactile—In your day-to-day life, what are the things you come into *contact* with most often? Your list might include one or two faucets in the bathroom, the car door and steering wheel, your bag, pens, the computer keyboard, or the remote control. You get a **tactile** response from each of the things in the aforementioned list. Come up with the two or three things you *touch* most often, and this will help you to remember that tactile means *producing a sensation of touch*.

PRACTICE ANSWERS AND EXPLANATIONS

Practice 1

1. Julia liked the **cadence**, or rhythmic flow, of the marching band.

2. Miss Mayall disapproved of the gum chewing, so she looked **askance** at the boys.

3. Jerry had to get sick before realizing how **deleterious**, or harmful, alcohol can be to the body.

4. Coach Dennis was **avuncular** in that he was kind to his players.

5. Like professional politicians, the candidates gave speeches about, or **declaimed**, their positions before the election.

Practice 2

6. To **discern** is to *perceive* or notice and not to *overlook*. It isn't to *describe*, either, although this is not an antonym.

7. **Effluvia** is *odoriferous* and *air pollution* may qualify as such. *Fragrant* is the antonym.

8. If something is described as **ersatz** it is *artificial* and fake and certainly not *genuine*. *Fascinating* is not an opposite.

9. To be **incongruous** is to be inappropriate or *incompatible*, like a penguin in the desert. *Fitting* is the antonym. *Contemptuous* means disapproving, so is neither a synonym nor an antonym.

10. To **jeopardize** is to *endanger*: to *expose* to danger. To jeopardize is definitely not to *protect*.

Practice 3

11. Although *visceral* fits grammatically, **vociferous** (loud) is the better answer.

12. *Reputable*, or trustworthy, behavior doesn't get you suspended. Behavior that is disreputable, **reprehensible**, and blameworthy does.

PRACTICE ANSWERS AND EXPLANATIONS *(cont'd)*

13. As **vapid** means tasteless and dull, Principal Brown took offense. Needless to say, the use of the word *vestige* (trace or mark) would not garner such a reaction!

14. Regina's parents were **resolute**, or firmly determined, about grounding her. Their reaction was anything but fake (*ersatz*).

15. Gerry wasn't **wanton** (undisciplined and reckless) as his teachers suspected. *Tactile* relates to the sense of touch.

CHAPTER 10 QUIZ

Take your time, not only with the questions, but in reading the answer explanations that follow. Set a goal for yourself—80% (16 correct answers) is recommended—and if you don't reach that goal, go back and read through the chapter again. Good luck!

DIRECTIONS: For questions 1–8, circle T for True or F for False.
For questions 9–20, circle the synonym.

1. **T F**   **vociferous**—loud
2. **T F**   **nefarious**—wicked
3. **T F**   **incandescent**—vapid
4. **T F**   **ersatz**—legitimate
5. **T F**   **declaim**—to speak loudly
6. **T F**   **deleterious**—harmful
7. **T F**   **blanch**—to belch
8. **T F**   **acrid**—harsh

9. **askance:**	disapprovingly	approvingly	questioningly
10. **discern:**	act sincerely	differentiate	act vengefully
11. **visceral:**	instinctive	dull	naïve
12. **incongruous:**	compatible	inappropriate	pathetic
13. **olfactory:**	taste	touch	smell
14. **cadence:**	nefarious	lexicon	rhythm
15. **palpable:**	fleeting	doubtful	substantial
16. **reprehensible:**	disreputable	reputable	scrupulous
17. **resplendent:**	improper	brilliant	uninteresting
18. **turpitude:**	pleasantness	vileness	decency
19. **venerable:**	esteemed	reviled	ventilated
20. **insidious:**	unappealing	blatant	harmful

CHAPTER 10 QUIZ ANSWERS AND EXPLANATIONS

1. **True.** To be **vociferous** is to be noisy and overly enthusiastic.

2. **True.** To be **nefarious** is to be wickedly vicious.

3. **False.** If an object is **incandescent** it shines brightly. It is not vapid or dull.

4. **False.** If something is described as **ersatz** it isn't legitimate, but artificial to the point of being an inferior substitute or imitation.

5. **True.** To **declaim** is to speak loudly.

6. **True.** To be **deleterious** is to be harmful.

7. **False.** To **blanch** is not to belch, but to turn pale.

8. **True.** If something is **acrid** it is harsh or bitter.

9. **Askance** is synonymous with *disapprovingly*. *Approvingly* is an antonym and *questioningly* is incorrect.

10. To **discern** is to *differentiate*. It has nothing to do with *acting sincerely* (honestly) or *vengefully*.

11. If something can be considered **visceral**, then it has happened *instinctively*. It took place on a deep, emotional level. It is not something *dull* or *naïve*.

12. If something is **incongruous**, it is *inappropriate*. *Compatible* (well matched) and *pathetic* (sad) are incorrect.

13. **Olfactory** relates to the sense of *smell* and not the senses of *taste* or *touch*.

14. If music has **cadence** it has a certain *rhythm* and tempo. A *lexicon* is a dictionary, and *nefarious* is wicked.

15. Something **palpable** is *substantial;* one can touch it or at least understand it. *Fleeting* and *doubtful* are near-antonyms.

16. To be **reprehensible** is to be *disreputable*. Obviously, *reputable* is the opposite, as is *scrupulous* (conscientious).

CHAPTER 10 QUIZ ANSWERS AND EXPLANATIONS *(cont'd)*

17. **Resplendent** is synonymous with *brilliant. Uninteresting* is an antonym and *improper* is inappropriate.

18. **Turpitude** is a noun meaning inherent *vileness. Pleasantness* and *decency* are near-antonyms.

19. To be **venerable** is to be *esteemed;* it is to have earned respect over the years. It is not to be *reviled.* And *ventilated* (allowing air in and out) is a trick answer based on the *ven-* prefix.

20. To be **insidious** is to be sneakily *harmful.* Although this kind of behavior may be *unappealing* and *blatantly* wrong, neither of those words is the best answer.

CHAPTER 11

Positive Emotions

*Vocabulary that falls
on the sunny side of the street*

BUILDING BLOCK QUIZ

By answering the 12 questions below, you will get a sense of how closely you should study this chapter in order to master all of that vocabulary! And if you choose incorrect answers for the final two questions, you'll want to go back to chapter 10 for some review.

DIRECTIONS: Fill in the blanks, using the most appropriate of the four multiple-choice answers. The correct answer will always fit into the sentence grammatically.

1. There's just something about a _____ child actor that makes for a good, uplifting movie.

   (A) vindictive   (B) plucky

   (C) becalm   (D) wanton

2. When Carrie was able to walk just two weeks after the accident, everybody credited her athleticism and _____ nature.

   (A) resilient   (B) amorous

   (C) virulent   (D) consummate

3. When Marquis _____ his love for Tamara with an engagement ring, both families immediately began to talk about the wedding.

   (A) alleviated   (B) cavorted

   (C) avowed   (D) confiscated

4. Miya pursued her college degree with _____ and was able to graduate within four years.

   (A) vim   (B) approbation

   (C) turpitude   (D) lethargy

5. Jake's mother always said that the difference between a job and a career comes from the _____ with which you work.

   (A) synergy   (B) parch

   (C) chortle   (D) ardor

6. As Mrs. Harris was _____ to a transfer, the whole family would be moving to Japan for a year.

   (A) amenable   (B) wry

   (C) sportive   (D) obstructive

7. Matt's fingers were _____ and this helped to make him an excellent typist and guitar player.

   (A) tout   (B) lithe

   (C) winsome   (D) appalling

8. Miss Eggert was a schoolwide favorite because she was never hesitant to _____ her students.

   (A) surmount   (B) proscribe

   (C) nullify   (D) extol

9. Although Mr. Helene wasn't yet tenured, he was _____ in his requests for funding for a school photography club.

   (A) intrepid   (B) solicitous

   (C) amenable   (D) tactile

10. Mrs. Unger took the student council to the outdoor education center for an afternoon of teamwork training, in hopes that this would lead them to _____ and become more productive.

    (A) alleviate   (B) contradict

    (C) coalesce   (D) salvage

11. The athletic director decided that the pressure-filled tournament would be _____ to the young team and turned down the invitation.

    (A) deleterious   (B) resilient

    (C) facetious   (D) squalid

12. Everyone liked the fact that the new science teacher was so _____, despite having already published two books.

    (A) olfactory   (B) saccharine

    (C) mawkish   (D) unobtrusive

BUILDING BLOCK ANSWERS AND EXPLANATIONS

1. B. A **plucky** (spunky and courageous) child actor is sure to sell out theaters. *Vindictive* (vengeful) and *wanton* (undisciplined and reckless) actors probably make bad movies, as they are difficult to work with. To *becalm* is to rest or stop.

2. A. Carrie is **resilient**, which means she is able to recover quickly. She may be *amorous* (passionate) and *virulent* (dangerous), but neither explains her ability to recuperate. *Consummate* (accomplished) doesn't really make sense before "nature."

3. C. To **avow** is to state openly or declare, so this is correct. *Alleviated* (relieved), *cavorted* (frolicked), and *confiscated* (took) do not fit in the context of the sentence.

4. A. To pursue something with **vim** is to pursue it with great energy. *Lethargy* is the opposite, meaning laziness and lack of energy. *Approbation* (approval) and *turpitude* (moral depravity) are both incorrect.

BUILDING BLOCK ANSWERS AND EXPLANATIONS *(cont'd)*

5. D. The difference Jake's mother was referring to was passion or **ardor**. *Synergy* (cooperation) sounds right but doesn't really make sense, nor do *parch* (dry out) and *chortle* (laugh).

6. A. When her company asked about a transfer, Mrs. Harris was **amenable** (agreeable and cooperative). She was neither *wry* (sarcastic) nor *obstructive* (unhelpful). And although the move might have made her happy, she wasn't *sportive* (playful) about it, either.

7. B. **Lithe** means bending with ease and describes Matt's fingers perfectly. To *tout* is to hype, *winsome* is charming, and *appalling* is frightful, so all three of those are out.

8. D. The correct answer is **extol**, as it means to praise. The other three words are too negative: to *surmount* is to conquer, to *proscribe* is to forbid, and to *nullify* is to cancel.

9. A. In the context of the sentence, only **intrepid** (meaning fearless) fits perfectly. The key to this question is the contrast, indicated by "Although," between Mr. Helene's lack of tenure and his efforts to start a new club. *Amenable* is too friendly and agreeable, while *solicitous* is too considerate. *Tactile* refers to the sensation of touch.

10. C. The student council has to **coalesce**; to unite and band together so as to be more productive. Although *alleviate* (ease or lessen) and *salvage* (save) are close, they aren't close enough. And the last thing Mrs. Unger wants is for members of the student council to *contradict* (disagree with) one another.

11. A. The pressure would be **deleterious**, or harmful, to the team. It would not be *resilient* (flexible and hardy), *facetious* (joking), or *squalid* (filthy). If you answered this question incorrectly, you might want to go back to chapter 10 for some review.

12. D. Despite having published three books, the teacher was **unobtrusive**, which means modest and unassuming. *Saccharine* and *mawkish* both mean sickeningly sweet or sentimental. *Olfactory* relates to the sense of smell, so it's completely irrelevant here. If you answered this question incorrectly, you might want to go back to chapter 10 for some review.

PART ONE

affable adj. (AH fah buhl)—friendly, easy to approach, fun
*Since she was so **affable**, Jessie was named "Most Huggable" in the yearbook, to nobody's surprise.*

alacrity n. (ah LAK rah tee)—cheerful willingness, eagerness; speed
*Mancha jumped for the Frisbee with agility and **alacrity** that Dave had never before seen in a dog.*

alleviate v. (ah LEEV ee ayt)—to relieve, improve partially
*For Isabelle, nothing **alleviated** the stress of teaching like seeing a student improve.*

amenable adj. (ah MEHN ah buhl)—agreeable, cooperative
*Hector's reputation wasn't good, but by the end of the first week, everybody at the radio station found him to be **amenable**.*

amorous adj. (AH mehr uhs)—strongly attracted to love; showing love
*All of the greetings cards were way too **amorous** for Glenn, so he just wrote his own.*

approbation n. (ah pro BAY shun)—praise, official approval
***Approbation** came for Billy in the form of a college recommendation from Principal Unger.*

ardor n. (AHR dur)—great emotion or passion
*Beth's **ardor** for gardening was evident in the colorful spread of her yard.*

assignation n. (ah sihg NAY shun)—appointment for lovers' meeting; assignment
*Juliet and Romeo had many secret **assignations**.*

avow v. (ah VOW)—to state openly or declare
*In speaking their vows, Neil and Macy publicly **avowed** their love for one another.*

blithe adj. (BLIYTH)—joyful, cheerful, carefree
*Michelle **blithely** assumed that her coworkers would be as happy as she was about the promotion.*

cavort v. (ka VOHRT)—to frolic, frisk, play
*The puppies looked adorable as they **cavorted** in the grass.*

chortle v. (CHOR tuhl)—to chuckle
*Santa **chortled** as Rudolph led the team of reindeer through the clouds.*

Practice 1

DIRECTIONS: Match the word (left column) with its definition (right column).

1. **approbation**		great passion
2. **affable**		praise
3. **ardor**		friendly
4. **alacrity**		carefree
5. **blithe**		enthusiasm

Your Words, Your World

Alleviate—If you think about what it is you want to do most this weekend, about what it is that *improves* your mood, you will be thinking of how you **alleviate** your stress. You will be *relieving* yourself of the tension and pressure that comes with school and/or work.

Chortle—Think of what makes you laugh. Maybe it's a movie or maybe it's one of your friends. Remember these things—and also the fact that **chortle** and *chuckle* both begin with *ch*—and you'll surely remember that to **chortle** is to *laugh, chuckle*, or *giggle*.

PART TWO

cloying adj. (KLOY ing)—overly sweet
*Kids today enjoy making fun of the **cloying** TV shows of previous decades.*

coalesce v. (KOH ah less)—to grow together or cause to unite as one
*Both sides of the family **coalesced** to celebrate Wendy's 16th birthday.*

consummate adj. (KON suh mit)—accomplished, complete, perfect
*Karen skated a **consummate** routine, winning the gold medal with ease.*

cordial adj. (KOR juhl)—warm and sincere, friendly, polite; from Latin *cord* or *cor,* meaning heart
*Before getting down to business, Matthew extended his hand in a **cordial** manner.*

elate v. (ee LAYT)—to make joyful; exhilarate
*Nothing **elates** children like the announcement of a snow day.*

euphoria n. (yoo FOR ee uh)—great happiness or well-being
***Euphoria** swept through the crowd as Oprah handed out the car keys.*

extol v. (ehk STOL)—to praise
*The salesman **extolled** the virtues of the used car.*

facetious adj. (fuh SEE shuhs)—witty, humorous, in jest
*Quinn's **facetious** remarks made the meeting more lively and interesting.*

frolicsome adj. (FRO lihk sum)—frisky, playful
*The **frolicsome** kitten entertained them for hours.*

gregarious adj. (greh GAAR ee uhs)—outgoing, sociable
*Unlike her introverted friends, Susan was very **gregarious**.*

indefatigable adj. (in de FAH tee gu buhl)—never tired
*Theresa seemed **indefatigable**, running from one meeting to another.*

intrepid adj. (in TREH pid)—fearless
*The **intrepid** kayak team went into the rapids and over the waterfall.*

jocular adj. (JAH kyoo luhr)—playful, humorous
*Ever **jocular**, Grandpa Hughes told stories for hours that night.*

lithe adj. (LIYTH)—moving and bending with ease; marked by grace
*Edy's **lithe** movements led her parents to believe that she would be a dancer.*

mawkish adj. (MAW kihsh)—sickeningly sentimental
*Mr. Goldberg let Myles know, as gently as possible, that his poem was more **mawkish** than romantic.*

Practice 2

DIRECTIONS: Consider the definition and then circle T for True or F for False.

6. **T F**   **cloying**—overly sweet

7. **T F**   **consummate**—accomplished

8. **T F**   **euphoria**—unhappiness

9. **T F**   **indefatigable**—never tired

10. **T F**   **lithe**—moving with ease

Your Words, Your World

Jocular—Although you may have athletic friends called "jocks," to be **jocular** has nothing to do with sports. It is to be *playful* or *humorous*. Who is the most **jocular** person you know?

Gregarious—And who is the most **gregarious** person you know? To be **gregarious** is to be *extroverted* and *outgoing*, so think of the most *sociable* person you know.

PART THREE

purport v. (puhr POHRT)—to profess, suppose, claim
*Brad **purported** to be an opera lover, but he fell asleep when Francine took him to see* The Barber of Seville.

resilient adj. (rih SIHL ee uhnt)—able to recover quickly after illness or bad luck; able to bounce back
*Psychologists say that being **resilient** is one of the keys to happiness.*

saccharine adj. (SAA kuh ruhn)—excessively sweet or sentimental
*Lucy loved **saccharine** movies, so at least once a month Paul had to watch one.*

solicitous adj. (suh LIH sih tuhs)—concerned, caring, eager
*Dory's overly **solicitous** questions made her father wonder what she wanted.*

sportive adj. (SPOHR tihv)—frolicsome, playful
*Because they wanted a more **sportive** vacation, the Hendersons decided to visit Disney World instead of going antiquing in Vermont.*

surmount v. (suhr MOWNT)—to conquer, overcome
*The blind woman **surmounted** great obstacles to become a well-known trial lawyer.*

tenacious adj. (ten AY shuhs)—determined, keeping a firm grip on
*Becky was **tenacious** when it came to determining a budget for the school's art programs.*

tout v. (TOWT)—to praise or publicize loudly or extravagantly
*Principal Velanueva **touted** his choice of assistant principal, discussing the man's background as a police officer.*

vim n. (VIHM)—vitality and energy
*The **vim** with which Andy worked was awe-inspiring.*

vindicate v. (vihn dih KAYT)—to clear of blame; support a claim
*Tess felt **vindicated** when the newspaper reported a rise in unemployment.*

winsome adj. (WIHN suhm)—charming, happily engaging
*Dawn gave the police officer a **winsome** smile, and he let her go without writing a speeding ticket.*

Practice 3

DIRECTIONS: Read the three possible synonyms, then circle the one you think best defines the word in bold.

11.	**purport:**	to claim	insignificant	to frolic
12.	**saccharine:**	merciless	wanton	sentimental
13.	**solicitous:**	begging	considerate	uncaring
14.	**tenacious:**	indeterminate	infirm	determined
15.	**vim:**	vitality	mellow	whim

Your Words, Your World

Vindicate—Picture a shady-looking guy named Vin, sitting up on the stand during the trial of the century. Fortunately for Vin, there isn't any evidence against him, and this is because Vin is *innocent*. Imagine the look on his face when he is found *not guilty* and he is *cleared of all blame*. He has been **vindicated**.

Surmount—To *conquer* a mountain is a tremendous feat. As the second syllable of **surmount** is *mount,* picture yourself atop Mt. Everest, the world's highest peak. To **surmount** is to *overcome*.

Tout—As **tout** rhymes with *shout*, think of someone shouting your *praises* in public. Imagine your mother or father standing on a street corner, *yelling* about your good grades or good job to anyone who'll listen! When something is **touted**, it must be praised *loudly* and *extravagantly*.

PRACTICE ANSWERS AND EXPLANATIONS

Practice 1

1. **Approbation** is praise or official approval.

2. If someone is **affable**, he or she is friendly and approachable.

3. **Ardor** is a noun that means great emotion and passion.

4. **Alacrity** is defined as enthusiasm.

5. To be **blithe** is to be carefree.

Practice 2

6. **True.** To be **cloying** is to be overly sweet.

7. **True.** If someone is considered **consummate**, he or she is skilled and highly accomplished in his or her field.

8. **False. Euphoria** is a great feeling of happiness.

9. **True.** To be **indefatigable** is to never be tired.

10. **True.** To be **lithe** is to be able to move with ease.

PRACTICE ANSWERS AND EXPLANATIONS *(cont'd)*

Practice 3

11. To **purport** is *to claim* or profess. It is not *to frolic* (play) or be *insignificant* (unimportant).

12. If someone is **saccharine,** he or she is excessively sweet or *sentimental*. He or she is not *wanton* (reckless) or *merciless* (without sympathy).

13. To be **solicitous** is to be caring and *considerate*. Begging is a trick answer, playing off of the word *soliciting* (begging for business). *Uncaring* is an antonym.

14. To be **tenacious** is to be *determined*. On the other hand, *infirm* means to be sickly, while *indeterminate* means undefined.

15. **Vim** is a noun synonymous with *vitality* and energy. A *whim* is an impulse. To be *mellow* is to be calm.

CHAPTER 11 QUIZ

Take your time, not only with the questions, but in reading the answer explanations that follow. Set a goal for yourself—80% (16 correct answers) is recommended—and if you don't reach that goal, go back and read through the chapter again. Good luck!

DIRECTIONS: For questions 1–10, circle T for True or F for False.
For questions 11–20, circle the synonym.

1. **T F** **consummate**—incomplete

2. **T F** **vindicate**—persecute

3. **T F** **tout**—praise

4. **T F** **resilient**—unable to recover

5. **T F** **purport**—claim

6. **T F** **gregarious**—outgoing

7. **T F** **cloying**—without fragrance

8. **T F** **ardor**—great passion

9. **T F** **solicitous**—concerned

10. **T F** **euphoria**—happiness

11.	**cavort:**	to frolic	to drive	to devise
12.	**amenable:**	stubborn	winsome	cooperative
13.	**blithe:**	cheerful	lithe	cynical
14.	**chortle:**	to gag	to praise	to chuckle
15.	**facetious:**	witty	honest	pious
16.	**winsome:**	charming	victorious	elated
17.	**avow:**	to shock	to declare	to be friendly
18.	**tenacious:**	vicious	lonely	determined
19.	**surmount:**	to overcome	to praise	to bemuse
20.	**affable:**	laughable	euphoric	friendly

CHAPTER 11 QUIZ ANSWERS AND EXPLANATIONS

1. False. If a person is considered **consummate**, he or she is accomplished and in no way incomplete.

2. False. To **vindicate** is to clear of blame, which is the opposite of persecute.

3. True. To **tout** is to praise extravagantly.

4. False. To be **resilient** is actually to be able to recover quickly.

5. True. To **purport** is to claim, profess, or suppose.

6. True. If a person is **gregarious**, he or she is outgoing and sociable.

7. False. To be **cloying** is to be overly sweet. It is not to be without fragrance.

8. True. To do something with **ardor** is to do it with great emotion or passion.

9. True. To be **solicitous** is to be anxious and concerned.

10. True. The state of **euphoria** is one of great happiness!

11. To **cavort** is *to frolic* and have fun. This has nothing to do with *driving* or *devising*.

12. To be **amenable** is to be *cooperative*. *Stubborn* is an antonym, and *winsome* means charming, but not necessarily *cooperative*.

13. To be **blithe** is to be *cheerful*, which is nearly the opposite of *cynical*. And although *lithe* rhymes, it is a distracter and means flexible.

14. To **chortle** is to *chuckle*. It is not to *gag* or *praise*.

15. To be **facetious** is to be *witty* in a tongue-in-cheek sort of way. It is definitely not to be *honest* or *pious* (religious).

16. To be **winsome** is to be *charming*. To be *elated* is to be overjoyed and to be *victorious* is to be the winner.

17. To **avow** is *to declare*. It is neither *to shock* nor *to be friendly*.

CHAPTER 11 QUIZ ANSWERS AND EXPLANATIONS *(cont'd)*

18. To be **tenacious** is to be *determined*. It should not be confused with *vicious,* and it is not to be *lonely*.

19. To **surmount** is *to overcome:* to conquer, prevail, and triumph. It is not *to praise* or *to bemuse* (confuse).

20. To be **affable** is simply to be *friendly*. *Euphoric* means overjoyed, while *laughable* means funny in a somewhat critical way.

CHAPTER 12

Grumpy, Crabby, Mean

Words to describe the down and depressed

BUILDING BLOCK QUIZ

By answering the ten questions below, you will get a sense of how closely you should study this chapter in order to be able to recall all of these negative words.

DIRECTIONS: Fill in the blanks, using the most appropriate of the four multiple-choice answers. The correct answer will always fit into the sentence grammatically.

1. Rebecca's poor report card was _____, as she was usually an A student.

   (A) plaintive   (B) jaded
   (C) enigmatic   (D) torpid

2. Mr. Walters knew that the surprise quiz would _____ his class, but gave it anyway.

   (A) pique   (B) alleviate
   (C) bellicose   (D) brandish

3. Nurse Greene noted how _____ Peter's face was and called his mother.

   (A) austere   (B) wan
   (C) contentious   (D) choleric

4. Alex treated all of his teachers with _____ and so none of them were shocked or sad to hear that he'd been expelled.

    (A) respect (B) disconcert

    (C) malaise (D) disdain

5. Over the year, Kelly became more and more _____ until finally her guidance counselor called her parents in for a meeting.

    (A) morose (B) gregarious

    (C) sportive (D) winsome

6. The entire school was _____ upon learning of the student's death in that morning's accident.

    (A) elated   (B) plaintive

    (C) flagrant (D) oscillate

7. Usually cheerful and energetic, Natalie felt _____ because of her flu.

    (A) torpid   (B) plucky

    (C) jocular (D) indefatigable

8. A(n) _____ person and a by-the-book teacher, Miss Lopez taught the least popular class in school.

    (A) saccharine (B) ignoble

    (C) bilious (D) opprobrious

9. The class stared in awe as Mike's mother _____ him in front of everybody for his rude remarks.

    (A) chided (B) extolled

    (C) baned (D) brandished

10. Mr. Tompkins had a talent for _____ upset students and getting to the heart of the matter.

    (A) counteracting (B) demeaning

    (C) beleaguering (D) mollifying

BUILDING BLOCK ANSWERS AND EXPLANATIONS

1. C. Rebecca's report card was not the usual, so it was **enigmatic**, or puzzling. *Plaintive* (expressing woe) is incorrect as are *jaded* (weary) and *torpid* (lazy).

2. A. The quiz would **pique** (arouse anger, or at least interest) the class and this seems to be, at least in part, what Mr. Walters wanted. Although it was an aggressive move, *bellicose* (warlike) is not the answer. Nor is it *alleviate* (ease or lessen) or *brandish* (wield or wave).

3. B. Peter was sickly pale (**wan**) and not angry, so *contentious* (quarrelsome) and *choleric* (easily angered) are ruled out, as is *austere* (strict).

4. D. Alex treated his teachers with **disdain**, which is to say with scorn and contempt. It was definitely not with *respect. Disconcert* (ruffle or upset) and *malaise* (depression or unease) are also incorrect.

5. A. The guidance counselor wouldn't have called home if Kelly were *gregarious* (outgoing), *sportive* (frolicsome), or *winsome* (charming). It was because she was **morose** (gloomy or sullen) that the guidance counselor called for a meeting.

6. B. The entire school was feeling **plaintive** in that students and staff were expressing their woe and suffering. They certainly weren't *elated* (ecstatic). *Flagrant* (blatant) and *oscillate* (swing back and forth, physically or emotionally) are both incorrect as well.

7. A. Natalie was feeling **torpid**, or lethargic (lacking energy). The other three choices are near-antonyms: *plucky* (spunky), *jocular* (playful), and *indefatigable* (never tired). The word "usually" sets up a contrast with Natalie's typical "energetic" behavior, and **torpid** is the only choice that has this meaning.

8. C. Miss Lopez was **bilious** (bad-tempered) and this was, in part, why students didn't like her. Although *ignoble* (having low moral standards), *opprobrious* (disgraceful, shameful), and *saccharine* (excessively sentimental) all fit—the first two better than the third—the most likely choice remains **bilious**.

BUILDING BLOCK ANSWERS AND EXPLANATIONS *(cont'd)*

9. A. Mike's mother **chided**, or scolded, him in front of everybody. Although she may have *brandished* something (waved something menacingly) while doing this, **chided** is the better choice. *Extolled* (praised) doesn't make sense. *Bane* (nuisance) is a word but "baned" is not.

10. D. The best choice is **mollifying**, which means soothing in temper or disposition. *Demeaning* (humiliating) and *beleaguering* (harassing) are the opposite. *Counteracting* (offsetting) has a similar meaning, but doesn't really make sense here (how do you "offset" a student?).

PART ONE

adversarial adj. (ahd ver SAR ee uhl)—competitive or antagonistic
*The brothers' **adversarial** relationship made it impossible for their parents to enjoy a meal.*

affront n. (ah FRONT)—personal offense, insult
*Clyde took the waiter's insulting remark as an **affront** to his family.*

appalling adj. (uh PAW lihng)—causing dismay; frightful
*Fern argued that the amount of cheating in today's high schools was absolutely **appalling**.*

aversion n. (ah VER shun)—intense dislike
*Laura had an instant **aversion** to Mike because of his obnoxious personality.*

bane n. (BAYN)—cause of harm or ruin; source of annoyance
*Traffic was the **bane** of Tori's existence; she couldn't stand all that wasted time in her car.*

beleaguer v. (bee LEE guhr)—to harass, plague
*Mickey's **beleaguered** parents finally gave in to his request for a Nintendo.*

bellicose adj. (BELL uh kohs)—warlike, aggressive
*The **bellicose** Chief Eaglehawk surprised everyone when he called for a truce.*

> **FLASHBACK**
>
> In the first chapter, you learned that the word root **bell** means *war*.
> **Belligerent** and **bellicose** both mean *aggressive*, but **bellicose** goes
> a step farther, meaning *warlike*.

bemuse v. (bee MUZ)—to confuse, stupefy; plunge deep into thought
*Helen was **bemused** and certainly not amused at the computer problems.*

berate v. (bee RAYT)—to scold harshly
*When Coach Reed got his team into the locker room, he **berated** them
for their sloppy playing.*

bilious adj. (bihl EE uhs)—ill-tempered; sickly, ailing
*Uncle Jack's **bilious** complaining about his health ruined every holiday.*

brandish v. (BRAN dish)—wave menacingly
*Wyatt Earp could make outlaws surrender by simply **brandishing** his
revolver.*

cantankerous adj. (kaan TAANG kuhr uhs)—having a difficult, unco-
operative, or stubborn disposition
*Haley couldn't stand to be around Wendall when he was being
cantankerous.*

chide v. (CHIYD)—to scold, express disapproval
*Florence **chided** her poodle for licking the icing off of the birthday cake.*

choleric adj. (KOL er ik), (koh LEER ik)—easily angered,
short-tempered
*Ms. West was **choleric** and her students quickly figured out when to
keep quiet.*

confound v. (kuhn FOWND)—to baffle, perplex
*Vince, **confounded** by the difficult algebra problems, threw his math book
at the wall and stormed out.*

Practice 1

DIRECTIONS: After reading the three choices, circle the one that you think is the *antonym*.

1. **affront**:   behind   compliment   insult

2. **beleaguer**:   harass   delight   ignore

3. **berate**:   scold   tardy   praise

4. **choleric**:   easygoing   gabby   short-tempered

Your Words, Your World

Chide—To **chide** is to *scold* or to *express disapproval*. If you have a teacher, manager, or parent who does this to you, you will surely remember what **chide** means.

Brandish—Movies, music videos, and video games often show people **brandishing** weapons. To **brandish** is to *wave menacingly*, so if you picture a gun in the hands of a gangster, you will be able to recall this definition.

Aversion—Think of your *least favorite* thing, activity, or person and you will remember what **aversion** means. If you have an *intense dislike* for anchovy pizza, for example, you have an **aversion** to it.

PART TWO

consternation n. (KAHN stuhr nay shuhn)—intense fear or dismay
*Tony, a seasoned hunter, showed a surprising amount of **consternation** when the black bear lumbered too close to camp.*

contentious adj. (kuhn TEHN shuhs)—controversial, always ready to argue, quarrelsome
*Jay was known to be **contentious** and after a while, nobody bothered to argue with him anymore.*

counteract v. (kown ter ACT)—to oppose the effects by contrary action
*Dr. Byron started administering antibiotics to **counteract** the sickness.*

demean v. (dee MEEN)—to degrade, humiliate, humble
The editor constantly tried to **demean** *Betsy and her writing, but Betsy stuck with her job as a reporter.*

disconcert adj. (dis kuhn SURT)—ruffle; distress; disturb; disappoint
David was **disconcerted** *to find his locker left open after class.*

disparage v. (diss PAHR ij)—to belittle, speak disrespectfully about
Gregorio loved to **disparage** *his brother's dancing skills, pointing out every mistake he made on the floor.*

doleful adj. (DOHL fuhl)—sad, mournful
Looking into the **doleful** *eyes of the lonely puppy, Lynn yearned to take him home.*

enigmatic adj. (en ihg MA tik)—puzzling
The class was even more confused after Professor Noble's **enigmatic** *answers about his final exam.*

flagrant adj. (FLAY grent)—outrageous, shameless
Joan's **flagrant** *disregard for the rules led to her eventual removal from the ethics commission.*

frenetic adj. (freh NEH tihk)—frantic, frenzied
The **frenetic** *schedule of the school day suited some of the teachers' personalities just fine, while other teachers would have preferred a more relaxed pace.*

ignoble adj. (IHG noh buhl)—having low moral standards, not noble in character; mean
Tabloids like The National Enquirer *may have an* **ignoble** *reputation, but their sales numbers couldn't be better.*

irascible adj. (ih RAA suh buhl)—easily angered, hot tempered
One of the most **irascible** *barbarians in history, Attila the Hun ravaged much of Europe during his time.*

irreverent adj. (ir REHV er ehnt)—disrespectful; gently or humorously mocking
Kevin's **irreverent** *attitude in Sunday school annoyed the priest, but it amused the other children.*

Practice 2

DIRECTIONS: In completing the sentences, use four of the seven words below. Use each of the words just once.

consternation   demeaning   flagrant   contentious
disparage   irascible   ignoble

5. Although she was often too argumentative, being _____ made Mrs. Bishop a good choice as advisor to the debate club.

6. Willie's _____ violations of his parole led to yet another arrest.

7. Tim was so _____ toward everyone that Linda found it easy to ignore his taunts.

8. Kenneth's parents were in such a state of _____ about his weight loss and drop in grades that they brought him to see a psychologist.

Your Words, Your World

Counteract—Think of something that is a part of your daily life that you have an aversion to. Maybe it's hearing your alarm clock in the morning. Now think of a way to **counteract** this thing. Can you *undo* the annoyance of your alarm clock by setting your stereo to turn on first thing in the morning?

Disconcert—Imagine paying $40 to see your favorite band, only to have the band not show up, or leave after playing for just one hour. Imagine how *distressed*, *disturbed*, and *displeased* you would be. You probably would feel **disconcerted** about this *disappointing concert*.

Enigmatic—Picture a puzzle, plain and simple. As **enigmatic** means *puzzling* (as well as *mysterious* and *unfathomable*), the image of a puzzle should trigger your memory.

Frenetic—**Frenetic** shares the same root with *frantic* and *frenzied*, which also happen to be synonyms. And if that trick doesn't work, you can always picture a *frantic*, *frenzied*, **frenetic** cartoon character—one like the Tasmanian Devil, perhaps.

PART THREE

jaded adj. (JAY dehd)—tired by excess or overuse; slightly cynical
The musician played more than 20 jaded love songs and scowled the whole time, making it hard to enjoy the show.

lampoon v. (laam POON)—to ridicule with satire
Mayor McNichols hated being lampooned by the press for trying to improve people's manners.

malaise n. (MAA layz)—a feeling of unease or depression
During his presidency, Jimmy Carter spoke of a "national malaise" and was subsequently criticized for being too negative.

misanthrope n. (MIHS ahn throhp)—a person who hates or distrusts humankind
Scrooge was such a misanthrope that even the sight of children singing made him angry.

mollify v. (MAAL uh fiy)—to soothe in temper or disposition
A small raise and an extra vacation day mollified Mickey after he failed to get the promotion.

morose adj. (muh ROHS)—gloomy, sullen
After hearing that the internship had been given to someone else, Lenny was morose for days.

obfuscate v. (AHB fyoo skayt)—to confuse, make obscure
Benny tends to obfuscate his own point by bringing in irrelevant facts.

MEMORY TIP

To remember **obfuscate**, think of the *ob* and associate it with *obscure;* and also, think of the *fus* and associate it with *confuse.* To **obfuscate** is to *make obscure* and to *confuse.*

---

opprobrious adj. (uh PROH bree uhs)—disgraceful, shameful
The singer's new song was an opprobrious plea for money, and record sales were disappointing.

oscillate v. (AH sih layt)—to swing back and forth like a pendulum; to vary between opposing beliefs or feelings
Because they are out of touch with young people, politicians tend to oscillate on education legislation.

ostracize v. (ah struh SIYZE)—to exclude from a group
Feeling ostracized by her friends, Tabitha couldn't figure out what she had done.

pique v. (PEEK)—to arouse anger in; to arouse interest in; provoke
It seemed that Farley's one joy in life was piquing his father's anger.

precarious adj. (prih CAA ree uhs)—lacking in security or stability; dependent on chance or uncertain conditions
War is always a precarious time, at home and abroad.

rancor n. (RAAN kuhr)—bitter hatred
Having been teased for years, Hal was filled with rancor for his classmates.

rankle v. (RAANG kuhl)—to cause anger and irritation
At first the babysitter found the children's television show adorable, but after half an hour it began to rankle.

saturnine adj. (saat uhr NIYN)—cold and steady in mood; slow to act
Tim's saturnine responses made him seem unapproachable.

truculent adj. (truhk YUH lehnt)—disposed to fight, belligerent
Quentin was truculent when he first enrolled at Washington High, but quickly realized he didn't need to be so defensive.

vex v. (VEHKS)—to irritate, annoy; confuse, puzzle
Herbert, who loved his peace and quiet, was vexed by his neighbor's loud music.

vitriolic adj. (VIH tree AH lik)—spiteful; caustic; bitter
It had been a long time since anyone had seen such a vitriolic review of a Julia Roberts film.

wan adj. (WAHN)—sickly pale
In the midst of her cold, Melody's usually rosy cheeks looked wan.

Practice 3

DIRECTIONS: Consider the two word choices in the parentheses, and circle the one that best fits in the context of the sentence.

9. Theo's behavior was (**wan** OR **opprobrious**), but his apology was heartfelt and soon all was forgotten.

10. After students started referring to "(**Morose** OR **Misanthrope**) Mondays," the staff used the nickname as well.

11. No one could believe the (**rancor** OR **surmount**) with which Mr. DeLeon gave his resignation.

12. Norm (**disparaged** OR **lampooned**) the school's staff and students in his weekly cartoon, but he did it so well that nobody seemed to mind!

Your Words, Your World

Vex—Does it seem like life was better when you were a kid, with no *worries*? Well, that's because life's questions really begin to **vex** people once they become teenagers, and it only continues into adulthood. People are constantly *perplexed* and *irritated* by those questions they just can't answer.

Rankle—What really **rankles** you? What really gets your *blood boiling*? Is it people who cheat? What is it that causes *anger* and *irritation*?

PRACTICE ANSWERS AND EXPLANATIONS

Practice 1

1. An **affront** is an *insult,* so the antonym is *compliment. Behind* is an irrelevant distracter.

2. To **beleaguer** is to *harass. Delight* is the correct choice. *Ignore* is unrelated.

3. To **berate** is to *scold,* while *praise* is the antonym. *Tardy* means late and is neither the antonym nor the synonym.

PRACTICE ANSWERS AND EXPLANATIONS *(cont'd)*

4. A person who is **choleric** has a *short temper*. Choleric people definitely are not *easygoing*. Nor are they *gabby*, but *easygoing* is the antonym.

Practice 2

5. Mrs. Bishop was **contentious**, meaning she was quick to debate or argue.

6. Willie's violations were **flagrant**, which means outrageous or shameless.

7. To **demean** is to degrade and humiliate.

8. To be in a state of **consternation** is to feel intense fear or dismay.

Practice 3

9. Theo's behavior was not *wan* (sickly pale), but **opprobrious**, which means disgraceful and shameful.

10. "**Morose** Mondays" is a nickname for the gloomiest day of the week. A *misanthrope* is a person who hates humanity.

11. The answer is **rancor**, which means bitter hatred. *Surmount* is not the answer as it is grammatically incorrect and means to overcome.

12. If Norm were to *disparage* (belittle) everyone, they certainly would mind. To be **lampooned** (ridiculed in a humorous way) on the other hand, might be acceptable to students and maybe even staff.

CHAPTER 12 QUIZ

Take your time, not only with the questions, but in reading the answer explanations that follow. Set a goal for yourself—80% (16 correct answers) is recommended—and if you don't reach that goal, go back and read through the chapter again. Good luck!

DIRECTIONS: For questions 1–10, circle T for True or F for False. For questions 11–20, circle the synonym.

1. **T F** **counteract**—to pretend

2. **T F** **ignoble**—immoral

3. **T F** **precarious**—insecure

4. **T F** **ostracize**—to exclude

5. **T F** **malaise**—a joyful feeling

6. **T F** **consternation**—state of fear

7. **T F** **disconcert**—to upset

8. **T F** **affront**—an insult

9. **T F** **jaded**—fed up

10. **T F** **vitriolic**—kind

11.	**vex:**	pacify	annoy	invigorate
12.	**beleaguer:**	harass	crescendo	accretion
13.	**saturnine:**	aloof	friendly	resilient
14.	**demean:**	augment	humiliate	abate
15.	**contentious:**	disagreeable	contestant	agreeable
16.	**brandish:**	to brand	to abuse	to wield
17.	**aversion:**	dislike	penchant	fondness
18.	**confound:**	to find	to soothe	to baffle
19.	**opprobrious:**	joyful	shameful	full
20.	**choleric:**	irreverent	irritable	cantankerous

CHAPTER 12 QUIZ ANSWERS AND EXPLANATIONS

1. **False.** To **counteract** is to oppose by contrary action and not to pretend.

2. **True.** To be **ignoble** is to have low moral standards or to be immoral.

3. **True.** If something is in a **precarious** position it is lacking in security and stability.

4. **True.** To **ostracize** is to exclude from a group by common consent.

5. **False.** A **malaise** is a feeling of unease or depression and not a joyful feeling.

6. **True.** A feeling of **consternation** is an intense state of fear or dismay.

7. **True.** To **disconcert** is to ruffle or upset.

8. **True.** An **affront** is a personal offense or insult.

9. **True.** To feel **jaded** is to be tired of something because of its excess or overuse. It is to be fed up.

10. **False.** To be **vitriolic** is to be spiteful, caustic, and bitter. It is definitely not to be kind.

11. To **vex** is to irritate or *annoy*. It is not to *pacify* (calm someone down) or *invigorate*.

12. To **beleaguer** is to *harass*. To *crescendo* is to increase and an *accretion* is an accumulation.

13. To be **saturnine** is to be *aloof* and cold toward others. It is neither *friendly* nor *resilient*.

14. To **demean** is to degrade or *humiliate*. To *augment* is to supplement and to *abate* is to decrease, both of which are incorrect.

15. To be **contentious** is to be *disagreeable*. The antonym is *agreeable*. *Contestant* is also incorrect.

16. To **brandish** is *to wield* (wave menacingly). It is neither *to brand* nor *to abuse*.

CHAPTER 12 QUIZ ANSWERS AND EXPLANATIONS *(cont'd)*

17. An **aversion** is an intense *dislike* of something. *Penchant* and *fondness* are synonyms of one another, but antonyms of **aversion** as they mean a liking for something.

18. To **confound** is *to baffle* or stupefy. *To find* is a distracter based on the appearance of "found" in **confound**. *To soothe* means to mollify.

19. **Opprobrious** means *shameful* and definitely not *joyful* or *full*.

20. To feel **choleric** is to feel *irritable* and short-tempered. It is not to be *irreverent* (disrespectful), nor *cantankerous* (crabby).

CHAPTER 13

Sizing It Up

Bigger, smaller, shorter, taller; it's all here

BUILDING BLOCK QUIZ

By answering the 12 questions below, you will get a sense of how closely you'll have to study this chapter in order to master the vocabulary used to describe differences in size. Should you happen to choose incorrect answers for the final two questions, you'll want to go back to chapter 12 for some review.

DIRECTIONS: Fill in the blanks, using the most appropriate of the four multiple-choice answers. The correct answer will always fit into the sentence grammatically.

1. Whenever Jan's weight began to _____, she quickly switched from cookies to fruit after lunch and dinner.

   (A) wane   (B) abate

   (C) wax   (D) allay

2. Mrs. Grady reminded the class that _____ words in a research paper can often lower its grade.

   (A) finite   (B) infusion

   (C) superstar   (D) superfluous

3. Vince liked to _____ his fruit with his Swiss Army knife.

   (A) pare   (B) eradicate

   (C) proliferate   (D) inundate

4. Mick _____ the empty potato chip bag as he'd told his little brother that he didn't have any food left.

   (A) mitigated   (B) jettisoned
   (C) razed   (D) chided

5. Ken knew that unlike his mother, his father had _____ patience, so he stopped arguing.

   (A) finite   (B) capacious
   (C) behemoth   (D) superfluous

6. The crowd began to _____ after the security guards dragged the two girls away.

   (A) collage   (B) surfeit
   (C) remnant   (D) dissipate

7. As there was a(n) _____ of talent at the talent show, most people went home early.

   (A) abundance   (B) legion
   (C) dearth   (D) inflation

8. Lila could see Ursula _____ at the offer of dessert and knew that she would want to leave the dinner party soon.

   (A) burgeon   (B) balk
   (C) augment   (D) allay

9. Kara gave her little sister a Band-Aid to _____ the paper cut.

   (A) assuage   (B) debase
   (C) wax   (D) augment

10. In order to _____ the class's anxiety before the SAT, Miss Harmon turned her review classes into a mini-Olympics.

   (A) faux pas   (B) crescendo
   (C) vex   (D) allay

11. Mr. Jackson hoped to _____ the disgruntled employees by offering behavior incentives.

    (A) rankle   (B) mollify

    (C) degrade   (D) jettison

12. Jean's _____ to school lunches was almost comical, except to her mother who had to pack a lunch every day.

    (A) voracious   (B) zenith

    (C) aversion   (D) partiality

BUILDING BLOCK ANSWERS AND EXPLANATIONS

1. C. Jan would have fruit for dessert when her weight started to **wax,** or increase gradually. The opposite is to decrease, or lessen, which is the definition for *wane, abate,* and *allay.*

2. D. Superfluous means extra or more than necessary, and is the best choice. *Finite* (limited) doesn't make quite as much sense in context: a paper can't have an infinite number of words. An *infusion* is a mix or combination and makes as little sense here as *superstar.*

3. A. To **pare** is to trim, as in the skin of fruit, which is how Vince used his knife. To *eradicate* (eliminate) is incorrect as is *proliferate* (multiply or grow) and *inundate* (overwhelm).

4. B. Jettisoned means discarded. *Mitigated* (lessened), *razed* (destroyed), and *chided* (scolded) are all inappropriate choices.

5. A. Ken's father's patience was limited, or **finite.** It was neither *capacious* nor *behemoth,* both of which mean large. *Superfluous,* which means more than necessary, also fails to fit the sentence's intended meaning.

6. D. The crowd began to **dissipate,** or vanish. The other three answers don't fit grammatically or in context, as *surfeit* means an excessive amount, *remnant* means left over, and *collage* means assemblage.

7. C. There was a **dearth,** or lack, of talent, so people were not motivated to stay. There certainly wasn't an *abundance,* a *legion* (crowd), or an *inflation* (increase).

BUILDING BLOCK ANSWERS AND EXPLANATIONS *(cont'd)*

8. B. Ursula **balked** at the offer of dessert, meaning she refused it. *Burgeon* means multiply, *augment* means supplement, and *allay* means dispel, none of which makes sense here.

9. A. Kara wanted to ease, or **assuage**, her sister's pain. She did not want to *debase* (demean) it, *augment* (increase) it, or cause it to *wax* (gradually increase).

10. D. Only **allay** (to lessen or ease) makes sense. A *faux pas* is a social error, to *crescendo* is to increase, and to *vex* is to annoy.

11. B. He hoped to **mollify**, or soothe in temper and disposition, his employees with the rewards. He certainly didn't want to *rankle* (irritate) or *degrade* (humiliate) them, nor did he want to *jettison* (get rid of) them. If you answered this question incorrectly, you might want to go back to chapter 12 for some review.

12. C. Jean had an **aversion** to, or intense dislike of, school lunches. *Voracious* is an adjective meaning huge or insatiable, while the sentence calls for a noun. *Zenith* means peak, but you can't have a "zenith to" something. *Partiality* means bias towards and it conveys the opposite of the sentence's intended meaning. If you answered this question incorrectly, you might want to go back to chapter 12 for some review.

PART ONE

accretion n. (uh KREE shuhn)—a growth in size, an increase in amount
The accretion of the college's endowment meant more scholarships could be offered.

allay v. (uh LAY)—to lessen, ease, reduce in intensity
Nurse Fanny sat with Sally all night, trying to allay Sally's fears.

amenity n. (uh MEN it tee)—pleasantness; something increasing comfort
After his third massage of the week, Joel really began to appreciate the resort's amenities.

amortize v. (uh MORE tiyze)—to diminish by installment payments
*Jess would **amortize** her debt with automatic deductions from each paycheck.*

assuage v. (uh SWAGE)—to make less severe, to ease, to relieve
*After a bad day at work, Phil liked to go to the movies to **assuage** his stress.*

attenuate v. (uh TEN oo ate)—to soothe; to lessen; to make thin or slender; to weaken
*To make sure that states ratified the Constitution, the framers **attenuated** the power of the federal government.*

balk v. (BAWK)—to refuse, shirk; prevent
*The horse **balked** at jumping over the high fence, going so far as to throw his rider off.*

behemoth n. (buh HEE muhth)—something of monstrous size or power; huge creature
*The Ford LTD was a **behemoth** and took up half the driveway.*

bereft adj. (bee REHFT)—deprived or lacking of something
*The reality show was **bereft** of anything resembling dignity or intelligence.*

blight v. (BLIYT)—to afflict, destroy
*The locusts **blighted** the crop in a matter of hours.*

burgeon v. (BER gehn)—to sprout or flourish
*The size of suburban schools **burgeoned** as more and more people moved out of the city.*

capacious adj. (kah PAY shus)—large, roomy; extensive
***Capacious** houses quickly constructed in the suburbs are often called "McMansions."*

colossal n. (kuh LAH suhl)—immense, enormous
*Joseph made a **colossal** error by skipping school; he failed the final exam and was forced to retake the course.*

Practice 1

DIRECTIONS: In completing the sentences, use five of the eight words below. Use each of the words just once.

amortize	assuage	behemoth	bereft
burgeoned	capacious	colossal	amenity

1. The teacher tried to _____ the class's fear of exams by reviewing with a game of Hangman.

2. Participation in the Spanish Club _____ after the piñata party.

3. The new cafeteria was _____ and well lit, and Mr. Drake knew the students were going to love it.

4. Carol felt _____ of an advisor and friend when Miss Fenwick retired.

5. For the class, the poster project was a _____ of an assignment that would be impossible to complete over the weekend.

Your Words, Your World

Amenity—Recall the *nicest* hotel you ever stayed in, and try to remember the **amenities**. These might include a swimming pool, a gym, a *comfortable* bed, or the *pleasant* staff. Think of that hotel, and you will remember that an **amenity** is anything to *improve your experience*.

Balk—In baseball, the term **balk** refers to a pitcher *stopping* in the middle of his motion. This is a useful image, as balk means to *refuse, shy away from, shirk,* or *prevent*. When the pitcher shies away from delivering the pitch, that's called a **balk**.

Colossal—Picture an *immense* blimp floating through the sky. Or a *huge* cruise ship, **colossal** compared to all the other boats around it. There is also the idea of a *tremendous* mistake, as **colossal** doesn't just describe things in the physical world.

PART TWO

crescendo n. (kruh SHEN doh)—gradual increase in volume, force, or intensity
*Due to the way the song **crescendoed**, the audience was left emotionally exhausted.*

dearth n. (DUHRTH)—a lack, scarcity, insufficiency
*The **dearth** of teachers made it difficult for principals to staff their classrooms.*

debase v. (dee BAYS)—to degrade or lower in quality or stature
*The Governor's embezzlement **debased** the stature of his office.*

debilitating adj. (dee BIL uh tay ting)—impairing the strength or energy
*The 25 percent cut in staff proved **debilitating** to IntelliCo, and within a month profits had suffered.*

degradation n. (deh gruh DAY shun)—reduction in worth or dignity
*When Sarah broke up with Charlie at the dance, he had never felt such **degradation**.*

> **MEMORY TIP**
>
> The **de-** in the preceding four words indicates a *lessening* or a *de*crease.

distract v. (dihs TRAKT)—to cause to lose focus, to divert attention
*Music didn't **distract** Jeremy from his studies; it actually helped him to stay focused.*

eradicate v. (ee RAHD ih kayt)—to erase or wipe out
*Evan's economics thesis involved **eradicating** poverty in a Costa Rican village.*

hindrance n. (HIN drehns)—impediment, clog; stumbling block
*Not wishing to be a **hindrance**, Gary played outside while his father cleaned up for the party.*

inflation n. (in FLAY shun)—undue amplification, often economic
*Mr. Ogelvie's example of **inflation** was the increase in the cost of a
cheeseburger over five years.*

infusion n. (in FYOO zhun)—the introduction of, the addition of
*The United States has benefited from the **infusion** of many different
cultures.*

inundate v. (IN uhn dayt)—to cover with a flood; to overwhelm as if
with a flood
*These days, college students are **inundated** with credit card offers.*

> **MEMORY TIP**
>
> The **in-** in the previous three words indicates an *increase*
> or *growth*.

Practice 2

DIRECTIONS: After reading the three choices, circle the one that you
think is the *antonym*.

6. **dearth:**   scarcity   insufficiency   adequacy

7. **hindrance:**   assistance   impediment   clog

8. **debilitating:** impairing   helping   debating

9. **crescendo:**   augment   increase   decrease

10. **infusion:**   dispersal   increase   absolute

Your Words, Your World

Inflation—Think of a fully **inflated** balloon to remind yourself that **inflation** means *increase, rise,* or at its worst, *unnecessary amplification*. As an
adult, you know that **inflation** means an increase in prices such that one
dollar buys less than it did before.

Distract—A concert or movie may *sidetrack* you from your work or studies. A friend may look to *divert*, or entertain, you when you're feeling
down, and there's nothing wrong with that. Just be sure to avoid getting
too **distracted** from this book!

PART THREE

jettison v. (JEHT ih zuhn) (JEHT ih suhn)—to discard, to get rid of as unnecessary or encumbering
The sinking ship jettisoned its cargo in a desperate attempt to reduce weight.

legion n. (LEE jun)—a great number, a multitude
As soon as Lester got his first big role, he had legions of fans.

Lilliputian adj. (lihl ee PYOO shun)—very small
Amy looked Lilliputian next to her roommate, a former basketball star.

mitigate v. (MIHT ih gayt)—to make less severe, make milder
Judge Leland decided to mitigate the first-timer's sentence.

modicum n. (MAHD ih kuhm)—a small portion, limited quantity
Bebe asked for even a modicum of a raise, and her boss agreed to give her $2 more per hour.

palatial adj. (puh LAY shuhl)—relating to a palace; magnificent
After the cramped studio apartment, the one-bedroom apartment seemed palatial.

pallid adj. (PAHL id)—lacking color or liveliness
Tyler often exaggerated his illnesses, but his pallid skin color was a sure sign that he was sick.

pare v. (PAYR)—to trim off excess, reduce
Mrs. Rodgers could pare down the essays in the writing contest by eliminating the ones with spelling and punctuation mistakes.

proliferate v. (proh LIH fuhr ayt)—to grow by rapid production of new parts; increase in number
The cancer cells proliferated so quickly that even the doctor was surprised.

raze v. (RAYS)—to tear down, demolish
When Ricky returned, the house had been razed and there was nothing left on the lot.

superfluous adj. (soo PUHR floo UHS)—extra, more than necessary
The job counselor told Georgio that the extra reference letters were **superfluous***, and he should pick just three.*

surfeit n. (SUR fiht)—excessive amount
Because of the **surfeit** *of pigs, pork prices fell to record lows.*

voluminous adj. (vah LOO mehn us)—large, having great volume
The bachelor's **voluminous** *mug was filled with root beer, as he no longer drank alcohol.*

voracious adj. (vor AY shus)—having a great appetite
The **voracious** *boys ate three pizzas all by themselves.*

wax v. (WAAKS)—to increase gradually; to begin to be
The moon was in its **wax** *phase, after waning.*

zenith n. (ZEE nihth)—the point of culmination; peak
The singer considered her appearance at the Metropolitan Opera House to be the **zenith** *of her career.*

Practice 3

DIRECTIONS: Consider the two word choices in the parentheses, and circle the one that best fits in the context of the sentence.

11. Izzy thought that the standing ovation was (**voracious** OR **superfluous**), but thanked the crowd, nonetheless.

12. Dr. Harvey hoped to (**proliferate** OR **mitigate**) the effects of the teacher strike by using assistant teachers and substitutes.

13. The (**zenith** OR **modicum**) of Verna's high school soccer career came with the win at the state championship.

14. There was a (**surfeit** OR **dearth**) of pizza after the dance, and the class president decided to donate it to the homeless.

15. Usually (**pallid** OR **Lilliputian**), Tina was darkly tan after her Caribbean vacation.

Your Words, Your World

Lilliputian—Is there a *miniaturized* version of something in your house? Maybe you have a *tiny* replica of an antique car or a *very small* portrait of an ancestor in a locket? Anything *super small* is considered **Lilliputian**.

Jettison—The next time you clean out your room, what will be the first thing to get *thrown out*? Will you get *rid* of old clothing or books? Will you have a hard time **jettisoning** anything?

PRACTICE ANSWERS AND EXPLANATIONS

Practice 1

1. To **assuage** is to ease or make less severe, and the teacher was hoping to calm the class with some Hangman. (NOTE: allay, abate, and attenuate are all acceptable answers, as well.)

2. Participation in the Spanish Club **burgeoned**, or flourished.

3. The new cafeteria was **capacious**, which means large and roomy.

4. Carol felt **bereft**, which means deprived.

5. The assignment was a **behemoth** in that it seemed monstrous—too large to complete in a weekend.

Practice 2

6. *Adequacy* is the antonym of **dearth**. The synonyms are *scarcity* and *insufficiency*, so neither of those answers is correct.

7. The antonym of **hindrance** is *assistance*, while *impediment* and *clog* are synonyms.

8. The antonym of **debilitating** is *helping*. One synonym is *impairing*. *Debating* is irrelevant.

9. The antonym of **crescendo** is *decrease*. *Augment* and *increase* are synonyms.

10. The antonym of **infusion** is *dispersal*. The synonym is *increase* (as a noun). *Absolute* has no relation to **infusion**.

Practice 3

11. Izzy was being humble in that he thought the standing ovation was **superfluous**, or more than necessary. *Voracious* means insatiable, which doesn't make as much sense as **superfluous**.

12. Dr. Harvey hoped to **mitigate**, or lessen the severity of, the teacher strike. He did not want to *proliferate* (reproduce, increase, or spread) it.

13. The **zenith** is the peak, or culmination, and the state championship was the high point of Verna's high school soccer career. A *modicum* is a small amount, so that's incorrect.

14. A **surfeit** (excessive amount) of pizza means there was a lot left over for the homeless. A *dearth,* or shortage, would mean no pizza.

15. Before her vacation, Tina was **pallid** (lacking color or liveliness), but not afterward. She may have been small, but it is doubtful she was *Lilliputian.*

CHAPTER 13 QUIZ

Take your time, not only with the questions, but in reading the answer explanations that follow. Set a goal for yourself—80% (16 correct answers) is recommended—and if you don't reach that goal, go back and read through the chapter again. Good luck!

DIRECTIONS: For questions 1–10, circle T for True or F for False. For questions 11–20, circle the synonym.

1. **T F   behemoth**—something tiny

2. **T F   debase**—to raise in quality or stature

3. **T F   zenith**—point of culmination

4. **T F   proliferate**—to shrink due to decreased production

5. **T F   voracious**—having a great appetite

6. **T F   palatial**—magnificent

7. **T F   crescendo**—a gradual increase

8. **T F   infusion**—the addition of

9. **T F   capacious**—large

10. **T F   debilitating**—impairing the strength

11. **augment:**	to reduce	to withdraw	to expand
12. **eradicate:**	to construct	to mitigate	to wipe out
13. **attenuate:**	to increase	to soothe	to wax
14. **mitigate:**	less severe	more severe	to crescendo
15. **pallid:**	effervescent	colorful	lacking color
16. **assuage:**	to ease	to burden	to increase
17. **raze:**	to burgeon	to demolish	to assemble
18. **hindrance:**	an assist	an impediment	an aid
19. **distract:**	to divert	to focus	to debase
20. **bereft:**	prosperous	affluent	deprived of

CHAPTER 13 QUIZ ANSWERS AND EXPLANATIONS

1. False. A **behemoth** is something monstrously huge, like an elephant, and not something tiny.

2. False. To **debase** is to belittle or humiliate (demean is a synonym). It is not to raise in quality or stature.

3. True. The **zenith** is the point of culmination. Think of the **zenith** of the sun in the sky at noon.

4. False. To **proliferate** is to grow due to increased production, the opposite of the given answer (to shrink due to decreased production).

5. True. To be **voracious** is to have a great appetite. Some people, for example, are voracious eaters.

6. True. **Palatial** means magnificent.

7. True. A **crescendo** is a gradual increase.

8. True. An **infusion** is the addition of something, but the word isn't used in mathematical contexts. It refers to things like color, light, taste, scent, or fun.

9. True. To be **capacious** is to be large, as in the size of a room.

10. True. When something is **debilitating** it is impairing the strength of something else.

11. To **augment** is *to expand*. It is not *to reduce* or *to withdraw*.

12. To **eradicate** is *to wipe out*, which is the opposite of *to construct* and nearly the opposite of *to mitigate* (to ease or lessen).

13. To **attenuate** is *to soothe* or lessen. It is not *to increase*, which is synonymous with *to wax*.

14. To **mitigate** is to make *less severe*. *More severe* and *to crescendo* (increase) are both incorrect.

15. If something is **pallid** it is *lacking color*. *Effervescent* (shiny and bubbly) and *colorful* are antonyms of **pallid**.

CHAPTER 13 QUIZ ANSWERS AND EXPLANATIONS *(cont'd)*

16. To **assuage** is *to ease*. It is not *to burden* or *to increase*. **Assuage** is most often used regarding people's emotions, like **assuaging** someone's fears.

17. To **raze** is *to demolish*. *To burgeon* means to flourish, and *to assemble* is to construct, the opposite of **raze**.

18. A **hindrance** is *an impediment*. *An assist* and *an aid* are both antonyms of **hindrance**.

19. To **distract** is *to divert*, especially attention. *To focus* is the opposite. *To debase* is to humiliate.

20. To be **bereft** is to be *deprived of* something. *Prosperous* and *affluent* both mean wealthy.

Foreign Words

Vocabulary from the melting pot

BUILDING BLOCK QUIZ

By answering the 12 questions below, you will get a sense of how closely you'll have to study this chapter in order to master the vocabulary you'll need to navigate the global village. If you choose incorrect answers for the final two questions, you'll want to go back to chapter 13 for some review.

DIRECTIONS: Fill in the blanks, using the most appropriate of the four multiple-choice answers. The correct answer will always fit into the sentence grammatically.

1. Eduardo had a _____ for General Tsao's Chicken.

   (A) bing   (B) bang

   (C) yen   (D) yang

2. Mr. Pauling asked the superintendent for a _____ regarding the funding for field trips.

   (A) tea-to-tea   (B) tête-à-tête

   (C) two-à-two   (D) tête

3. The judge informed the two debate clubs that loyalty and the Marine Corps code of _____ was the day's topic.

   (A) temper fatalis   (B) siempre fidalis

   (C) simper infidelis   (D) semper fidelis

4. In finalizing their plans to elope, Helen and Gabe made the lake their _____.

   (A) rendezvous   (B) voulez vous

   (C) voilà   (D) vestibule

5. Part of the comedian's appeal was the way he interrupted himself with silly _____ throughout the routine.

   (A) nonsensicals   (B) nonrefundables

   (C) non sequiturs   (D) nonplusseds

6. The principal was not pleased when Zabrina promised that the administrators would have to be more _____ if she were student body president.

   (A) lazy-fair   (B) laissez-faire

   (C) savoire faire   (D) lackadaisical

7. Jan tried to convince her father to buy the prom dress by saying it was _____ to spend no less than $500.

   (A) du jour   (B) de rigeur

   (C) de rigorous   (D) du ponte

8. The class quickly tired of Mr. Winterbottom's old _____.

   (A) passés   (B) clicky

   (C) cliques   (D) clichés

9. All of the teachers noticed the amazing sense of _____ shared by the senior class.

   (A) concoctory   (B) camaraderie

   (C) camouflagery   (D) imparity

10. When Freddy was suspended, even his friends had to admit that the punishment was _____.

    (A) à propose   (B) à pro bono

    (C) à professionale   (D) à propos

11. The math teachers all admitted to the students that the additional statewide test was more of a _____ than a help.

    (A) hindrance   (B) hind leg

    (C) reference   (D) hypocritical

12. The elementary school was _____ of musical instruments until the anonymous donation of $3,000.

    (A) cleft   (B) deft

    (C) bereft   (D) bedraggled

BUILDING BLOCK ANSWERS AND EXPLANATIONS

1. C. A **yen** is a strong desire or craving, and Eduardo had one for General Tsao's Chicken. *Bing, bang,* and *yang* are all silly answers. In this Building Block Quiz, most of the incorrect answers are nonsensical!

2. B. A **tête-à-tête** is a situation in which two people talk in private. In this case, the two people were Mr. Pauling and the superintendent. *Tea-to-tea, two-à-two,* and *tête* are all incorrect.

3. D. **Semper fidelis** is a Latin phrase—and the motto of the United States Marine Corps—that means to always be loyal. *Siempre fidalis, simper infidelis,* and *temper fatalis* are made-up answers.

4. A. A **rendezvous** is a place where a meeting has been arranged. *Voulez vous* (would you like?), *voilà* (ta da!), and *vestibule* (entrance hall) are all incorrect in this situation.

5. C. **Non sequiturs** are statements that do not logically follow what was said before. In this case, a comedian was using them to be funny. He was not using *nonrefundables. Nonsensicals* and *nonplusseds* are not real words, although *nonsensical* (meaningless) and *nonplussed* (puzzled) are adjectives.

6. B. Zabrina was saying she would make the administrators be more **laissez-faire** (a governmental position of noninterference), which means they wouldn't make as many rules for the students. What a politician! It goes without saying that *lazy-fair* and *lackadaisical* (also meaning lazy) are way off. *Savoire faire* means ability gained from having experienced something.

BUILDING BLOCK ANSWERS AND EXPLANATIONS *(cont'd)*

7. B. **De rigeur** means required by tradition or fashion. Do you think Jan's father fell for it? *Du jour* means of the day, and *de rigorous* and *du ponte* are made-up answers.

8. D. Mr. Winterbottom's **clichés** (overused expressions) might have been passé, but *passés* isn't a word, nor is *clicky*. *Cliques* are groups of friends, but that doesn't make sense in this context.

9. B. **Camaraderie** is a sense of comfort and trust shared between people. *Imparity* means inequality. *Concoctory* and *camouflagery* are concocted (made-up, artificial) words.

10. D. To say that something is **à propos** is to say that it is appropriate. The other three choices—*à propose, à pro bono, à professionale*—don't mean anything in French or English!

11. A. The math teachers thought the testing was more **hindrance** (impediment; trouble) than help. *Hind leg, reference*, and *hypocritical* (deceitful) are all incorrect. If you answered this question incorrectly, you might want to go back to chapter 13 for some review.

12. C. **Bereft** means deprived of or lacking. *Cleft* (partially split or divided), *deft* (dexterous), and *bedraggled* (disheveled) are all irrelevant. If you answered this question incorrectly, you might want to go back to chapter 13 for some review.

PART ONE

à propos adj. (ah pruh POH)—pertinent; appropriate; French for "to the purpose"
*The punishment of washing cars was **à propos** as Heidi had spray-painted several cars.*

ad hoc adj. (ad HAHK)—for a certain purpose; Latin for "for this"
*An **ad hoc** committee formed with the goal of raising money for a new playground.*

aficionado n. (uh fish ee yuh NAH doh)—a fan, usually of sports; Spanish for "affectionate one"
Catherine considered herself a baseball **aficionado** *and had the statistical knowledge to prove it.*

al fresco adj. (al FRES koh)—out in the fresh air; Italian for "in the fresh"
Tim preferred to dine **al fresco** *and asked for a table on the patio.*

au courant adj. (oh koo RAWN)—to be informed; knowledgeable of current events; French for "in the current"
Mitch read the paper every day and was considered **au courant** *by all his friends.*

avant-garde adj. (AH vant GARD)—a radically new or original movement, especially in the arts; French for "advance guard"
Maya Deren's **avant-garde** *films broke the rules of classical cinema.*

bourgeois adj. (boor ZHWAH)—middle-class; French for "of the town"
The **bourgeois** *family was horrified when the lower-class family moved in next door.*

camaraderie n. (kahm RAH da ree)—trust, sociability among friends; French for "comrade"
The photo clearly shows the **camaraderie** *as the team sits smiling at the airport.*

carte blanche n. (kahrt BLANCH)—full authority and freedom to do whatever one wants; French for "blank card"
When Mr. Thomas returned from Florida, he told his class that Disney World was **carte blanche** *for kids.*

cliché n. (klee SHAY)—overused expression or idea
The movie wasn't very original, as the characters continually uttered **clichés***.*

collage n. (ko LAZH)—assemblage of diverse elements; French for "pasting"
Dean Wintner used a **collage** *of newspaper clippings to decorate the wall of her office.*

déjà vu n. (DAY zhah vu)—the illusory feeling of having been in a situation before; French for "already seen"
Standing on the deck of the cruise ship, Renee had an overwhelming sense of déjà vu.

de rigeur adj. (duh ri GUHR)—required by tradition or fashion; French for "indispensable"
The limousine and corsage had become de rigeur for the prom.

Practice 1

DIRECTIONS: Match the foreign word (left column) with its translation or English meaning (right column).

1. **de rigeur**   pasting

2. **collage**   indispensable

3. **ad hoc**   middle-class

4. **bourgeois**   for a certain purpose

Your Words, Your World

Carte blanche—Picture a *blank card*. Can you see it? A business card without any print? Well, if you can see it, you can remember it. **Carte blanche** is a *blank card*. More specifically, it is like having a *blank check*, meaning if you have it, you can help yourself to whatever you would like. Picture not just the *blank card* (or *blank check*), but the fun you would have using it.

Avant-garde—Put more emphasis on the *advance* than the *guard*. When something is **avant-garde**, it is a *glimpse of the future*. It is an indicator of something *up and coming*, usually in the art world. Think of *advance* and you'll remember this definition.

Aficionado—Remember these words: "*official fan.*" **Aficionado** almost sounds like "*official fan,*" doesn't it? Can you see this person, wearing the team's full uniform, with his or her face painted in the team's colors, carrying a sign in each hand? **Aficionado** is Spanish for "*affectionate one*" and is most often applied to a *die-hard fan* of a certain team (though the meaning isn't limited to sports). Are you an **aficionado**?

PART TWO

faux pas n. (foh PAH)—an embarrassing mistake in a social setting; French for "false step"
When Missy dropped the baked beans all over her skirt at the cocktail party, it was the worst faux pas of her life.

joie de vivre n. (zhwah duh VEE vruh)—the enjoyment of life, usually shared with others; French for "joy of living"
Dr. Bingham always reminded her students that family, not work, was the way to achieve joie de vivre.

laissez-faire n. (lah zay FAIR)—a governmental position of noninterference, most often in terms of business; French for "let do"
The president's laissez-faire policies temporarily aided the economy.

> **MEMORY TIP**
>
> The *laissez* of **laissez-faire** is pronounced "lazy." Let this remind you that, in a way, *a position of noninterference* is . . . lazy.

non sequitur n. (nahn SEK wi tur)—a statement that does not logically follow what was said before; Latin for "it does not follow"
Mr. Edham's non sequiturs made his math lessons hard to follow.

outré adj. (oo TRAY)—bizarre; French for "carried to excess"
Liza's outré outfits were ridiculous and her friends told her so.

panache n. (puh nahsh)—flamboyance or dash in style and action; French for "plume"
Leah's panache made her very well known within her department.

raison d'être n. (ray zohn DET ruh)—the reason for living or existing; French for "reason to be"
As soon as his daughter was born, Calvin knew his raison d'être.

rendezvous n. (RAHN day voo)—a place where a meeting has been arranged; a meeting at such a place; French for "present yourself"
The lake was a popular summer rendezvous.

savoire faire n. (sav wahr FEHR)—the ability gained from having experienced something; French for "to know how to do"
Everybody said Kirk came back from his term abroad with a surprising maturity and savoire faire.

tête-à-tête n. (TET ah TET)—two people talking in private; French for "head-to-head"
Neil wouldn't tell anybody what was said in his tête-à-tête with Principal Lowell.

vis-à-vis prep. (VEE zah VEE)—as compared with or in relation to; French for "face-to-face"
Bernie was slow in finding his first job, vis-à-vis his go-getter of a brother.

yen n. (yehn)—a strong desire, craving; Cantonese for "smoke"
Pregnant women commonly have a yen for pickles.

zeitgeist n. (ZIYT giyst)—in the spirit of the times; German for "time spirit"
At the 1950s theme dance, the girls wore poodle skirts for fun and in accordance with the zeitgeist.

Practice 2

DIRECTIONS: In completing the sentences, use four of the seven words below. Use each of the words just once.

vis-à-vis   zeitgeist   faux pas   laissez-faire
raison d'être   non sequiturs   joie de vivre

5. Rapping was part of the _____, so Miss McGill agreed to do it for the talent show.

6. Derek's classroom was across the hall _____ Lilly's classroom.

7. Miss Masters told anyone who asked that the works of Jane Austen were her _____.

8. Mr. Pasquali advised Ben to avoid _____ when speaking publicly.

Your Words, Your World

Faux pas—If you have never, ever made a **faux pas**, congratulations. Chances are, though, there is at least one *social blunder* on your mind right now. At some point, you did something *foolish* in front of other people. Put that *embarrassing* memory to use now, and in a way, your **faux pas** will have been worth it.

Panache—If you know someone who has **panache**—*style, grace,* a socially acceptable *flamboyance*—let that person be your guiding light when confronted with this word. Think of how you look up to this person, whether you'd like to admit it or not. This could be due to his or her *sense of fashion*, ability to *hold the attention* of a group of people, or *confidence*. . . . Oh, to have **panache**!

Practice Answers and Explanations

Practice 1

1. **De rigeur** means *indispensable*.

2. A **collage** is an assemblage of diverse elements (literally *pasting*).

3. **Ad hoc** means *for a certain purpose*.

4. Something **bourgeois** is related to the *middle class* (literally "of the town").

Practice 2

5. Rapping seemed to be part of the **zeitgeist**, or spirit of the times.

6. Derek's classroom was across the hall in relation to (**vis-à-vis**) Lilly's.

7. Jane Austen's books were her **raison d'être**, or reason for living.

8. Ben needed to avoid all **non sequiturs**, or random digressions, when speaking publicly.

CHAPTER 14 QUIZ

Take your time, not only with the questions, but in reading the answer explanations that follow. Set a goal for yourself—80% (8 correct answers) is recommended—and if you don't reach that goal, go back and read through the chapter again. Good luck!

DIRECTIONS: For questions 1–7, circle T for True or F for False. For questions 8–10, circle the synonym.

1. **T F**   **zeitgeist**—trust

2. **T F**   **non sequitur**—an illogical statement

3. **T F**   **ad hoc**—Latin for "always loyal"

4. **T F**   **collage**—an artistic assemblage

5. **T F**   **déjà vu**—a nice view

6. **T F**   **joie de vivre**—the enjoyment of life

7. **T F**   **avant-garde**—unoriginal

8.	**faux pas:**	past tense	blunder	false friend
9.	**bourgeois:**	upper-class	middle-class	lower-class
10.	**panache:**	a dessert	humility	flamboyance

CHAPTER 14 QUIZ ANSWERS AND EXPLANATIONS

1. **False.** **Zeitgeist** is the spirit of the times and not trust.

2. **True.** A **non sequitur** is an illogical statement in that it does not fit with what was said before.

3. **False.** **Ad hoc** means for a certain purpose. *Semper fidelis* is Latin for "always loyal."

4. **True.** A **collage** is an artistic assemblage.

5. **False.** **Déjà vu** is the illusory feeling of having been in a situation before. It is definitely not French for "a nice view."

CHAPTER 14 QUIZ ANSWERS AND EXPLANATIONS *(cont'd)*

6.   True.   Joie de vivre means the enjoyment of life.

7.   False.   If something is **avant-garde** it is not unoriginal. Quite the opposite, it is radically original.

8.   A **faux pas** is a social *blunder.* It is neither a *false friend* nor the *past tense.*

9.   Bourgeois is French for "related to the *middle class.*" *Upper-class* and *lower-class* are both incorrect.

10. Panache means *flamboyance.* It is not a *dessert,* and *humility* has a strongly opposed meaning.

Most Frequently Tested SAT Words

The words you need to ace the SAT

BUILDING BLOCK QUIZ

By answering the ten questions below, you will get a sense of how closely you'll have to study this chapter in order to master the vocabulary that commonly shows up on the SAT!

DIRECTIONS: Fill in the blanks, using the most appropriate of the four multiple-choice answers. The correct answer will always fit into the sentence grammatically.

1. Jeff didn't realize how much his little brother _____ him until his mother pointed it out.

   (A) rescinded   (B) supplanted

   (C) emulated   (D) rejected

2. Lezlie was a(n) _____ expert on all things MTV and VH1.

   (A) veritable   (B) bogus

   (C) excoriate   (D) amalgamate

3. The _____ way the kitten hid behind the chair instantly won everyone's heart.

   (A) abstruse   (B) courageous

   (C) tremulous   (D) plucky

4. The photos really captured the baby's _____ face.

   (A) devilish   (B) seraphic

   (C) unsightly   (D) insular

5. Maureen was _____ with her teachers and not always in a good way.

   (A) timid   (B) timorous

   (C) audible   (D) audacious

6. Dean's _____ mind made him a good research scientist.

   (A) credulous   (B) incredulous

   (C) naïve   (D) incorrigible

7. Bert's _____ attitude earned him no friends, but plenty of enemies.

   (A) haughty   (B) emphatic

   (C) incredulous   (D) viscous

8. Michelle's singing style was _____ of Mariah Carey.

   (A) unwarranted   (B) unwitting

   (C) derivative   (D) prodigal

9. The boy's _____ ways made all the teachers wonder if he was a victim of abuse.

   (A) precocious   (B) chary

   (C) loquacious   (D) facile

10. Lenny enjoyed _____ the other players, as it made him feel better about his skills.

    (A) compounding   (B) adroiting

    (C) unavailing   (D) abasing

BUILDING BLOCK ANSWERS AND EXPLANATIONS

1. C. Jeff's little brother **emulated** (copied and imitated) him. He did not *reject*, *supplant* (displace), or *rescind* (cancel) him.

2. A. Lezlie was a **veritable** (without question) expert. She was not an *amalgamate* (combine), *excoriate* (criticize), or *bogus* (fake) expert.

3. C. **Tremulous**, or trembling, is appropriate for describing the scared kitten. *Plucky* is synonymous with *courageous* and both are inappropriate, as the kitten was hiding. *Abstruse* means obscure, so that doesn't fit either.

4. B. The baby's face was **seraphic** (angelic) and not *insular* (narrow-minded), *unsightly*, or *devilish*.

5. D. Maureen was **audacious**, or bold. Although she might have been *audible*, this is an incorrect choice, as are *timorous* and *timid*, both of which are antonyms to **audacious**. It's hard to see how any of the incorrect answers could apply "not in a good way."

6. B. As a researcher, Dean must have had an **incredulous** (skeptical) mind. It wouldn't have helped his research if his mind had been *incorrigible* (incapable of being corrected), *naïve* (overly trusting), or *credulous* (a synonym of naïve).

7. A. Bert was unpopular because he was **haughty**, or arrogant and condescending. This is a better choice than *viscous* (syrupy), *incredulous* (skeptical), or *emphatic* (forceful).

8. C. To be **derivative** is to have copied or adapted from someone else. It is to be unoriginal. Michelle was not *prodigal* (wasteful), *unwitting* (unsuspecting), or *unwarranted* (unnecessary).

9. B. The boy was **chary**, which means cautious and extremely shy. There is no evidence of his having been *facile* (superficial), *loquacious* (wordy), or *precocious* (intelligent).

10. D. Lenny enjoyed **abasing** (disgracing) the other players. *Unavailing* and *compounding* are irrelevant, and *adroiting* isn't a word.

PART ONE

abase v. (ah BEYS)—to demean; humble; disgrace
John's immature behavior abased him in my eyes.

aberration n. (ab er A shun)—something different from the usual
Due to the bizarre aberrations in the author's behavior, her publicist decided that the less the public saw of her, the better.

acuity n. (uh KYOO ih tee)—sharp vision or perception
With unusual acuity, she was able to determine that the masterpiece was a fake.

adroit adj. (uh DROYT)—skillful; accomplished; highly competent
The adroit athlete completed even the most difficult obstacle course with ease.

allusion n. (uh LOO shun)—indirect reference
The player was sometimes referred to as The Slugger, an allusion to his ability to hit the baseball very hard.

anachronistic adj. (uh NAK ru NISS tik)—outdated; occurring out of its proper time
The hippie's clothes, with their beads and dangling tassels, were anachronistic in style.

> **FLASHBACK**
>
> In Chapter 1, Word Roots, you learned that **chron** means *time*. Remembering this will help you to recall that **anachronistic** means *out of time* or *outdated*.

audacious adj. (ah DAY shus)—bold, daring, fearless
The audacious freshman ignored the senior's request.

banal adj. (bah NALL)—trite, overly common
Corey often used banal phrases that made people think he was less intelligent than he really was.

bucolic adj. (byoo CAH lihk)—pastoral, rural
*My aunt likes the hustle and bustle of the city, but my uncle prefers a more **bucolic** setting.*

chary adj. (CHAHR ee)—watchful, cautious; extremely shy
Mindful of the fate of the Titanic, *the captain was **chary** of navigating the iceberg-filled sea.*

circuitous adj. (suhr KYOO ih tuhs)—indirect, roundabout
*The venue was only a short walk from the train station, but due to a roadblock, I had to take a **circuitous** route.*

commodious adj. (kuh MODE ee us)—roomy, spacious
*Raeqwan was able to stretch out fully in the **commodious** bathtub.*

compound v. (kom POWND)—to combine, augment
*After spitting out his food, Marv **compounded** the insult to the hostess by giving his plate to the dog to finish.*

derivative adj. (di RIV uh tiv)—copied or adapted; not original
*The TV show was so obviously **derivative** of* Seinfeld *that viewers were not interested in watching it.*

Practice 1

DIRECTIONS: After reading the three choices, circle the *antonym.*

1.	**aberration**:	different	ordinary	unusual
2.	**acuity**:	naïve	insight	perception
3.	**banal**:	unique	trite	common
4.	**bucolic**:	pastoral	urban	rural
5.	**circuitous**:	undeviating	indirect	roundabout

Your Words, Your World

Adroit—Who is the most *skillful* person you know? And what is his or her *skill*? When a person is **adroit**, he or she is *accomplished* (*highly competent*) in a certain area. Who comes to mind when you think of this word?

Commodious—Everybody has a favorite room: what's yours? Is it in your house or is it someplace else? Is it a tiny little space or is it *roomy*? A *spacious*, or **commodious**, room might be your favorite if you're a fan of *wide-open*, *ample* spaces. What room will you think of to remind yourself that **commodious** means *large*?

Derivative—Who is your favorite singer or band? Is that person or group completely original or **derivative** of another singer or band? Whose style was a major *influence*? Think of either the original artist or your favorite, and you will remember that **derivative** means *copied* or *unoriginal*.

PART TWO

dilapidated adj. (dih LAAP ih day tihd)—in disrepair, run-down
*The architect saw great potential in the **dilapidated** house.*

emphatic adj. (em FAT ik)—forceful and definite
*When asked if they wanted to come to school over the weekends, the students answered with an **emphatic** "NO!"*

emulate v. (EM yoo layt)—to copy, imitate
*Heather tried to **emulate** her mother in every way possible.*

exacting adj. (eg ZAK ting)—requiring a lot of care or attention; demanding
*Baking bread is an **exacting** task because too much or too little attention can kill the yeast.*

feral adj. (FEHR ul)—suggestive of a wild beast, not domesticated
*Though the animal-rights activists did not want to see the **feral** dogs harmed, they offered no solution.*

implausible adj. (im PLAWS uh bul)—improbable, inconceivable
*Max found his neighbor's claim that he'd seen a UFO highly **implausible**.*

impudent adj. (ihm PYUH duhnt)—marked by cocky boldness or disregard for others
*Considering the judge had been lenient in her sentence, it was **impudent** of the defendant to refer to her by her first name.*

> **FLASHBACK**
>
> In Chapter 1, Word Roots, you read about **im-** and how it means *not*. In **implausible**, the negative emphasis is on *not being conceivable or probable*. In **impudent**, the negative emphasis is on *not regarding others* and *not being humble*.

haughty adj. (HAW tee)—arrogant and condescending
*The teacher resented Sally's **haughty** attitude and gave her a D for the semester.*

hubris n. (HYOO brihs)—excessive pride or self-confidence; Greek for "to rush into"
*Nathan's **hubris** spurred him to say things that many considered insensitive.*

incorrigible adj. (ihn KOHR ih juh buhl)—incapable of being corrected or amended; difficult to control or manage
*Bobby's mother complained all the time about how **incorrigible** he was.*

indiscriminate adj. (in dis KRIM uh nit)—haphazard; random; chaotic
*John didn't want to make an **indiscriminate** choice, so he visited ten different colleges before applying.*

insuperable adj. (ihn SUH puhr uh buhl)—incapable of being surmounted or overcome
***Insuperable** as Quinchon's problems seemed, he refused to be grumpy or pessimistic.*

Practice 2

DIRECTIONS: Consider the definition, and then circle T for True or F for False.

6. **T F** **emulate**—to imitate

7. **T F** **exacting**—easy

8. **T F** **implausible**—inconceivable

9. **T F** **hubris**—a lack of confidence

10. **T F** **insuperable**—surmountable

Your Words, Your World

Insular—Insulation is pink and fluffy. And itchy! Picture insulation around a person, having surrounded that person for the past ten years. This *isolated* person would have *no idea* about politics, changes in technology, new music and fashions, or anything else current. This person would have a *narrow viewpoint* because he or she would *know nothing* about modern-day living. This is typical of **insular** people. NOTE: **Insular** is usually used in regards to a group of people; not to an individual.

Feral—**Feral** just sounds like a *wild* animal, doesn't it? If you love animals, picture a *wild* animal, but if you don't, simply think of the most *uncouth, untamed, uncultivated, undomesticated* person you know. He or she is **feral**.

Dilapidated—Every town has a haunted house, or, at least, a *decrepit* place where no one would ever think of living again. Imagine the place near where you live that is in the worst state of *disrepair* and let this serve as your reminder: **dilapidated** means *ramshackle* and *run-down*.

PART THREE

interminable adj. (in TER mi nu bul)—endless
*By the time the seemingly **interminable** school play ended, half the audience was gone.*

loquacious adj. (loh KWAY shuhs)—talkative
*Patty was **loquacious**, which was always a problem as she worked in the library.*

nebulous adj. (NEH byoo luhs)—vague, undefined
*Jerry's **nebulous** promise to get fast food for school lunches made many voters skeptical.*

precipitous adj. (PREE sih puh tuhs)—steeply; hastily
*The night before finals, John **precipitously** began to study.*

precocious adj. (pri KOH shiss)—unusually advanced or talented at an early age
*The fact that Beatrice got married at 18 shocked no one, as she'd always been a bit **precocious**.*

prodigal adj. (PRAH dih guhl)—recklessly extravagant, wasteful
*The **prodigal** spending of the class secretary earned her a suspension and removal from office.*

seraphic adj. (seh RAH fihk)—angelic, sweet
*Selena's **seraphic** appearance belied her bitter personality.*

stalwart adj. (STAHL wuhrt)—marked by outstanding strength and vigor of body, mind, or spirit
*Hank's 85-year-old grandmother went to the market every day, impressing everyone with her **stalwart** routine.*

timorous adj. (TIM uh rus)—timid, shy, full of apprehension
*A **timorous** child, Lois too often relied on adults to help her out.*

FLASHBACK

Often synonyms will have word roots in common. This is the case with **timorous**, which means *timid*. It is also true of the next word: **tremulous** means *trembling*.

---

tremulous adj. (TREM yoo luss)—trembling, quivering; fearful, timid
*The **tremulous** boy was found in the staff bathroom, hiding from the bullies.*

unwarranted adj. (uhn WAAR ehn ted)—groundless, unjustified
*The student art show received criticism that was **unwarranted** in its harshness.*

unwitting adj. (uhn WIH ting)—unaware; unintentional
*The **unwitting** students had no idea that Mr. Brady was planning a pop quiz.*

utilitarian adj. (yoo TIL eh TAR ee uhn)—efficient, functional, useful
*The school website became even more **utilitarian** when the students began to maintain it.*

viscous adj. (VIHS kus)—thick, syrupy, and sticky
*The **viscous** sap trickled slowly down the trunk of the tree.*

Practice 3

DIRECTIONS: Read the three possible synonyms, then circle the word you think best defines the word in bold.

11.	**interminable**:	predetermined	finite	endless
12.	**nebulous**:	vague	defined	distinct
13.	**timorous**:	timid	audacious	impudent
14.	**tremulous**:	fearless	courageous	trembling
15.	**unwitting**:	unsuspecting	wary	cautious

Your Words, Your World

Loquacious—If someone were to describe you as **loquacious**, you might take offense. That's because you are being accused of being *long-winded*. The other person might mean to say that you are a good *communicator*, but **loquacious** does have a negative connotation. It means *overly talkative*.

Stalwart—Now, if someone were to call you **stalwart**, you might also take offense, but you'd be misunderstanding the compliment. If you are stalwart, you possess a *strength of body, mind, and spirit*; this word is also used to describe someone who is *rugged* and *athletic*. So if somebody notices your **stalwart** nature, be happy!

Utilitarian—Don't be upset if someone calls you **utilitarian** either. It simply means that you are *highly efficient*. Usually, this word is used to describe organizations, groups, or systems that are *functional* and *useful*.

PRACTICE ANSWERS AND EXPLANATIONS

Practice 1

1. An **aberration** is something *different* or *unusual*. So *ordinary* is correct.

2. **Acuity** is a noun that means *insight* and *perception* and not *naïve*.

3. If something is **banal**, it is *trite* and *common*. **Unique** is the antonym.

PRACTICE ANSWERS AND EXPLANATIONS *(cont'd)*

4. **Bucolic** is used to describe a place that is *pastoral* and *rural*, so *urban* (relating to the city) is the opposite.

5. To go somewhere or do something in a **circuitous** manner is to be *indirect* about it. *Roundabout* is a synonym, while *undeviating* is an antonym.

Practice 2

6. **True.** To **emulate** is to imitate.

7. **False.** When a task is **exacting**, it requires great care. It is anything but easy.

8. **True.** If something is **implausible** it is improbable and inconceivable.

9. **False.** **Hubris** is excessive pride and confidence.

10. **False.** If a task is **insuperable**, it isn't easy or surmountable. The task is insurmountable or impossible.

Practice 3

11. **Interminable** is synonymous with *endless*, so *predetermined* and *finite* are antonyms.

12. **Nebulous** is synonymous with *vague*, while *defined* and *distinct* are antonyms.

13. **Timorous** means *timid*. An *audacious* and *impudent* person is not timid!

14. **Tremulous** is synonymous with *trembling*. *Fearless* and *courageous* are both antonyms.

15. **Unwitting** is synonymous with *unsuspecting*; *wary* and *cautious* are its antonyms.

CHAPTER 15 QUIZ

Take your time, not only with the questions, but in reading the answer explanations that follow. Set a goal for yourself—80% (16 correct answers) is recommended—and if you don't reach that goal, go back and read through the chapter again. Good luck!

DIRECTIONS: For questions 1–12, circle T for True or F for False.
For questions 13–20, circle the synonym.

1. **T F** **aberration**—unusual

2. **T F** **derivative**—original

3. **T F** **feral**—sterile

4. **T F** **impudent**—humble

5. **T F** **incorrigible**—uncorrectable

6. **T F** **precocious**—immature

7. **T F** **stalwart**—strong and brave

8. **T F** **unwarranted**—justified

9. **T F** **insuperable**—insurmountable

10. **T F** **dilapidated**—renovated

11. **T F** **bucolic**—pastoral

12. **T F** **implausible**—conceivable

13. **unwitting**:	unintentional	conscious	intentional
14. **nebulous**:	vague	defined	concrete
15. **interminable**:	restricted	endless	predetermined
16. **circuitous**:	indirect	electrical	direct
17. **anachronistic**:	avant-garde	outdated	couture
18. **banal**:	trite	uncommon	original
19. **adroit**:	novice	skillful	incompetent
20. **tremulous**:	fearless	assertive	trembling

CHAPTER 15 QUIZ ANSWERS AND EXPLANATIONS

1. **True.** An **aberration** is unusual.

2. **False.** To be **derivative** is to imitate and copy; it is to be unoriginal.

3. **False.** When something is **feral** it is characteristic of a wild animal.

4. **False.** **Impudent** means marked by disregard for others. It is not synonymous with humble.

5. **True.** To be **incorrigible** is to be uncorrectable.

6. **False.** To be **precocious** is not to be immature. It is to be unusually advanced at an early age.

7. **True.** If someone is **stalwart**, he or she is strong and brave.

8. **False.** When something is **unwarranted** it is not justified. It is groundless and unjustified.

9. **True.** To be **insuperable** is to be insurmountable.

10. **False.** When a building is **dilapidated** it is anything but renovated. It is run-down and in a state of disrepair.

11. **True.** A **bucolic** scene is pastoral and rural (related to the country-side).

12. **False.** To be **implausible** is not to be conceivable. It is to be improbable and inconceivable.

13. **Unwitting** is *unintentional*. *Conscious* and *intentional* are its antonyms.

14. To be **nebulous** is to be *vague* and not *defined* or *concrete*.

15. **Interminable** means *endless*, which is contrary to *restricted* and *predetermined*.

16. When something is done in a **circuitous** way, it is done in an *indirect* manner, making *direct* an incorrect choice. *Electrical* is a distracter based on the confusion of circuit (electrical) and **circuitous**.

CHAPTER 15 QUIZ ANSWERS AND EXPLANATIONS *(cont'd)*

17. The adjective **anachronistic** means *outdated. Avant-garde* and *couture* are two French words associated with up-to-the-minute art and fashion, respectively.

18. To be **banal** is to be common or *trite*, so *uncommon* and *original* are both wrong.

19. When someone is **adroit**, that person is neither a *novice*, nor *incompetent*. Quite the opposite, when someone is adroit, he or she is *skillful*.

20. If someone is **tremulous**, that person is *trembling* and neither *fearless* nor *assertive*.

CHAPTER 16

Most Frequently Tested GRE Words

The words you need to ace the GRE

BUILDING BLOCK QUIZ

By answering the 12 questions below, you will get a sense of how close-ly you should study this chapter in order to master the vocabulary you'll need for the GRE! Keep in mind, should you happen to choose incorrect answers for the final two questions, you'll want to go back to chapter 15 for some review.

DIRECTIONS: Fill in the blanks, using the most appropriate of the four multiple-choice answers. The correct answer will always fit into the sentence grammatically.

1. The speech Dean Finch gave after the tragic events of September 11, 2001, was _____ and provided everyone a bit of relief.

    (A) disparate   (B) felicitous

    (C) didactic   (D) chimerical

2. When the football team won the first game, it was a(n) _____ after four losing seasons.

    (A) normality   (B) anonymity

    (C) juxtaposition   (D) anomaly

3. Gina finally ended her _____ relationship with Rich after he punched her car and dented it.

   (A) prodigy   (B) tempestuous

   (C) vernal   (D) cathartic

4. Lynn's one fault was that she lived life in a _____ way and was always surprised by changes.

   (A) myopic   (B) assiduous

   (C) fallacious   (D) abstruse

5. Even though Francine and Shaniqua came from _____ backgrounds, they were the best of friends.

   (A) didactic   (B) ambidextrous

   (C) ephemeral   (D) disparate

6. What Dave lacked in _____, he had in street smarts, so he rarely got into trouble.

   (A) continence   (B) continents

   (C) malapropisms   (D) circumlocution

7. Mrs. Reagan _____ her daughter to get married, which only made dating more difficult.

   (A) scolded   (B) aplombed

   (C) beseeched   (D) amalgamated

8. After graduating from business school, Jeffrey _____ his academic success to his grandfather.

   (A) blamed   (B) disparated

   (C) excoriated   (D) imputed

9. For her 21st birthday, Meg's parents sent her on a _____ to Europe.

   (A) confluence   (B) continence

   (C) sojourn   (D) celerity

10. At the _____ of the school year, the highways near the university became filled with packed cars covered in college stickers.

   (A) cessation   (B) acumen

   (C) celerity   (D) presage

11. Alberto's little brother was _____, so they were able to do a lot of things together.

   (A) obdurate   (B) precocious

   (C) salacious   (D) propagate

12. When Nick's father called his A+ a(n) _____, it almost made him cry.

   (A) volition   (B) pundit

   (C) aberration   (D) platitude

BUILDING BLOCK ANSWERS AND EXPLANATIONS

1. B. The speech Dean Finch gave after the September 11, 2001, attacks was **felicitous**, meaning suitable and appropriate (with a secondary meaning of pleasurable). *Disparate* means dissimilar, *didactic* means instructive, and *chimerical* means fanciful, none of which is appropriate.

2. D. The victory was an **anomaly**, or irregularity. *Normality* (ordinariness), *anonymity* (the state of being unknown or unnamed), and *juxtaposition* (combination) are all incorrect.

3. B. The relationship was **tempestuous**, meaning stormy and turbulent. *Prodigy* (genius), *vernal* (springtime), and *cathartic* (therapeutic) are all poor choices in context.

BUILDING BLOCK ANSWERS AND EXPLANATIONS *(cont'd)*

4. A. Lynn lived life in a **myopic** way, meaning she lacked foresight and so was surprised by change. *Assiduous* (persevering), *fallacious* (misleading), and *abstruse* (obscure) are all incorrect.

5. D. The girls came from **disparate** (dissimilar) backgrounds. None of the other answers—*didactic* (instructive), *ambidextrous* (able to use either the left or right hand), and *ephemeral* (short-lived)—makes sense.

6. A. Dave lacked **continence**, which means self-control. *Continents* makes no sense in this context. *Malapropisms* (mistaking one word for another in a comic way) and *circumlocution* (the act of doing something in a roundabout way) are both incorrect.

7. C. Mrs. Reagan **beseeched** (begged and pleaded) her daughter, which probably sounded a lot like *scolding*, but that answer is incorrect. *Aplombed* is not a real word, and *amalgamated* (compounded) doesn't fit.

8. D. Jeffrey **imputed** (credited) his success to his grandfather. He didn't *blame* his grandfather, nor did he criticize (*excoriate*) him. Disparate mean dissimilar, but *disparated* isn't a word.

9. C. Meg went on a **sojourn**, which is a temporary stay or visit. *Confluence* (coming together), *continence* (self-control), and *celerity* (rapidity) are all incorrect.

10. A. Those packed cars marked the **cessation**, or end, of the school year. *Acumen* (insight), *celerity* (speed), and *presage* (to foretell) don't work in the context of the sentence.

11. B. Alberto's little brother was **precocious**, which means he was unusually advanced for his age. He was neither *obdurate* (stubborn) nor *salacious* (scandalous in a sexual way), and *propagate* (reproduce and spread) does not fit grammatically. If you answered this question incorrectly, you might want to go back to chapter 15 for some review.

12. C. An **aberration** is something different from the norm, and it hurt Nick's feelings when his father said that about his good grade. *Volition* is a wish, a *pundit* is an expert, and a *platitude* is a cliché. If you answered this question incorrectly, you might want to go back to chapter 15 for some review.

PART ONE

abstruse adj. (ahb STROOS)—difficult to comprehend; obscure
*Stan's presentation was so good that he turned an **abstruse** subject into one the rest of the class could understand.*

acumen adj. (AH kew men)—sharpness of insight
*Charlie's literary **acumen** helped him to do very well on the Advanced Placement exam, so he got to skip Freshman English.*

amalgamate v. (ah mal gah MATE)—to mix, combine
*Giant Industries **amalgamated** with Mega Products to form Giant-Mega Products Incorporated.*

ambidextrous adj. (am bih DEX truss)—able to use both hands equally well
*The **ambidextrous** chef was able to chop vegetables with both hands, simultaneously.*

anonymity adj. (ah noh NIHM eh tee)—condition of having no name or an unknown name
*The actor said he wanted to return to the **anonymity** of his school days.*

aplomb n. (uh PLAHM), (uh PLUHM)—self-confidence, assurance
*For such a young dancer, Daria had great **aplomb**, making her perfect to play the young princess.*

arduous adj. (AR joo uhs)—extremely difficult, laborious
*Amy thought she would pass out after completing the **arduous** hike.*

assiduous adj. (uh SIH joo ihss)—diligent, persistent, hardworking
*The chauffeur scrubbed the limousine **assiduously** on the morning of the wedding.*

beseech v. (bah SEECH)—to beg, plead, implore
*Taylor **beseeched** Mr. Jones to give her a second chance at the music store, but he refused.*

catharsis n. (KAH thar sis)—purification, cleansing
*Plays can be more satisfying if they end in some sort of emotional **catharsis** for the characters involved.*

celerity n. (seh LEH rih tee)—speed, haste
*The track team practiced with great **celerity**.*

cessation n. (se SAY shun)—termination, halt, end
*The **cessation** of the attacks meant that people could start using the park again at night.*

chimerical adj. (kie MEHR ih kuhl), (kie MEER ih kuhl)—fanciful; imaginary, impossible
*The inventor's plans seemed **chimerical** to the conservative venture capitalist.*

circumlocution n. (SIR kuhm low KYOO shin)—roundabout, lengthy way of saying something
*Ogden used endless **circumlocutions** to avoid discussing emotional issues.*

FLASHBACK

Circum means *around*, so remember this word root when asked about **circumlocution**. It's a lengthy word that refers to a *lengthy way of saying something*, usually to *talk around* an issue.

Practice 1

DIRECTIONS: Consider the two word choices in the parentheses, and circle the one that best fits in the context of the sentence.

1. Mary wrote a series of (**chimerical** OR **assiduous**) poems on the theme of lost love.

2. Because only his rap name was famous, G Boy enjoyed (**ambidextrous** OR **anonymity**) when making dinner and hotel reservations under his given name.

3. The memorial service provided (**catharsis** OR **anonymity**) for everyone involved.

4. The (**aplomb** OR **cessation**) of the soccer season meant Yol had more time for her nonathletic friends.

5. Gary's political (**acumen** OR **abstruse**) always impressed his teachers.

Your Words, Your World

Abstruse—What is the most *confusing* class you have ever taken? What subject matter was the most *difficult for you to comprehend*? Well, if you think of that nightmarish year—all of that *perplexing, puzzling, obscure* information—you will remember what **abstruse** means.

Aplomb—Do you know someone who does everything with **aplomb**? Does someone come to mind when you think of *self-confidence, assurance,* and *poise*? Hopefully, the answer is yes. Because if that person can help you to remember what **aplomb** means, all of his or her *style* and *composure* will have helped you, as well.

Beseech—When was the last time you had to *beg* for something? And what was it you *pleaded* for or *implored* another person to do for you? To *grovel* like that is to **beseech** and it never feels very good, so if you can remember that feeling at least you'll also remember the meaning of **beseech**.

PART TWO

confluence n. (KAHN floo uhns)—the act of two things flowing together; the junction or meeting place of two things
*At the Young Democrats meeting, the head of the Young Independents signed an agreement, leading to a **confluence** of ideas between the two organizations.*

continence n. (KAHN tih nihns)—self-control, self-restraint
*Lucy exhibited impressive **continence** in steering clear of fast food, and she quickly lost ten pounds.*

didactic adj. (di DAK tik)—excessively instructive
*Helen's father was overly **didactic**, turning every family activity into a lesson.*

> **MEMORY TIP**
>
> **Didactic** rhymes with *tactic* and to be *excessively instructive* is a tactic some people take. Somewhat boring in the classroom, it is especially lethal in a book or movie. Remember, it is a mistake to take a tactic that's **didactic**.

disparate adj. (DIS par it)—dissimilar, different in kind
*Although the two sisters looked like identical twins, their personalities were quite **disparate**.*

ephemeral adj. (eh FEM ehr ihl)—momentary, transient, fleeting
*The lives of mayflies seem **ephemeral** to us, since the flies' average life span is a matter of hours.*

excoriate v. (ehk SKOHR ee ayt)—to censure scathingly; to express strong disapproval
*The three-page letter to the editor **excoriated** the magazine for printing the rumor without verifying it.*

extrapolation n. (ihk STRAP uh lay shuhn)—the use of known data and information to determine what will happen in the future; prediction
*Through the process of **extrapolation**, the study group was able to develop a theory.*

fallacious adj. (fuh LAY shuhs)—tending to deceive or mislead; based on incorrect logic (a fallacy)
*The **fallacious** statement "the earth is flat" was the subject of Matthew's essay.*

felicitous adj. (feh LIH sih tus)—suitable, appropriate; well-spoken
*The father of the bride made a **felicitous** speech at the wedding, contributing to the overwhelming success of the evening.*

imperturbable adj. (IHM puhr TUHR buh buhl)—unshakably calm and steady
*No matter how disruptive the children became, the babysitter remained **imperturbable**.*

impute v. (im PYOOT)—to attribute, to credit
*When Greg found the puddle, he quickly **imputed** it to his puppy.*

juxtaposition n. (juks ta po ZISH un)—side-by-side placement for comparison
*Marty's presentation included the **juxtaposition** of an acorn and a walnut.*

laudable adj. (LAW du buhl)—deserving of praise
*Kristin's dedication was **laudable**, but she just didn't have the skills to be a professional soccer player.*

malapropism n. (MAAL uh prahp ihz uhm)—the accidental, often comical use of a word that resembles the one intended but has a different, often contradictory meaning
*Everybody laughed at the **malapropism** when the announcer said "public boredcasting" instead of "public broadcasting."*

myopic adj. (mie AHP ihk), (mie OH pihk)—lacking foresight, having a narrow view or lack of long-range perspective
*The **myopic** business owner didn't want to spend money on advertising, and as a result, his store went out of business.*

Practice 2

DIRECTIONS: Match the word (left column) with its definition (right column).

6.	**excoriate**	momentary
7.	**fallacious**	comical use of the wrong word
8.	**ephemeral**	determining what will happen
9.	**malapropism**	to censure harshly
10.	**extrapolation**	misleading

Your Words, Your World

Disparate—When two people are *different*, they are **disparate**. Think of twins who don't look alike (fraternal). They are probably *dissimilar* in a number of ways. Even identical twins have *contrasting* traits.

Juxtaposition—A **juxtaposition** is a *side-by-side comparison* of two things. Imagine two different iPods held up for *evaluation* and *judgment*. Imagine looking at a magazine article *comparing* them as you try to decide which you want to buy. The image in that magazine, one iPod next to the other, should symbolize the word **juxtaposition** for you. (Also realize that the word **juxtaposition** contains *position*.)

PART THREE

obdurate adj. (AHB door it)—stubborn, hardhearted; inflexible
Professor Raimes was obdurate on the issue and no amount of persuasion could change his mind.

perfunctory adj. (pir FUNK tu ree)—done in a routine manner; indifferent; automatic
The secretary listened to the boy's story, gave a perfunctory smile, and told him to sit and wait.

platitude n. (PLAA tuh tood)—overused and trite remark
Instead of voicing the usual platitudes in his commencement remarks, the comedian gave a memorable and inspiring speech to the graduating class.

presage n., v. (PREH sihj)—something that foreshadows, a feeling of what will happen in the future; to predict or foretell
The Persian Gulf War was a presage to the fall of Saddam Hussein.

prodigy n. (PRAHD ih jee)—person with exceptional talents
Her parents noticed very early in her childhood that Lezlie was a math prodigy, capable of doing the most complex computations in her head.

propagate v. (PROP uh gayt)—to spread out; to have offspring
While Gary only told one person about his new girlfriend, news of the relationship propagated around the school within an hour.

pundit n. (PUHN diht)—one who gives opinions in an authoritative manner
Victor wanted to be a pundit of the arts when he grew up, and he practiced by writing reviews in the campus paper.

revile v. (rih VEYE uhl)—to criticize with harsh language, verbally abuse
The new plant manager had several plans in the works, all of which were reviled by the workers' union.

salacious adj. (suh LAY shuhs)—appealing to sexual desire
The audience was shocked by the comedian's salacious routine.

sojourn n. (SOH jurn)—a temporary stay, visit
After graduating from college, Iliani embarked on a sojourn to China.

stasis n. (STAY sihs)—a state of static balance or equilibrium; stagnation
*The rusty World War II tank in the town park had obviously been in **stasis** for years.*

> **MEMORY TIP**
>
> The first syllable of **stasis** is pronounced *stay* and this might help you to remember that **stasis** means to *stay in balance* or to be in a *sta(y)te of equilibrium*.

supersede v. (soo puhr SEED)—to cause to be set aside; to force out of use as inferior; replace
*Ellen's computer was still running version 2.0 of the software, which had long since been **superseded** by three more versions.*

supplant v. (suh PLAANT)—to replace (another) by force, to take the place of
*After the military officers overthrew the government, a dictator **supplanted** the democratically elected president.*

tempestuous adj. (tehm PEHS choo uhs)—stormy, turbulent
*The camping trip was cut short when the drizzle turned into a **tempestuous** downpour.*

transitory adj. (TRAAN sih tohr ee)—short-lived, existing only briefly
*The football team's championship victory was **transitory** because it was disqualified when officials discovered that players had used steroids.*

vernal adj. (VUHR nuhl)—related to spring; fresh
*Bea basked in the balmy **vernal** breezes, happy that winter was coming to an end.*

volition n. (vole ISH un)—free choice, free will; act of choosing
*Of his own **volition**, Darius admitted to cheating on the test.*

zephyr n. (ZEH furh)—a gentle breeze; something airy or insubstantial
*The **zephyr** from the ocean made the intense heat on the beach bearable.*

Practice 3

DIRECTIONS: In completing the sentences, use five of the eight words below. Use each of the words just once.

perfunctory	platitude	obdurate	propagate
sojourn	stasis	presage	superseded

11. On Jill's _____ to Africa, she came to see the world in a different light.

12. For Jamal, studying for the science exam _____ studying for the math quiz.

13. Professor Lieberson's _____ had little effect on her students as they had heard her give others the exact same compliment.

14. To _____ word of the school orchestra's appearance at the mall, the group posted flyers around the campus.

15. By October things had calmed down, and the professors felt the university had reached a point of acceptable _____.

Your Words, Your World

Vernal—Just saying the word **vernal** should trigger a memory of how the *first warm breeze* of the year feels. And if you need more than a physical reminder, just think of the **vernal** equinox (usually March 20th or 21st), when the hours of daylight and darkness are of equal length. *Vernus* is Latin for "belonging to spring," and **vernal** always *relates to spring*.

Zephyr—The first *vernal* breeze might be a **zephyr**. The root of the word **zephyr** can be found in the Greek *Zephyrus*, a god personified by the western *wind*. Most of the time, **zephyr** is used in reference to a *gentle breeze*, but it can also mean something *light* and *insubstantial*.

Presage—**Presage** means *to foreshadow* or to give *a feeling of what will happen in the future*. There is always a day or two in the winter when the sun comes out, a warm wind blows (perhaps a vernal zephyr), and the birds begin to sing. And this **presages**, or *signifies*, the coming spring.

PRACTICE ANSWERS AND EXPLANATIONS

Practice 1

1. Mary wrote **chimerical**, or fanciful, poems. While she may have worked hard to write them, the poems themselves can't be *assiduous* (hardworking).

2. G Boy appreciated his **anonymity**, or ability to go unrecognized, under his given name. *Ambidextrous* means being able to use both hands equally well, so it is irrelevant in this context.

3. The memorial service provided **catharsis**—a cleansing release of emotions—for the mourners. The other choice, *anonymity,* would mean that the mourners were unrecognized, which doesn't make sense.

4. **Cessation** means termination or end, while *aplomb* means self-assurance and doesn't work in the sentence. Yol had more time because her soccer season ended, so **cessation** is the answer.

5. Gary's political **acumen** (insight) earned him the respect of his teachers. *Abstruse* means difficult to comprehend or obscure, and is incorrect.

Practice 2

6. To **excoriate** is to censure harshly.

7. Someone or something **fallacious** is misleading and tending to deceive.

8. **Ephemeral** means momentary, fleeting, or brief.

9. A **malapropism** is a comical misuse of a word or phrase. Yogi Berra is famous for his malapropisms.

10. An **extrapolation** is a way of determining what will happen.

Practice 3

11. Jill's trip to Africa was merely a **sojourn**, or temporary stay, but it had a big impact on her.

12. Preparing for the exam **superseded** (took the place of or overruled) reviewing for the quiz.

PRACTICE ANSWERS AND EXPLANATIONS *(cont'd)*

13. A **platitude** is an overused remark, and Professor Lieberson seems to have been using her compliments a bit too much. *Tired* is a current phrase that refers to something overused, such as a **platitude**.

14. To **propagate** is to spread and in this case, the orchestra was spreading word of its gig.

15. **Stasis** is a state of balance or equilibrium and when the university calmed down, it had reached this state.

CHAPTER 16 QUIZ

Take your time, not only with the questions, but in reading the answer explanations that follow. Set a goal for yourself—80% (16 correct answers) is recommended—and if you don't reach that goal, go back and read through the chapter again. Good luck!

DIRECTIONS: For questions 1–12, circle T for True or F for False.
For questions 13–20, circle the synonym.

1. **T F**   **myopic**—lacking foresight

2. **T F**   **sojourn**—a long vacation

3. **T F**   **fallacious**—tending to mislead

4. **T F**   **acumen**—lacking insight

5. **T F**   **excoriate**—to censure

6. **T F**   **platitude**—original remark

7. **T F**   **presage**—to foreshadow

8. **T F**   **revile**—to criticize

9. **T F**   **volition**—free will

10. **T F**   **didactic**—lacking instruction

11. **T F**   **zephyr**—a storm

12. **T F**   **juxtaposition**—an upside-down position

13. **supersede**:	to take over	to cede	to be great
14. **celerity**:	celebrity	slothfulness	speed
15. **transitory**:	short-lived	severe	permanent
16. **chimerical**:	fanciful	realistic	possible
17. **obdurate**:	stubborn	flexible	compliant
18. **supplant**:	to support	to replace	to concede
19. **imperturbable**:	calm	impulsive	high-strung
20. **aplomb**:	aghast	insecurity	self-confidence

CHAPTER 16 QUIZ ANSWERS AND EXPLANATIONS

1. **True.** To be **myopic** is to be lacking foresight. Associate "opic" with optical to help recall the sight part of this definition.

2. **False.** A **sojourn** is actually a short stay or visit, so a long vacation is wrong.

3. **True.** To be **fallacious** is to tend to deceive or mislead. A con man is **fallacious**.

4. **False.** **Acumen** refers to a sharpness of insight and not a lack of insight. John Madden has athletic acumen and thus is one of the most popular football analysts ever.

5. **True.** To **excoriate** is to censure scathingly.

6. **False.** A **platitude** is not original. It is an overused remark. Cliché is a synonym.

7. **True.** To **presage** is to foreshadow.

8. **True.** To **revile** is to criticize with harsh language.

9. **True.** If one does something by one's own **volition**, it is an act of free will.

10. **False.** To be **didactic** is not to be lacking instruction, but to be excessively instructive. A novel might be criticized as being overly didactic.

11. **False.** A **zephyr** is a gentle breeze and not a storm.

12. **False.** A **juxtaposition** is a side-by-side placement for comparison and has nothing to do with an upside-down position.

13. To **supersede** is to take the place of something or *to take over,* and not *to cede* (yield) or *to be great.*

14. **Celerity** is *speed*, so *slothfulness* is an antonym. *Celebrity* is a look-alike distracter.

15. To be **transitory** is to be *short-lived. Severe* (extreme, harsh) is incorrect, while *permanent* is an antonym of **transitory**.

CHAPTER 16 QUIZ ANSWERS AND EXPLANATIONS *(cont'd)*

16. **Chimerical** means *fanciful*, therefore *realistic* and *possible* are its antonyms.

17. To be **obdurate** is to be *stubborn*, so *flexible* and *compliant* are its antonyms.

18. To **supplant** is *to replace*. *To support* and *to concede* are incorrect because they are near-antonyms of **supplant**.

19. **Imperturbable** means *calm*, definitely not *impulsive* or *high-strung*!

20. **Aplomb** is *self-confidence* and poise. *Insecurity* suggests the opposite, while *aghast* means horrified.

Most Commonly Misused Words

You'll never mix up "affect" and "effect" again

BUILDING BLOCK QUIZ

By answering the ten questions below, you will get a sense of how closely you should study this chapter in order to master the vocabulary words that people commonly mispronounce, misspell, and confuse with other words.

DIRECTIONS: Fill in the blanks, using the most appropriate of the four multiple-choice answers. The correct answer will always fit into the sentence grammatically.

1. When the bully tried to _____ Jimmy's lunch money, Jimmy wisely told the teacher.

    (A) abject   (B) expropriate

    (C) equivocate   (D) expatriate

2. Laura looked really _____ after Gabe broke up with her.

    (A) object   (B) fulsome

    (C) abject   (D) incipient

3. Hillary was a bright girl, but for some reason she told the most _____ lies.

    (A) patent   (B) obscure

    (C) temporal   (D) titular

4. *Schindler's List* _____ the class in ways Mr. Verrone hadn't predicted.

   (A) disassembled   (B) dissembled

   (C) effected   (D) affected

5. Xavier's constant _____ was a source of anger and upset for his parents.

   (A) duplication   (B) Spartan

   (C) propensity   (D) duplicity

6. When Heather and Jack stopped arguing in public, it was a(n) _____ sign that their marriage counseling was working.

   (A) ostensible   (B) discomfit

   (C) apathetic   (D) osteoporosis

7. The newspaper's refusal to publish the environmentalist's editorial about global warming _____ him.

   (A) exacerbated   (B) excoriated

   (C) exasperated   (D) unadulterated

8. Mrs. Klein had to admit that her class was indeed _____ when only three of its members showed up for the car wash fundraiser.

   (A) pathetic   (B) empathetic

   (C) salient   (D) apathetic

9. At the wedding, Nina's parents were impressed with how _____ all her friends were.

   (A) urbane   (B) urban

   (C) querulous   (D) abject

10. Dr. Jennings quickly tired of Sandra's _____ ways and canceled all future appointments with her, citing the importance of honest communication in therapy.

    (A) frank   (B) inveterate

    (C) surreptitious   (D) intemperate

BUILDING BLOCK ANSWERS AND EXPLANATIONS

1. B. To **expropriate** is to forcibly take property (just what you'd expect from a bully). *Equivocate* (be evasive), *expatriate* (live abroad), and *abject* (hopeless) are all incorrect.

2. C. If someone is **abject**, like Laura, then she is miserable and not *incipient* (just beginning), *fulsome* (flattering), or an *object*.

3. A. A **patent** lie is an obvious lie. An *obscure* lie would be vague and although that's close, **patent** is better. *Temporal* means sequential and *titular* means supposed, neither of which works.

4. D. Not to be confused with an *effect* (a consequence), **affect** means to produce an emotional response, as *Schindler's List* did. *Effect* can be used as a verb meaning to bring about, but it has nothing to do with emotions. *Dissembled* (pretended) and *disassembled* (taken apart) are both incorrect.

5. D. Xavier's deception, or **duplicity**, upset his parents. *Duplication* (repetition), *Spartan* (simple, sparse), and *propensity* (tendency) make no sense in context, even if Xavier had a propensity to lie.

6. A. Heather and Jack had reached an **ostensible** (apparent, but possibly hiding a deeper meaning) resolution of their differences: they no longer argued, at least not in public. *Discomfit* (to embarrass) and *apathetic* (uninterested) are both incorrect, while *osteoporosis* (a health condition in which the bones become brittle) is just a distracter.

7. C. The environmentalist was **exasperated**, or frustrated, because the newspaper would not publish his opinion. The newspaper's decision did not *exacerbate* him (make him worse), *excoriate* him (harshly criticize him), or *unadulterate* him (an adjective meaning absolutely pure, not a verb).

BUILDING BLOCK ANSWERS AND EXPLANATIONS *(cont'd)*

8. D. Mrs. Klein had to admit that her students were **apathetic**, meaning they had little care, or feeling, for others. Although their turnout was *pathetic* (pitiful), they were not personally pathetic. Neither were they *salient* (outstanding) nor *empathetic* (understanding the feelings of others).

9. A. Nina's parents thought her friends were **urbane**, which means courteous and refined and not *urban* (related to a city), *querulous* (argumentative), or *abject* (hopeless).

10. C. Sandra's **surreptitious** (sneaky) ways ruined Dr. Jennings's trust in her. To be *intemperate* is to be extreme, to be *frank* is to be honest (thus an antonym), and to be *inveterate* is to be confirmed.

PART ONE

abject adj. (AAB jekt)—miserable, pitiful
*After finding the **abject** bird on the ground, we took it inside and called the Audubon Society.*

apprise v. (uh PRIYZ)—to inform; French for "to teach" or "to inform"
*Emanuel had to **apprise** his boss when a package arrived.*

enjoin v. (ehn JOYN)—to direct or impose with urgent appeal, to order with emphasis; to forbid
*Patel explained that he is **enjoined** by his culture from eating the flesh of a cow, which is sacred in India.*

enmity n. (EN mih tee)–hostility, antagonism, ill will
*After the car accident, there was so much **enmity** between the two families that the Bells decided to move away.*

equivocate v. (ih KWIHV uh kayt)—to avoid committing oneself in what one says; to be deliberately unclear
*Officer Cardea had no patience for suspects who wasted his time **equivocating**.*

expropriate v. (eks PRO pree ayt)—forcibly take one's property; to seize
*Missy explained she'd missed the past two weeks of school because her family's apartment and car had been **expropriated** by the government for taxes owed.*

fulsome adj. (FOOL suhm)—abundant; flattering in an insincere way
*Right before grades were given, many **fulsome** students stopped by Mrs. Leibowitz's office.*

> **MEMORY TIP**
>
> Sometimes compliments come with strings attached. Chock-full of strings! So let the "ful" in **fulsome** remind you that this word describes someone who gives compliments, but in an insincere way (because he or she wants something).

incipient adj. (ihn SIHP ee uhnt)—beginning to exist or appear; in an initial stage
*The **incipient** idea seemed brilliant, but the Spanish Club officers knew it needed much more development.*

intemperate adj. (in TEM per ut)—not moderate
*The **intemperate** climate in the desert meant boiling hot days and bitter cold nights.*

inveterate adj. (ihn VEHT uhr iht)—firmly established, especially with respect to a habit or attitude; unchangeable
*An **inveterate** risk-taker, Lori tried her luck at bungee jumping.*

malingerer n. (muh LIN gehr ehr)—one who evades responsibility by pretending to be ill
*Andrew had the reputation of being a **malingerer** just because his older brother was one.*

patent adj. (PAA tehnt)—obvious, evident
*Moe could no longer stand Frank's **patent** fawning over Heather and told him so.*

portentous adj. (pohr TEHN tuhs)—self-important; arrogant
*The minister always spoke in a **portentous** way, which irritated many congregants.*

propensity n. (proh PEHN suh tee)—a natural inclination or preference
Natalie had a propensity for lashing out at others when stressed, so her family and friends stayed away at exam time.

Practice 1

DIRECTIONS: After reading the three choices, circle the one that you think is the *antonym*.

1. **abject:**   joyous   unhappy   miserable

2. **apprise:**   to inform   to conceal   to tell

3. **fulsome:**   critical   overgenerous   flattering

4. **incipient:**   developing   established   initial

5. **inveterate:**   adaptable   established   unchangeable

Your Words, Your World

Enmity—When was the last time a story in the news made you angry? When did something upset you to the point of *hostility*? Is this a regular occurrence? Do you often find yourself in a state of **enmity** as you fling the remote control in disgust? Hopefully not! **Enmity** equates to a state of *antagonism*. If the news makes you feel this way, if it's so bad that you feel *irritated* after watching, maybe you should turn off the TV and spend some more time with this book!

Equivocate—What chore, errand, or job do you **equivocate** about more than any other? What is it that you hate so much, you *beat around the bush*, *make excuses*, and *avoid doing it at all costs*? What, more than anything else in the world, makes you want to *avoid committing yourself*? To be *deliberately unclear* when giving your answer? Perhaps it's baby-sitting, having lunch with a certain friend or relative, or walking the dog.

Propensity—If given the *choice*, what is your *preference*? What do you *like* to do when you have free time? What is your *natural inclination*? Do you have a **propensity**, or *preference*, when it comes to activities? Perhaps your **propensity** is for listening to music, talking to friends on the phone, using IM, visiting chat rooms, or watching TV. What are you *predisposed* to do with your free time?

PART TWO

querulous adj. (KWER uh lus)—complaining, grumbling
*Nick's boss was tired of his **querulous** attitude and threatened to dock an hour's pay if he complained again.*

replete adj. (rih PLEET)—abundantly supplied, complete
*Even though Tim's music collection was **replete** with over a thousand CDs, he decided to purchase an iPod.*

salient adj. (SAY lee uhnt)—prominent, of notable significance
*Joan finally told Hank that his most **salient** characteristic was his tendency to dominate every conversation.*

Spartan adj. (SPAHR tihn)—highly self-disciplined; careful, strict; marked by simplicity
*While training, Cheech preferred to live in a **Spartan** room so he could shut out all distractions.*

specious adj. (SPEE shuhs)—having the ring of truth but actually being untrue; deceptively attractive
*The students were disappointed to learn that the band's mention of a show in the auditorium was just a **specious** promise.*

surreptitious adj. (sir up TISH iss)—secret, stealthy
*George had to be **surreptitious** when he slipped the birthday card in Janet's handbag.*

tangential adj. (tan JEN shul)—digressing, diverting
*Dave's arguments were always **tangential** to the conversation, and people began to ignore him after a while.*

temporal adj. (TEHMP ore uhl)—having to do with time
*The history test would include a **temporal** fill-in-the-blank section, so Margaret studied a time line she'd created herself.*

titular adj. (TIHCH yoo luhr)—existing in title only; having a title without the functions or responsibilities
*Carla was thrilled to be voted Homecoming Queen until somebody explained that the **titular** honor didn't mean she could boss anybody around.*

tractable adj. (TRAK te bul)—easily managed or controlled
*During the second quarter, Francine's classes were **tractable**, so she decided to get a part-time job.*

MEMORY TIP

Ask a farmer if he'd prefer to go back to the days of having his plow pulled by oxen or horses, and he'll tell you . . . tractors make things much more **tractable**!

---

umbrage n. (UHM brij)—offense, resentment
*Becky took **umbrage** with the principal's accusation that she'd been smoking in the bathroom.*

unadulterated adj. (uhn ah DUL ter ay ted)—absolutely pure
*Jenny liked to tell people she only drank bottled water because it was **unadulterated**.*

unequivocal adj. (uhn eh KWEV ih kul)—absolute, certain
*The jury's verdict was **unequivocal**: the sadistic murderer would be locked up for life.*

urbane adj. (erh BANE)—courteous, refined, suave
*Although Tom thought of himself as an **urbane** college student, everybody at home just thought he was full of himself.*

veracious adj. (ver AH shus)—truthful, accurate
*Suspecting her son's excuse for coming home late wasn't **veracious**, Sue decided to check his story.*

Practice 2

DIRECTIONS: Consider the definition and then circle T for True or F for False.

6. **T F**   **salient**—insignificant

7. **T F**   **specious**—deceptively false

8. **T F**   **tangential**—digressing

9. **T F**   **umbrage**—inoffensive

10. **T F**   **unadulterated**—unchanged

Your Words, Your World

Temporal—If you are musical, you can keep *tempo*. Picture a metronome on top of a piano or even the snapping of fingers to keep *time*. This will help you to recall that **temporal** means *having to do with time*. **Temporal** refers more often to *chronological order* than to rhythm, but if music is your thing, use the association with *tempo* to help yourself out.

Urbane—Imagine the most *polite* city in the world. There is no crime and no one is rude. The streets are *clean* and the people are *courteous* and *kind*. In addition, they are all *highly educated, suave,* and *refined*. The inhabitants of this city, if it ever could exist, would be considered **urbane**. So to remember **urbane**, just think of this urban setting and its *cultured, sophisticated,* and *stylish* inhabitants.

Querulous—In your life, there is, more likely than not, a King of Complaining. This is someone who is always grumbling about something. This king's soul mate is the Queen of **Querulous**, who is always *argumentative* and *irritable*. Who would want to hang out with that kind of king and queen?

PART THREE

The following list pairs words commonly confused for one another.

access n. (AK ses)—ability to obtain or make use of
The student council president fought, unsuccessfully, to get Internet access in the cafeteria.

excess n. (ek SES)—overload, overindulgence; extra
Jill partied to excess and had to miss the family reunion the next day.

affect v. (ah FEKT)—to produce an emotional response; to influence
Manny was really affected by the play and couldn't stop thinking about it all week.

effect v. (eh FEKT)— to cause; to produce
Although many worried that the World Trade Center tragedy would drive people out of New York City, the terrorist attack did not effect this migration.

apathetic adj. (ahp ah THET ik)—having little feeling, emotion, or interest
Yulitza's joke made her mother fear that Yulitza was truly apathetic about poverty and hunger.

empathetic adj. (ehm pah THEH tihk)—sympathetic; compassionate; understanding the feelings of others
Kenny showed just how empathetic he was when he donated all of his graduation money to AIDS relief.

censor v. (SEN sir)—to examine in order to suppress or delete anything considered objectionable
It was clear the declassified government documents had been censored, as several paragraphs had been crossed out.

censure v. (SEN shur)—to find fault; to criticize; to find blameworthy
While Congress decided whether or not to censure the president, the reporters waited eagerly outside.

disassemble v. (dis ah SEM buhl)—to take apart
From a young age, Carmen liked to disassemble her toys and then put them back together.

dissemble v. (dih SEM bul)—to pretend, disguise one's motives
With his parents and the principal staring at him, Billy could only dissemble for so long.

discomfit v. (dis KUM fit)—to put into a state of embarrassment and humiliation
Darren liked to discomfit everyone with his dirty jokes, but one day a teacher overheard and sent him to detention.

discomfort v. (dihs KUM fort)—to make uneasy; embarrass
Sometimes the best books discomfort the reader, showing that person something about the world that he or she had never considered before.

MEMORY TIP

Discomfit and **discomfort** are sometimes confused with one another and this isn't just because they sound the same. Their definitions are actually quite similar. Just think of people being embarrassed and uncomfortable when you're asked about **discomfit** and **discomfort**, and chances are you'll get the question right.

---

duplicity n. (doo PLISS ih tee)—deception, dishonesty
*The two girls claimed to be best friends, but their relationship was always being tested by **duplicity**.*

duplication n. (dup li KAY shun)—the act of making an exact copy of something
*Henry used his artistic talents for **duplication**, and everyone was always impressed with his reproductions of famous paintings.*

exacerbate v. (ig ZAS ur bayt)—to aggravate, intensify the bad qualities of
*Oftentimes, when people try to self-medicate with illegal drugs, it only **exacerbates** the problem.*

exasperate v. (ex AHS per ate)—to cause irritation or annoyance to
*By December, the students had **exasperated** Mr. Meyers to the point that he was ready to quit.*

ostensible adj. (ah STEN sihbel)— apparent, perceived; for display
*Endorsed by the school paper, Tammy was the **ostensible** front-runner in the race for student council president; however, Ryan actually had more student support.*

ostentatious adj. (ahs sten TAY shus)—flamboyant and arrogant; eye-catching; pretentious
*The number of BMWs in the parking lot was an **ostentatious** display of the students' wealth.*

Practice 3

DIRECTIONS: Read the three possible synonyms, then circle the word you think best defines the word in bold.

11. **excess:**   entrance   necessary   indulgence

12. **effect:**   to cause   to incite   to sadden

13. **empathetic:**   pathetic   sympathetic   unfeeling

14. **dissemble:**   to pretend   to take apart   to follow through

15. **exacerbate:**   to aggravate   to improve   to enhance

Your Words, Your World

Don't have time to sit around repeating these words to yourself, over and over again, in order to remember them? Well, you don't have to! The following exercise tests your knowledge of the material . . . without requiring that you take a test! So your job now is to really *think* about the following words and how they apply to your everyday life. NOTE: You will notice that these are the words that are often confused with the ones in the previous synonym activity. After looking at them separately in two different activities, you should have an easier time telling them apart in the future.

Access—Internet **access**, **access** to that concert you're dying to see, **access** to the phone number of the pizza place, **access** to the information you need to finish your research paper: these days, it's not just about *being able to obtain* what you want or need, it's about being able to do it quickly and easily.

Affect—Think about what **affects** you most, about what *produces an emotional response*. Recall what **affects** you in a good way, what *makes you* sad, what *makes you* angry, and even what *makes you* hungry! These are all things that *influence how you feel*: things that **affect** you.

Discomfit—One common phrase these days is *diss* as in *disrespect*. If you have ever been *dissed* by somebody, you have been **discomfited**. You have been *embarrassed* in front of other people. You have been *humiliated* by another person. It's happened to everybody: just remember that to be *dissed* is to be **discomfited**.

PRACTICE ANSWERS AND EXPLANATIONS

Practice 1

1. The antonym of **abject** is *joyous*. *Miserable* and *unhappy* are synonymous with **abject**.

2. *Inform* and *tell* are synonymous with **apprise**, while *conceal* is the antonym. No one ever says "Keep me **apprised** of the situation" because he or she wants the truth of the matter to be concealed.

3. The antonym of **fulsome** is *critical*, while *overgenerous* and *flattering* are its synonyms.

4. The antonym of **incipient** is *established*. *Developing* and *initial* both refer to origins and are synonyms of **incipient**.

5. The antonym of **inveterate** is *adaptable*. *Established* and *unchangeable* are synonyms of **inveterate**.

Practice 2

6. False. **Salient** is defined as significant and is definitely not insignificant.

7. True. **Specious** means deceptively false.

8. True. **Tangential** is synonymous with digressing and diverting.

9. False. To take **umbrage** is to take offense. Inoffensive is incorrect.

10. True. **Unadulterated** means pure, untainted, and unchanged.

Practice 3

11. **Excess** is synonymous with *indulgence*, so *necessary* is an antonym. *Entrance* should be associated with access and not **excess**.

12. To **effect** is *to cause*. Although *to incite* and *to sadden* have similar meanings, they relate to emotions and therefore are more properly associated with affect, not **effect**.

13. To be **empathetic** is to be *sympathetic* and not *pathetic* (pitiful, sad) or *unfeeling*.

PRACTICE ANSWERS AND EXPLANATIONS *(cont'd)*

14. To **dissemble** is *to pretend* and not *to follow through. To take apart* is to disassemble and should not be confused with **dissemble**.

15. To **exacerbate** is *to aggravate* and not *to improve* or *to enhance.*

CHAPTER 17 QUIZ

Take your time, not only with the questions, but in reading the answer explanations that follow. Set a goal for yourself—80% (16 correct answers) is recommended—and if you don't reach that goal, go back and read through the chapter again. Good luck!

DIRECTIONS: For questions 1–9, circle T for True or F for False.
For questions 10–20, circle the synonym.

1. **T F**   **propensity**—a natural tendency

2. **T F**   **tangential**—quite important

3. **T F**   **inveterate**—new

4. **T F**   **exasperate**—to annoy

5. **T F**   **dissemble**—to pretend

6. **T F**   **access**—ability to obtain

7. **T F**   **fulsome**—excessive

8. **T F**   **salient**—prominent

9. **T F**   **apprise**—to inform

10. **enmity:**	enemy	hostility	cooperation
11. **patent:**	unclear	obscure	obvious
12. **querulous:**	complaining	tractable	amiable
13. **urbane:**	unrefined	courteous	uncouth
14. **veracious:**	hungry	truthful	inaccurate
15. **effect:**	to cause	to consume	to make emotional
16. **empathetic:**	unsympathetic	ambivalent	compassionate
17. **censor:**	to suppress	to sponsor	to promote
18. **unequivocal:**	ambivalent	ambiguous	absolute
19. **abject:**	miserable	optimistic	to protest
20. **umbrage:**	admiration	resentment	acclaim

CHAPTER 17 QUIZ ANSWERS AND EXPLANATIONS

1. True. A **propensity** is a natural inclination or preference. Every person has a **propensity** for something.

2. False. If something is **tangential**, it is a digression from the main topic and not quite important.

3. False. If something is **inveterate**, it is not new, but firmly established and set in its ways.

4. True. To **exasperate** is to annoy.

5. True. To **dissemble** is to deceive by pretending. Don't confuse this word with disassemble, to take apart.

6. True. To have **access** is to have the ability to obtain or make use of something. It's nice to have **access** . . . in excess!

7. True. The adjective **fulsome** means abundant or excessive, especially in terms of flattery.

8. True. To be **salient** is to be prominent and of notable significance.

9. True. To **apprise** is to inform.

10. Enmity means *hostility. Cooperation* is a near-antonym and *enemy* is a closely related word: an enemy is one who bears **enmity**.

11. If something is **patent**, it is blatant or *obvious*. It is definitely not *unclear* or *obscure* (vague).

12. A **querulous** person is always *complaining*, and not *amiable* (friendly) or *tractable* (easily managed).

13. To be **urbane** is to be *courteous* and sophisticated. *Unrefined* and *uncouth* are antonyms of **urbane**.

14. Veracious means *truthful. Voracious* describes a strong appetite, so *hungry* is a distracter. *Inaccurate* is an antonym.

15. To **effect** is *to cause. To make emotional* is to affect, so that is wrong. *To consume* is irrelevant.

CHAPTER 17 QUIZ ANSWERS AND EXPLANATIONS *(cont'd)*

16. If someone is **empathetic**, he or she is *compassionate. Unsympathetic* and *ambivalent* are near-antonyms of **empathetic.**

17. To **censor** is *to suppress.* It is the opposite of *to sponsor* and *to promote.*

18. **Unequivocal** means *absolute. Ambiguous* and *ambivalent* are defined as unclear and unsure, respectively.

19. **Abject** means *miserable. Optimistic* has an opposed meaning and *to protest* is the definition of object.

20. To take **umbrage** is to be in a state of *resentment. Admiration* and *acclaim* refer to positive feelings for something and are near-antonyms of **umbrage.**

CHAPTER 18

Fifty-Cent Words
You Can Actually Use

For the show-off in all of us

BUILDING BLOCK QUIZ

By answering the ten questions below, you will get a sense of how closely you should study this chapter in order to master the vocabulary that will help you even after you graduate from the school that accepted you upon learning that you aced the SAT or GRE!

DIRECTIONS: Fill in the blanks, using the most appropriate of the four multiple-choice answers. The correct answer will always fit into the sentence grammatically.

1. The Health Department would only reveal that there was a fear of _____ chemicals in the area, and that was why the nature preserve was being inspected.

    (A) pathetic   (B) pathogenic

    (C) anodyne   (D) altruism

2. Professor Wheatley tried to teach _____ and selflessness in addition to math.

    (A) altruism   (B) selfishness

    (C) alto   (D) compunction

3. Willy had always wanted a _____, but "Stinky" wasn't quite what he'd had in mind.

   (A) euphemism   (B) milieu

   (C) exhortation   (D) sobriquet

4. When Duane realized that his new doctor was completely _____ he asked his friends to recommend another physician.

   (A) inefficacious   (B) efficacious

   (C) competent   (D) effective

5. Larry joked about breaking into the credit card company's computer system to _____ all of his debt.

   (A) convalesce   (B) plunge

   (C) expunge   (D) adumbrate

6. It was Anne's _____ that led her to admit to taking the money from the fund-raiser.

   (A) conjunction   (B) amalgamation

   (C) compunction   (D) corruptibility

7. From a young age, Glenn had been a master of _____ so no one was surprised when he became a magician.

   (A) prestidigitation   (B) consanguineous

   (C) neonate   (D) inchoate

8. Mrs. Traylor told Gwen's parents that Gwen was one of the most _____ students she'd ever had the pleasure of teaching.

   (A) inefficient   (B) ineffective

   (C) inefficacious   (D) efficacious

9. Even though Miss Unger was in her first year of teaching, her _____ ways made her seem more mature and more in control than most rookies.

(A) abstemious   (B) absent

(C) alimentary   (D) anthropomorphic

10. Once Victoria decided that the school nurse was a(n) _____, she stopped going to her for bandages, advice, or anything else.

(A) interlocutor   (B) vicissitude

(C) palimpsest   (D) charlatan

BUILDING BLOCK ANSWERS AND EXPLANATIONS

1. B. There was a fear of **pathogenic** (disease-causing) chemicals, not *pathetic* (pitiful), *anodyne* (bland), or *altruism* (unselfishness) chemicals.

2. A. Professor Wheatley was concerned with **altruism**, or the unselfish concern for the welfare of others. An *alto* is a female singer with a low range. *Selfishness* is an antonym of selflessness, but the sentence calls for a synonym instead. *Compunction* means regret and is also incorrect.

3. D. Willy had always wanted a nickname (**sobriquet**). *Euphemism* is close in that it is a word substituted for another word, but it's not close enough. A *milieu* is a setting and an *exhortation* is a strong written or verbal appeal.

4. A. This doctor was **inefficacious**, which means ineffective and incompetent. *Efficacious*, *competent*, and *effective* are all antonyms of **inefficacious**, thus incorrect.

5. C. Larry wanted to **expunge** (erase completely) his debt from the system. *Convalesce* (recover from illness), *adumbrate* (give a hint), and *plunge* don't work in the context of the sentence.

6. C. It was Anne's **compunction**, or feelings of regret, that led her to admit her guilt. *Conjunction* and *amalgamation* both mean merger or combination, so they're not right. *Corruptibility* fits the theme but refers to someone who can be convinced to commit a crime. It's unlikely that such a person would feel any **compunction**.

BUILDING BLOCK ANSWERS AND EXPLANATIONS *(cont'd)*

7. A. Glenn had been a master of **prestidigitation**, which is a cleverly executed trick or deception. *Inchoate* means unclear, *consanguineous* means of similar lineage, and *neonate* means a newborn, so all three are incorrect.

8. D. Gwen was **efficacious**, which means effective and efficient. *Inefficient*, *ineffective*, and *inefficacious* are all antonyms of the correct answer. They're also not the kind of thing that would make a student a "pleasure" to teach.

9. A. Miss Unger was **abstemious** (moderate and in control). If she had been *absent*, she wouldn't have been a very good teacher. *Alimentary* (pertaining to food) and *anthropomorphic* (assigning human characteristics to animals and inanimate things) are also incorrect.

10. D. Victoria thought that the school nurse was a **charlatan**, which means a quack or a fake. An *interlocutor* is a partner in conversation, so that's wrong. A *vicissitude* is a change, and a *palimpsest* is an object that has been written on, erased, and written on again, so both of those answers are incorrect, as well.

PART ONE

abstemious adj. (aab STEE mee uhs)—done sparingly; consuming in moderation
*Roger advised his children to be **abstemious** spenders, rather than blowing their allowances on candy and comic books.*

adumbrate v. (AAD uhm brayt) (uh DUHM brayt)—to give a hint or indication of something to come
*Whenever Miss Frey **adumbrated** about a test with an after-school review session, all of her students attended.*

alimentary adj. (AAL uh mehn tuh ree) (AAL uh mehn tree)—pertaining to food, nutrition, or digestion
*Frederique decided she wanted to work in an **alimentary** field, possibly as a nutritionist.*

BUILDING BLOCK ANSWERS AND EXPLANATIONS *(cont'd)*

altruism n. (AL troo ihzm)—unselfish concern for others' welfare
*Mitchell decided to become an Eagle Scout because of the group's focus on **altruism**.*

amalgamation n. (ah MAL ga MAY shun)—consolidation of smaller parts
*The concert was an **amalgamation** of songs from different pop artists.*

anodyne n. (AAN uh diyn)—a source of comfort; a medicine that relieves pain
*After a long day at the office, classical music was just the **anodyne** Regina needed.*

anthropomorphic adj. (AAN thruh poh MOHR fihk)—suggesting human characteristics for animals and inanimate things
*Many children's stories feature **anthropomorphic** animals such as talking pigs and wolves.*

> **MEMORY TIP**
>
> To **morph** is a commonly used expression meaning to change and **anthro** means man, as in human. So it only makes sense that **anthropomorphic** refers to the *practice of assigning human characteristics* to animals and other nonhuman things.

charlatan n. (SHAR lah tan)—quack, fake
*The **charlatan** of a doctor prescribed the wrong medication for hundreds of patients and found himself the subject of a class action suit.*

compunction n. (kum PUHNK shun)—feeling of uneasiness caused by guilt or regret
*When the principal didn't see any **compunction** in Daniel, she called the police to report that Daniel had slashed the tires of three teachers' cars.*

consanguineous n. (kahn saang GWIHN ee uhs)—having the same lineage or ancestry; related by blood
*Often, best friends will act as if they are **consanguineous**.*

conundrum n. (ka NUHN druhm)—riddle, puzzle or problem with no solution
*To Adam, algebra was a **conundrum**, and he believed he had no hope of ever passing the class.*

convalesce v. (kahn vuhl EHS)—to recover gradually from an illness
*After her bout with malaria, Tatiana needed to **convalesce** for a whole month.*

convergence n. (kuhn VEHR juhns)—the state of separate elements joining or coming together
*Mrs. Friedmann taught that a **convergence** of factors led to the start of World War I.*

efficacious adj. (ef ih KAY shus)—effective, efficient
*Nurse Gina was quite **efficacious**, and by the third day of school, all of the student health files were in order.*

emollient adj. (ee MOHL yent)—having soothing qualities, especially for skin
*After using the **emollient** lotion on her sunburn, Dominique felt much more comfortable.*

Practice 1

DIRECTIONS: Consider the two word choices in the parentheses, and circle the one that best fits in the context of the sentence.

1. Kevin saved a lot of money because he was so (**alimentary** OR **abstemious**) in his spending.

2. Al's mother asked him to please just tell her what he wanted for lunch rather than (**adumbrate** OR **convalesce**).

3. The new band was an (**amalgamation** OR **anthropomorphic**) of two other bands that had just broken up.

4. Rakeem's strong feelings of (**compunction** OR **adumbrate**) kept him from ever doing drugs again.

5. Principal Yee's new discipline system was (**efficacious** OR **emollient**), and the teachers and parents were thrilled.

Your Words, Your World

Convalesce—When was the last time you had to *recover from an illness*? Or better yet, what was the worst sickness you ever had and how long did it take you to **convalesce**? To **convalesce** is to *gradually get over being sick*. Think of the *lengthiest recovery* you ever had, and you'll be sure to remember this word.

Emollient—When you think of something *soothing*, especially something *soothing on your skin*, do you think of a blanket or do you think of *moisturizer*? Do you have a favorite blanket, perhaps from your childhood? If so, think of it whenever faced with the word **emollient**, and you'll be able to recall the definition. If not, just think of *lotion* or *moisturizer*, particularly if you use either on a daily basis.

PART TWO

euphemism n. (YOO fuh mihz uhm)—an inoffensive and agreeable expression that is substituted for one that is considered offensive
*Mr. Herbert was a good health teacher because he used **euphemisms** to help the students feel more comfortable with the subject matter.*

exhortation n. (eg zor TAY shun)—speech that advises or pleads
*The minister's **exhortation** convinced the mayor to show mercy toward the juvenile delinquents.*

grandiloquence n. (graan DIHL uh kwuhns)—pompous talk; fancy but meaningless language
*The headmistress was notorious for her **grandiloquence** at graduation, and everybody feared having to sit through her speech.*

> **MEMORY TIP**
>
> **Grandiloquence** even sounds high and mighty! The word is defined as *pompous, fancy talk*, and the trick is to put together **grand** (magnificent and sometimes self-important) and **-loquence** (the last part of *eloquence*, which means expressiveness): **grandiloquence**.

immutable adj. (im MYOOT uh bul)—unchangeable, invariable
*Poverty seemed an **immutable** fact of life for the Wood family, but fortunately, Beverly earned an academic scholarship to college.*

implacable adj. (ihm PLAY kuh buhl) (ihm PLAA kuh buhl)—inflexible; not capable of being changed or pacified
*Despite complaints from students and parents, Mr. Jacobsen was **implacable** about having the test the day before vacation.*

inchoate adj. (ihn KOH iht)—being only partly in existence; unformed
*Jessie had an **inchoate** first draft of her novel, with a couple of characters and scenes roughly sketched.*

inefficacious adj. (in ef ih KAY shus)—ineffective, incompetent
*Miss Collins's attempts to quiet the class were **inefficacious** as they ignored her and continued to yell.*

invariable adj. (in VAR ee uh bul)—constant, unchanging
*The university switched to the quarter system, despite the fact that trimesters had been an **invariable** aspect of the school for years.*

interlocutor n. (in ter LAHK yu tur)—someone taking part in a dialogue
*Everybody knew that Stew was a willing **interlocutor** with a real gift of gab.*

FLASHBACK

Inter means *between*—given the fact that a conversation happens between two people, this word root should remind you of the meaning of **interlocutor**.

---

macabre adj. (muh KAA bruh) (muh KAA buhr)—having death as a subject; dwelling on the gruesome
*Martin enjoyed **macabre** tales about werewolves and vampires.*

malleable adj. (MAAL ee uh buhl)—easily influenced or shaped, capable of being altered by outside forces
*Mr. Foster felt that all young minds were **malleable**, so he never, ever gave up on a student.*

milieu n. (mihl YOO)—the physical or social setting in which something occurs or develops; environment
*Quinchon was uncomfortable with the **milieu** at the club, so he left.*

Practice 2

DIRECTIONS: Match the word (left column) with its definition (right column).

6.	**euphemism**	environment
7.	**grandiloquence**	constant
8.	**implacable**	inflexible
9.	**invariable**	pompous talk
10.	**milieu**	an agreeable expression

Your Words, Your World

Interlocutor—Think of the person in the world you most enjoy talking to. Whether it's a best friend, a teacher, or one of your parents, picturing this certain somebody will help to remind you that an **interlocutor** is *someone taking part in a dialogue.* Just think, you may be somebody's favorite *conversationalist!*

Macabre—Stephen King is an author of **macabre** books. Clive Barker is a film producer who always makes *horror* movies that use *death* as a subject. Even if you don't enjoy such *gruesome* stories, keeping them in mind can help you remember this word.

PART THREE

neonate n. (NEE uh nayt)—a newborn child
*With all the talk of **neonates** in science class, Jerry began to imagine life as a father.*

obstreperous adj. (ahb STREP uh res)—troublesome, boisterous, unruly
*The **obstreperous** boys lost their bathroom privileges and had to be escorted by an adult.*

palimpsest n. (PAHL ihmp sehst)—an object or place having diverse layers or aspects beneath the surface
*When paper was expensive, people would just write over existing writing, creating a **palimpsest**.*

pathogenic adj. (paa thoh JEHN ihk)—causing disease
*Bina hoped her research of **pathogenic** microorganisms would help stop the spread of disease in developing nations.*

perspicacious adj. (pur spi KAY shuss)—shrewd, astute, keen-witted
*In Arthur Conan Doyle's stories, Sherlock Holmes uses his **perspicacious** mind to solve mysteries.*

phlegmatic adj. (flehg MAA tihk)—having a sluggish, unemotional temperament
*Waylon's writing was energetic but his **phlegmatic** personality wasn't suited for television, so he turned down the interview.*

prestidigitation n. (PREHS tih dih jih TAY shuhn)—a cleverly executed trick or deception; sleight of hand
*Denise's father was known for his practical jokes and **prestidigitation**, but she was a very serious young lady.*

> **MEMORY TIP**
>
> At six syllables, **prestidigitation** is one of longest words in this book and certainly the most difficult to pronounce. So remember, if you can pronounce **prestidigitation**, that's a *cleverly executed trick*.

seminal adj. (SEH muhn uhl)—influential in an original way, providing a basis for further development; creative
*Randall's graduate work was considered **seminal** in the area of quantum physics, inspiring many other scientists.*

sobriquet n. (SOH brih KAY) (SOH brih KEHT)—a nickname
*Before becoming president, Ronald Reagan was an actor. One of his roles earned him the **sobriquet** "The Gipper."*

variegated adj. (VAAR ee uh GAYT ehd)—varied; marked with different colors
*Mrs. Quinlon showed the class that the **variegated** foliage of the rain forest allows it to support thousands of animal species.*

verisimilitude n. (VEHR ah sih MIHL ih tood)—quality of appearing true or real
*Because they achieved a level of **verisimilitude**, reality TV shows saw their ratings soar.*

vicissitude n. (vih SIHS ih tood)—change or variation; ups and downs
*In his economics class, Allen learned that the key to stable investing is waiting out the **vicissitudes** of the stock market.*

Practice 3

DIRECTIONS: In completing the sentences, use five of the seven words below. Use each of the words just once.

verisimilitude   obstreperous   vicissitudes   neonate

variegated   palimpsest   sobriquet

11. Dean always flattered his teachers, but he had such skills of _____ that his teachers never realized it.

12. Mr. Thomas brought the _____ to the front office as proof that Janice had erased her paper and added the correct answers after the test was done.

13. Tim tired of the _____ of the stock market and decided to keep all of his money in his mattress instead.

14. The sophomores had the reputation of being _____, but their behavior was surprisingly good all year.

15. The diagram in the science book showed the _____ soil sample from ground level to 20 feet beneath the surface.

Your Words, Your World

Sobriquet—In your group of friends, there are probably a few *nicknames*, right? Well, simply think of your favorite *nickname*—maybe even your own, if you have one—and use it as a reminder: a **sobriquet** is a *nickname*.

Seminal—Has there been a **seminal** book, movie, song, or band in your life that has *influenced* you? Has it *shaped your future*? When something is *influential in an original way*, it is **seminal**. The world is full of people who chose a career because of a **seminal** movie; people who moved to a certain place because of a **seminal** book; and artists and writers who were *influenced* by a **seminal** work.

PRACTICE ANSWERS AND EXPLANATIONS

Practice 1

1. Kevin was **abstemious**, which means he did things sparingly. *Alimentary* refers to food and is incorrect.

2. Rather than give hints (**adumbrate**), Al should just have told his mother what he wanted. To *convalesce* is to recover from illness, so that is an irrelevant answer.

3. An **amalgamation** is a consolidation or joining together, which is what the bands did. *Anthropomorphic* describes the assignment of human characteristics to nonhuman things.

4. Rakeem's **compunction**, or feeling of guilt or regret, helped to keep him off drugs. To *adumbrate* means to hint and makes no sense in context.

5. The system was **efficacious**, which means effective, and not *emollient*, which means soothing to the skin.

Practice 2

6. A **euphemism** is *an agreeable expression* used to replace a distasteful expression.

7. **Grandiloquence** is *pompous talk*.

PRACTICE ANSWERS AND EXPLANATIONS *(cont'd)*

8. To be **implacable** is to be *inflexible*.

9. **Invariable** is the opposite of variable and means *constant*.

10. Milieu means *environment*.

Practice 3

11. Dean's **verisimilitude** (quality of appearing true) helped him to get away with flattering his teachers.

12. A **palimpsest** is an object that has layers or a document that has been erased and written over. Through the layers, one can see what was originally written (in this case, Janice's original answers).

13. The **vicissitudes** (variation or ups and downs) of the stock market led Tim to give up on investing.

14. Obstreperous is the answer as it means troublesome, boisterous, and unruly.

15. The diagram of the **variegated** (marked with different colors) soil layers helped to teach the science students to distinguish the different strata.

CHAPTER 18 QUIZ

Take your time, not only with the questions, but in reading the answer explanations that follow. Set a goal for yourself—80% (16 correct answers) is recommended—and if you don't reach that goal, go back and read through the chapter again. Good luck!

DIRECTIONS: For questions 1–11, circle T for True or F for False. For questions 12–20, circle the synonym.

1. **T F** **verisimilitude**—appearing true

2. **T F** **vicissitude**—variation

3. **T F** **grandiloquence**—meaningful talk

4. **T F** **emollient**—not soothing

5. **T F** **interlocutor**—a conversationalist

6. **T F** **altruism**—selfish behavior

7. **T F** **amalgamation**—consolidation of smaller parts

8. **T F** **convergence**—a coming together

9. **T F** **compunction**—guilt-free

10. **T F** **unconscionable**—scrupulous behavior

11. **T F** **conundrum**—a problem with no solution

12. **adumbrate:**	to hint	to state	to berate
13. **charlatan:**	fake	chieftain	physician
14. **milieu:**	French food	environment	genre
15. **neonate:**	baby	senior citizen	octogenarian
16. **obstreperous:**	respectful	gracious	unruly
17. **sobriquet:**	bouquet	nickname	sobering
18. **exhortation:**	press conference	advisory speech	conversation
19. **malleable:**	shapeless	resistant	easily influenced
20. **invariable:**	inconsistent	erratic	unchanging

CHAPTER 18 QUIZ ANSWERS AND EXPLANATIONS

1. **True.** **Verisimilitude** means appearing true.

2. **True.** **Vicissitude** is synonymous with change, variation, and ups and downs.

3. **False.** **Grandiloquence** is actually meaningless, pompous talk, not meaningful talk.

4. **False.** An **emollient** is a source of comfort, most often in the form of a soothing lotion applied to the skin. Not soothing is therefore incorrect.

5. **True.** An **interlocutor** is a conversationalist, specifically someone taking part in a dialogue.

6. **False.** **Altruism** is unselfish concern for the welfare of others.

7. **True.** An **amalgamation** is the consolidation of smaller parts.

8. **True.** A **convergence** is a coming together of things.

9. **False.** **Compunction** is not guilt-free, but is distress caused by guilt or regret.

10. **False.** If an act is **unconscionable**, it is unscrupulous and shockingly unfair.

11. **True.** A **conundrum** is a problem with no solution.

12. To **adumbrate** is *to hint*. It is not *to state* or *to berate*.

13. A **charlatan** is a *fake* and is often used in reference to a phony *physician*. *Chieftain* (leader) is also incorrect.

14. A **milieu** is an *environment*. Like *genre*, the word is taken from the French, so *genre* (type or sort) and *French food* are both trick answers.

15. A **neonate** is a newborn *baby*, so *senior citizen* and *octogenarian* (someone in his or her eighties) are both incorrect.

16. **Obstreperous** means *unruly*, so *respectful* and *gracious* are its antonyms.

CHAPTER 18 QUIZ ANSWERS AND EXPLANATIONS *(cont'd)*

17. A **sobriquet** is a *nickname*. It is not a *bouquet*, nor is it *sobering* (a serious fact or incident that makes one thoughtful).

18. An **exhortation** is a catchphrase or an *advisory speech*. It is not a *press conference;* it isn't even a *conversation*, just a one-way speech.

19. To be **malleable** is to be *easily influenced*, so *resistant* is its antonym, and *shapeless* is irrelevant.

20. **Invariable** means *unchanging*, so *inconsistent* and *erratic* are both its antonyms.

Sharp Vocab
Cumulative Test

Before moving on to bigger and better things, such as conquering an important exam or impressing family, friends, and potential employers with your new vocabulary, take the time to double-check your comprehension. Below, you will find a final Cumulative Test comprised of at least two words from each chapter of this book. From word roots all the way to "fifty-cent" words, you'll have the chance to flex your vocabulary muscle! Aim for 100% correct, and best of luck to you!

1. **T F**   **stoic**—indifferent
2. **T F**   **discretion**—disability
3. **T F**   **gregarious**—introverted
4. **T F**   **impugn**—to question
5. **T F**   **declaim**—to speak loudly
6. **T F**   **cataclysmic**—indestructible
7. **T F**   **evanescent**—momentary
8. **T F**   **amalgamation**—merger
9. **T F**   **requisition**—acquisition
10. **T F**   **actuate**—activate
11. **T F**   **dogmatic**—flexible
12. **T F**   **avow**—to declare
13. **T F**   **precocious**—precious
14. **T F**   **apprise**—to misinform

15. **malleable**:	maddening	easily influenced	difficult to convince
16. **dis**, as in dissemble:	away from	close to	analyze
17. **mal**, as in malevolent:	mediocre	superior	bad
18. **cogent**:	convincing	illogical	weak
19. **augment**:	to secure	to depend	to extend
20. **mitigate**:	to ease	to sever	to relocate
21. **panache**:	illogical statements	flamboyance	overused phrase
22. **surreptitious**:	stealthy	celebratory	repetitious
23. **affect**:	to influence	to attend	to produce
24. **crescendo**:	gradual increase	rapid ascent	sparkle
25. **rankle**:	to anger	to mediate	to meditate

CUMULATIVE TEST ANSWERS AND EXPLANATIONS

1. True. To be **stoic** is to be indifferent. A **stoic** person is rarely affected by emotions.

2. False. Discretion does not equate to disability. When one uses **discretion** one demonstrates good judgment.

3. False. To be **gregarious** is not to be introverted. On the contrary, it is to be outgoing and sociable.

4. True. To **impugn** is to call into question.

5. True. To **declaim** is to speak loudly and vehemently, as in a dramatic recitation or a persuasive speech.

6. False. Cataclysmic does not mean indestructible. It describes an event that is severely destructive.

7. True. If something is **evanescent**, it is momentary or short-lived.

8. True. An **amalgamation** is a merger or a consolidation of smaller parts.

9. False. Acquisition is incorrect even though it rhymes with **requisition** and has a related meaning. **Requisition** describes a demand for something, while acquisition describes the act of actually obtaining it. The **requisition** is the request.

10. True. To **actuate** is to activate or to put into motion.

11. False. To be **dogmatic** is to be rigidly fixed in one's opinions. To be flexible is the opposite.

12. True. To **avow** is to state openly or declare.

13. False. A **precocious** child is unusually advanced for his or her age. He or she may be precious, but that is not the correct definition.

14. False. To **apprise** is to give notice or inform, while to misinform is the opposite.

CUMULATIVE TEST ANSWERS AND EXPLANATIONS *(cont'd)*

15. When someone is **malleable**, he or she can be influenced easily. Material things such as clay or molten glass can also be **malleable**, or easily shaped. *Difficult to convince* is the opposite and *maddening* is unrelated.

16. The word root **dis** means *away from*. To **dis**semble is to disguise one's motives under a false appearance, as those who dissemble try to stay away from the truth. *Close to* means the opposite of **dis**, and *analyze* is not correct.

17. **Mal** is a word root meaning *bad*, as in **mal**evolent, which means spiteful and vicious. Both *mediocre* (of average or poor quality) and *superior* (better than or above) express different meanings.

18. To be **cogent** is to be logically forceful and *convincing*. Neither *illogical* nor *weak* can be correct.

19. **Augment** means to expand or *extend*. Neither to *secure* nor *to depend* is correct.

20. **Mitigate** may sound harsh, but it actually means *to ease*. *To sever* (to cut off) and *to relocate* (to move) are both incorrect.

21. **Panache** is a French word that means *flamboyance*. The incorrect choices also come from the foreign words chapter. A *non sequitur* (Latin for "does not follow") is an illogical statement and a *cliché* (French) is an overused phrase.

22. **Surreptitious** means secret or *stealthy*. *Celebratory* describes a happy mood or setting, while *repetitious* refers to something that is repeating.

23. To **affect** is *to influence*. *To produce* is to effect and is incorrect. *To attend* is irrelevant.

24. A **crescendo** is a *gradual increase*, as in the volume of music. It is not a *rapid ascent* (rise or climb), and it has nothing to do with a *sparkle*.

25. To **rankle** is to cause *anger* and irritate. *To meditate* means to contemplate, and *to mediate* is to settle a dispute between two parties. Both wrong answers describe a cooling of anger and tension, the opposite of **rankle**.